MEDIEVAL ARCHITECTURAL DRAWING

MEDIEVAL ARCHITECTURAL DRAWING

ENGLISH CRAFTSMEN'S METHODS
AND THEIR LATER PERSISTENCE
(*c.*1200 - 1700)

ARNOLD PACEY

TEMPUS

First published 2007

Tempus Publishing
Cirencester Road, Chalford
Stroud, Gloucestershire, GL6 8PE
www.tempus-publishing.com

Tempus Publishing is an imprint of NPI Media Group

© Arnold Pacey, 2007

The right of Arnold Pacey to be identified as the Author
of this work has been asserted in accordance with the
Copyrights, Designs and Patents Act 1988.

All rights reserved. No part of this book may be reprinted
or reproduced or utilised in any form or by any electronic,
mechanical or other means, now known or hereafter invented,
including photocopying and recording, or in any information
storage or retrieval system, without the permission in writing
from the Publishers.

British Library Cataloguing in Publication Data.
A catalogue record for this book is available from the British Library.

ISBN 978 0 7524 4404 8

Typesetting and origination by NPI Media Group
Printed and bound in Great Britain

CONTENTS

	Preface	7
	Acknowledgements	9
	Abbreviations and Measurements	11
Chapter 1	Stone-carvers: identities and drawings (masons and carvers, c.1200-1360)	13
Chapter 2	Early architectural drawing (masons' drawings on walls and tracing floors to c.1360)	33
Chapter 3	Geometry in medieval drawing (drawings and wall paintings, c.1200-1420)	59
Chapter 4	Carpenters' markings (carpenters and joiners, c.1200-1400)	87
Chapter 5	Later medieval architectural drawings (masons' drawings for mouldings, sculpture and tracery, to 1550)	117
Chapter 6	House carpenters and church carvers (drawings and woodwork, c.1450-1550)	139
Chapter 7	Circles and scale drawings (masons, carpenters and surveyors, 1520-1620)	161
Chapter 8	Setting out carpentry and drawing in red (carpenters' lines and circles, 1500-1700)	187
Chapter 9	The persistence of medieval drawing techniques (full-size drawings after 1660)	213
	Appendix	229
	Glossary	234
	Notes	236
	Index	254

PREFACE

It was once thought that no architectural drawings survived in England from the most creative period in medieval architecture, when the great abbeys were being built, and when Salisbury Cathedral and Lincoln Minster were under construction. It was even occasionally suggested that buildings were designed without use of drawings. Then John Harvey, in the 1960s, pointed to the significance of the plaster tracing floors at Wells Cathedral and York Minster, while earlier work done at Cambridge had identified drawings on the walls of churches in that locality. Yet little progress was made in understanding the lines, curves and sketches seen on walls and tracing floors, nor in explaining how they were used.

In the last 20 years, more of the drawings at Wells and York have been deciphered and further drawings have been found, notably in Yorkshire (by Stuart Harrison and D.H. Heslop) in Hampshire (by John Crook) and at Lincoln (by Jenny Alexander). In a secular context 'constructional graffiti' from the mid-sixteenth century have been discovered at Acton Court in Gloucestershire (by Kirsty Rodwell). The present author has identified more individual drawings, often in places where Harvey and others had previously made surveys.

Putting mural and tracing-floor drawings together with the handful of drawings on parchment or paper already known provides a useful sample of architectural drawings by building craftsmen from the thirteenth century onwards. The majority of such drawings were made by masons rather than carpenters or other craftsmen. Moreover, in addition to drawings made while a building was being designed, many other marks are found on building fabrics, including geometrical diagrams of various kinds and setting-out lines, marked on both timber and stone, to guide the shaping of the material or to mark out joints. Three of the chapters in this book discuss carpenters and while drawings by carpenters are rarely found, setting-out lines on the components of timber frames or roofs are quite often seen and reveal much about the drawing methods of these craftsmen.

Discussion of carpenters is carried through to the end of the seventeenth century because traditional methods continued to be used up to this period. This was true also, in some degree, for masons and sculptors, including craftsmen working for Christopher Wren, as will be seen in the final chapter.

The book deals almost entirely with drawings by English craftsmen. Scotland and Wales raise other questions in rather different contexts. More particularly, though, the emphasis is on English craftsmen rather than their French counterparts, as there has been a tendency for writers on medieval craftsmen to illustrate their books using drawings by Frenchmen (especially Villard de Honnecourt) even when discussing English practice. The aim of this book is to show that there are more drawings in England than has previously been supposed and that it is possible to discuss some English craftsmen by reference to their own drawings, rather than relying on comparison with French examples. (That is not, of course, to deny a close relationship between England and France during much of the Middle Ages, which is often referred to).

This book may appear to be rather specialist in approach. Yet there is now widespread interest in the architectural heritage of England, which ought to mean more people asking questions about how particular houses or churches were designed, and in this book the evidence that can be seen on the buildings themselves is discussed in detail. One aim of the book is to raise awareness about the subject, in the belief that many more drawings will then be recognised, particularly in areas of southern England and the Midlands from which there is at present no material. Hence an appendix detailing buildings that may be visited to see drawings has been included. Many similar buildings ought to be examined afresh to assess what they can tell us about craftsmen's drawings.

ACKNOWLEDGEMENTS

This book is based on fieldwork – that is, on the examination and survey of buildings, with the particular aim of recording drawings on walls, floors and timbers, as well as setting-out lines, carpenters' numbers and other details. My greatest debt is to my fieldwork colleague of 20 years standing, Alison Armstrong, who has taught me much about observing and recording detail, has helped with the work in Lancashire and at York Minster, and who made some of the discoveries reported in Chapter 8. Others who have helped in a similar way have been David Cant in Lancashire and Shropshire, and David Farrar in Cheshire. Tony Barker has contributed very substantially by keeping me abreast of new publications and, most generously, by enabling me to see many more buildings than would otherwise have been possible, particularly in some western counties, and in eastern England and London. The really exceptional hospitality of Penny and Peter Jones made repeated visits to Wells Cathedral possible, and they also showed me many other buildings in Somerset and Wiltshire. Others who have facilitated and participated in my explorations have been Fiona Pacey, Pamela Maryfield, Chris Crosland, Malcolm Birdsall, and George and Sonia Pacey.

I am also personally indebted to people responsible in various capacities for the buildings visited, including houseowners, the incumbents of several churches and churchwardens at Ashwell (Hertforshire) and Sefton (Lancashire). I am especially grateful to John David at York Minster, Andrew Parker at Wells Cathedral, Ian Garwood at Middle Temple Hall, and Dr A.V. Grimstone at Pembroke College, Cambridge (where Jayne Ringrose devoted a great deal of time to helping with archives).

Many relevant buildings have been visited during a long friendship with Howard Erskine-Hill who also helped greatly with the work at Pembroke College.

Among many archivists, librarians and museum curators to whom I owe a debt, I am especially grateful to John Clark at the Museum of London, Anne Taylor in Cambridge, Jill Cooke and Abigail Skerrey at Addingham Public Library, and also many staff at the National Monuments Record and in the Brotherton Library, University of Leeds. For help of a more practical kind I am greatly indebted to Peter Hadfield of Addingham and Daniel Pacey of Edinburgh.

Some themes in the book have been discussed at a series of meetings held at different centres in Yorkshire during the years 2004-7, organised jointly with David Cant. I am indebted to Dr Kate Giles for masterminding one of these meetings centred on York Minster and to Dr Paul Barnwell for leading a similar project at Beverley Minster. Through these meetings and also through meetings of the Vernacular Architecture Group I have benefited greatly from conversation with Jenny Alexander, Beth Davis, Mark Girouard, Gwyneth Guy, John McCann, Sarah Pearson, Kirsty Rodwell, Brenda Watkin and others. Over a much longer period the encouragement of Malcolm Airs has contributed greatly to the completion of this book.

Special thanks are due to the Marc Fitch Fund and to the Society of Architectural Historians (Dorothy Stroud bursary) for grants supporting the project.

Acknowledgements regarding sources and copyright of illustrations are provided in the captions to each one. Where drawings are not otherwise acknowledged, they are the responsibility of the author. Every effort has been made to trace owners of copyright and apologies are offered to any copyright-holder who has inadvertently been overlooked.

ABBREVIATIONS AND MEASUREMENTS

Abbreviations in lists of bibliographical references at the ends of chapers:

AMS	Ancient Monuments Society
BAACT	British Archaeological Association Conference Transactions
BOE	Buildings of England
HSLC	Historic [sic] Society of Lancashire and Cheshire
JBAA	Journal of the British Archaeological Association
RCHME	Royal Commission on the Historical Monuments of England
RIBA	Royal Institute of British Architects
VA	Vernacular Architecture (journal)
YAS	Yorkshire Archaeological Society
YVBSG	Yorkshire Vernacular Buildings Study Group

County names

Locations of buildings are given in relation to historic counties, with boundaries as they existed before 1974, because many reference books continue to reflect them, including newly revised editions of the Pevsner architectural guides (BOE). Exceptions to this are the cities of London, Bristol and York, regarded as outside the county structure, and Peterborough, which was once the centre of a small county (or Soke) of its own, but was variously linked to Northamptonshire and Huntingdonshire in reference books and is now in Cambridgeshire. The main danger of confusion between historic counties and modern designations is that the counties into which Yorkshire is now divided do not always correspond well with the historic ridings (abbreviated as East, North and West Ridings) each of which had its own separate county administration. Extra explanation is inserted occasionally to clarify this. In particular, most places referred to here as within the Yorkshire Dales were originally in the West Riding and are now in North Yorkshire.

Measurements

Dimensions are usually given using the international form of the metric system in which millimetres (mm) are preferred to centimetres. However, the craftsmen whose drawings are discussed made their measurements in inches, feet, yards and perches (or rods). Although standards of length varied from place to place during the Middle Ages, in most instances where measurements are quoted, the foot corresponded quite closely to standards used in more recent times, so units of measurement have roughly the following values:

1 inch = 25.4 millimetres
1 foot = 12 inches = 305 millimetres (304.8mm)
1 yard = 3 feet = 914 millimetres (914.4mm)

22 yards = 1 chain
4 perches or rods = 1 chain which is about 20 metres
and 1 perch = 16½ feet or 5.03 metres

CHAPTER 1

STONE-CARVERS: IDENTITIES AND DRAWINGS

(masons and carvers, *c.*1200-1360)

CARVED FOLIAGE

Craftsmen typical of many who built medieval churches can be encountered in a particularly intimate way through the carved stonework of the chapter house at Southwell Minster, Nottinghamshire. The freshness of much of the carving, and the fact that it is untouched by later restorers, gives it an unusual immediacy. The chapter house is octagonal in plan with seats built into its walls along each of seven sides and the entrance occupying most of the eighth side. Each seat has a small blank arch above it supported by slender stone shafts on either side. Above the arches, steep gables reach up towards the large windows. These details are first glimpsed through a richly carved entrance arch (*Plate 1*).

Although the basic architecture has parallels elsewhere, when Southwell chapter house is compared with others, notably at Westminster or Salisbury, what one notices is its relatively modest size and the clear span of its stone-vaulted ceiling, with no central column to provide support. This gives the structure a clarity which is reflected also in the carved foliage that ornaments its architectural forms. As well as foliage, there are corbels supporting the gables, often carved to represent the head of a man or woman – sometimes a stone mason or his wife, but also the occasional king, queen or bishop. Some heads have been destroyed or damaged (*Plate 2*), which is where it is most noticeable that no restoration has been attempted. Yet the crispness of the carved foliage remains, and what is outstanding is its vivid naturalism. The leaves, although of stone, seem as alive as if they were in a hedgerow, and we can recognise hawthorn, oak and maple, and also hops and vines, commonly grown in England when the carvings were made.

There is more carving of a similar kind in the vestibule or corridor that links the chapter house to the church, and the most spectacular work of all is the entrance arch that opens from the vestibule into the chapter house. Here, two bands of vine leaves and grapes are carried right up the arch to the keystone, where a boy is seen picking the grapes.

The remarkable quality of this carving has been the subject of much comment, notably by Nikolaus Pevsner,[1] Jean Givens,[2] Lawrence Stone[3] and Norman Summers,[4] and their questions raise many of the issues that will be pursued in connection with other architectural work in the course of this book: who were the craftsmen (or very occasionally, craftswomen[5]) and how did they set about their work? Did they use drawings or patterns of some other sort? In carving such naturalistic portrayals of different plant species as we see at Southwell, did they perhaps work from life or were 'model drawings' of these plants available?

One possible answer is evident from Pevsner's observation about two capitals carved with the leaves and fruit of hops, that the composition of one is the mirror image of the other. Since the leaves are also the same size, he argues that this is clear evidence that a pattern or drawing was used.[6] If a pattern or template giving a silhouette of some of the leaves was being used, simply turning it over would give the reversed composition. More likely, however, it was a drawing on parchment whose lines would be transferred to the stone by 'pricking through' pin-holes, in which case the composition could be reversed by turning the drawing over and pricking through the holes (or sprinkling flour through them) from the back.

One of the capitals carved with hop leaves is illustrated in Plate 2 (on the left) and is shown more diagrammatically in Figure 1.1. An outline of some of the leaves, such as may have appeared in a parchment drawing, appears in Figure 1.2 (top) with a mirror image of the same outline immediately below. Also depicted in this illustration is another hop-leaf capital, showing the reversed composition of the top row of leaves. Other leaves on this capital have been broken off or damaged, however, and the comparison cannot be carried further.

This pair of examples illustrates how drawings (or patterns made from drawings) were probably used, but questions still arise about whether the carvers were making drawings of their own direct from nature, or whether they were copying drawings made elsewhere, perhaps depicting

Stone-carvers: identities and drawings

Figure 1.1 Capital carved with hop leaves in the Chapter House, Southwell Minster, Nottinghamshire. By comparison with the hop leaves illustrated in Figure 1.2, the carver has given these a smoother finish without indicating veins and folds in leaf surfaces. The different styles of carving are probably characteristic of the work of different craftsmen.

sculpture seen in other buildings. Commenting on Salisbury Cathedral, Pamela Blum notes that carvers working in the chapter house there were influenced by French work and identifies one particular head so similar to a carved head inside the west end of Reims Cathedral as to suggest that the Salisbury artist was working from a drawing made at that cathedral 'and may even have known Reims at first hand'.[7]

Reims Cathedral was influential in England at this time partly because of its close connection with Westminster Abbey, which can be seen in the style and proportions of the choir and transepts of the Abbey. The master mason there between 1245 and 1254 was Henry de Reyns and since 'Reyns' was a common Anglicisation of 'Reims', this name may indicate that Henry had worked at Reims.

Medieval Architectural Drawing

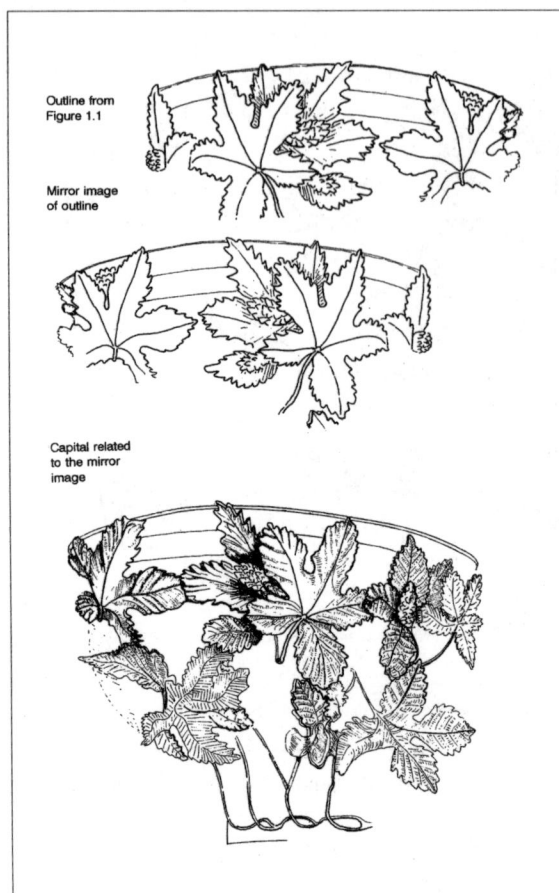

Figure 1.2 Southwell Minster: carving based on a mirror image of the capital illustrated in Figure 1.1. The lower part of the carving is damaged, and the comparison is only clear for the top row of leaves as shown in the two diagrams above.

Carving done at Reims from the 1240s included foliage depicted in a naturalistic, botanically accurate manner. The fashion for this kind of naturalism is subsequently presumed to have spread to Westminster, then to Lincoln and, in the 1280s, to York. The chapter house at York Minster, completed by 1288, has decorative foliage carved only a few years before that at Southwell (presumed to date from the early 1290s). It is similar in quality and style, but the leaves are smaller and the visual effect is rather different.

Southwell was one of the outlying minsters of the Archbishops of York, the others being at Ripon and Beverley, and the Southwell chapter house is clearly related in design to the one at York, most obviously in the fact that both dispense with a central support for their vaulted roofs.

Almost certainly some craftsmen moved from York to Southwell, but it is not clear to what extent similarities in style of carving between these places depended on the movements of skilled men, and to what extent they brought drawings with them. Of particular interest is whether drawings were brought to Southwell from York, from Lincoln, from Westminster or even Reims. Alternatively, did the carvers make their own drawings from living plants they found growing in the countryside near Southwell?

Pevsner was quite explicit about this. He thought that although the leading carvers at Southwell must have been trained in the traditions of York, they must also have been to Reims, 'returning with their sketchbooks full of ... careful drawings of realistic French capitals, which they reproduced when they came back.'[8] It is striking how the existence and regular use of sketchbooks is taken for granted in this statement, and it might perhaps be justified if it can be assumed that craftsmen in France and England followed similar practices. One man who definitely made sketches at Reims 50 years earlier and whose sketches are among the very few that survive from the thirteenth century, was Villard de Honnecourt. He sketched elevations of Reims Cathedral as well as details of machines, and showed different ways of carving human heads, animals and foliage. 'Such a man the master of Southwell must have been', concluded Pevsner.[9]

It is certainly possible that English craftsmen had travelled and had sketched carvings at Reims (and perhaps at the Sainte Chapelle in Paris). However, Jean Givens makes the important point that no matter how much carvers copied work by colleagues, there is a considerable difference between a carver copying a sculpture and copying a living plant.[10] Looking at a living plant, a sculptor starts with an immense amount of visual information from which to select details for making an image in stone. The leaves of the plant will be traversed by more veins than can be shown in stone, while the different textures of the top and underside of a leaf may have to be merely implied. Copying a sculpted plant, though, the carver is presented with pre-selected information. Somebody else has already made decisions about what can be represented in stone and what has to be ignored.

Thus, Givens concludes, the results of different craftsmen studying nature will be much more varied than if they were studying other craftsmen's carvings. If carvers always copy other carvings (or drawings of carvings) there is a loss of accuracy and detail each time. Yet, as Givens observes, the Southwell carvings are often more accurate than those at Reims, and are 'more descriptive'. This 'suggests the observation of life rather than exclusively the copying of images'. Plant species can more often be identified in the carvings at Southwell than at Reims or Westminster.[11]

This conclusion can seem to imply that the Southwell carvers worked directly from plant specimens. However, 'observation of life' by artists is not a matter of a one-off inspection. Repeated attempts are usually made to draw or model the object of interest, and in each attempt the detail of the object will be better understood and different decisions will be made about what to illustrate and what to ignore. Therefore, in addition to drawings made at other buildings where similar carving was done, the Southwell carvings definitely show evidence of drawing or carving from life.

Examples of masons' drawings that survive on the continent are often drawn using a stylus or leadpoint, to be inked in later, and may be on poor quality parchment, much reused.[12] But because parchment was expensive, it is possible that a stone-carver would go through the preliminary sketching phase using other media, perhaps working in chalk on a board or slate. Thus although drawings on parchment were certainly used at this time, there is a likelihood that other media also were used for rough sketches.

Despite such considerations, there have been several distinguished writers on medieval sculpture who have argued that the reason why no drawings seem to survive for carvings such as those at Southwell, is that sculptors made no drawings. They carved directly onto the stone.[13] To anybody personally accustomed to making drawings themselves, this view is not really credible. A skilled carver working directly on stone could certainly produce impressive works of art, but the creative achievement would usually be a response to the material and we would not expect naturalism. This latter kind of art arises from an *intimacy of observation* that comes from repeated attempts to sketch or model a particular subject, and from the visual thinking stimulated by drawing.[14] It even seems possible that the outburst of naturalistic carving that arose in the thirteenth century was made possible because more drawing was being done than earlier in the Middle Ages.

However, evidence for the use of drawings by carvers and sculptors remains disappointingly vague and indirect until almost 1500. In the case of other craftsmen, considered in later chapters, particularly masons designing window tracery and vaulting, drawings survive from a century before Southwell, while for carpenters and other woodworkers, the evidence is at first missing and becomes clear only later.

IDENTITIES OF CRAFTSMEN

When we turn from the question of absent drawings to the craftsmen who may (or may not) have made the drawings, hard evidence is again lacking. There are no surviving building accounts for the Southwell chapter house, and no other records of the number of craftsmen who did the carving. However, on the basis of the style of carving, Pevsner had a strong sense of the identity of the master carver mainly responsible for the archway at the entrance to the chapter house (*Plate 1*). This man did not carve everything on the archway, since at least two styles of carving can be seen there, but he must have been responsible for its overall design and for co-ordinating the work of the other craftsmen. For that reason, and in the absence of his name, he was referred to by Pevsner as the 'master of the entrance arch'[15] and, as already noted, he was considered to have worked previously at York, which was probably where he had learned his trade.

This man's carving of foliage on the archway and within the chapter house itself is vigorous and botanically accurate, but it has a crisp, clean finish that might be thought just a shade unnatural. By contrast, there is also work, clearly by a different carver, where leaves are shown with the ribbed or rippled surface sometimes seen in plants such as hops (as in *Figure 1.2* but not in *1.1*). Pevsner referred to this second carver as the 'dynamic master'.

Two other distinctive personal styles also attracted Pevsner's attention, and this seemed to suggest that most of the carving in the chapter house was done by just four men. However, the present author's observations suggest that although these four represent the main tendencies in carving styles, there are many individual groups of foliage that do not fit neatly into such categories, and there may have been additional carvers in addition to the distinct 'artistic personalities' that Pevsner identified.

Further insight into the number of craftsmen employed may be gained by looking at the carved heads that appear as corbels supporting the little gables above the chapter house seats. There are also head stops on the blank arcading in the vestibule. These are dismissed as of poor artistic quality by writers on sculpture[16] and Pevsner largely disregards them.

Figure 1.3 Carved heads from Southwell Minster (and York, bottom right) posed by the sculptor to include arms and hands, or the whole torso of the boy with the basket. The latter is at the apex of the entrance arch to the chapter house.

However, the heads are of considerable interest in other ways and display a similar range of styles in their carving as the foliage.

One group of heads, for example, is characterised by round, apparently expressionless faces. A good example is the boy picking grapes and putting them in a basket high above the entrance arch. This is a sculpture which is integral to the vine leaves and fruit which surround the figure, and was presumably the responsibility of the 'master of the entrance arch', regarded as the most gifted of the craftsmen here. Several details of this figure are worthy of comment apart from the face, for instance the prominent hands of the subject and the representation of the hair as a few short locks fringing the forehead (*Figure 1.3*, top right).

These details are to be seen in several other sculptured heads within the building, all of which may be the work of the same master. Since head stops do not usually offer scope for showing more than a hint of the shoulders, the way that hands are introduced into this carver's work is particularly striking. In one case, he combines a head stop with a second head below it, in the springing of the arch. Hands rest on the head of the second man below, as in some medieval representations of the devil taking possession of a person's soul (*Figure 1.3*, top left).

Another example of the same carver's work is a 'green man' relief, again having a rounded face without strong expression, although one may detect a suppressed grin in many of these faces and there is an element of humour which serious critics of the carvings tend to miss.

Figure 1.3 compares the several poses in which this carver placed his subjects in order to include the hands. Many other sculptors avoid showing hands, yet this one seems determined to invent ways of introducing them. However, one carving in Figure 1.3 (also in *Plate 3*) is from the chapter house at York, not from Southwell. It represents a man looking upwards to the ceiling with his hands extended downwards to support himself against the stonework over which he leans. Like most similar carving in the York chapter house this was damaged by reformation iconoclasts and was restored in the nineteenth century. Despite the head suffering in this way, the hands are original and suggest an affinity with Southwell. Indeed, this example is included among the Southwell poses in Figure 1.3 as a means of exploring the possibility that the leading carver at Southwell had previously worked in York.

On that basis, it might be argued that all the heads in Figure 1.3 are by this one carver, including the one at York. Not only the hands but also the humour in the carvings is distinctive and the artist responsible was certainly a master of the carving of hands. He can be called the Hands Master and it is likely that he was the same man that Pevsner calls the 'master of the entrance arch'.

In contrast to these light-hearted carvings there are a series of a dozen or more somewhat larger heads at Southwell. They are to be seen mainly on the north-west and north-east walls in the chapter house and are the work of a carver with at least some gift for portraying human features. However, the heads carved by this accomplished master and by the Hands Master account for only about half the sculptured head stops and corbels. The remainder are clearly the work of other carvers, and are so varied in quality that it is necessary to think that some half-dozen craftsmen may have worked on them, perhaps with the apprentices also being given the opportunity to do an occasional carving.

MASONS' MARKS

Efforts to identify carvers according to their style of carving may seem to be less than satisfactory. The contrast between the carvings which show their subjects' hands and the large, formally-sculpted heads may be clear-cut, but when estimates of the number of carvers working at Southwell vary from the four suggested by Pevsner to the six or more indicated above, this way of estimating the number of skilled masons must seem ambiguous and inexact.

When we turn from the carvings to the rectangular stone blocks from which the walls are built, some of these bear masons' marks, three or four of which can be seen in Plate 2 and are more clearly illustrated in Figure 1.4, where it will be noted that there are also two words on one of the stones. These are graffiti, written on the wall much later than when the carving was done. They are probably just names, but one word seems to be 'Mymaud' (mermaid?) and there is certainly a merman carved in the springing of the blank arcading nearby (*Figure 1.3*, centre).

Masons' marks such as these were made by 'banker masons' who cut the stones to shape on a bench known as the banker, usually located in the masons' lodge. The marks were needed where the workforce was being paid according to how many stones they cut and enabled the clerk responsible for wages to identify each individual mason's work. This

Stone-carvers: identities and drawings

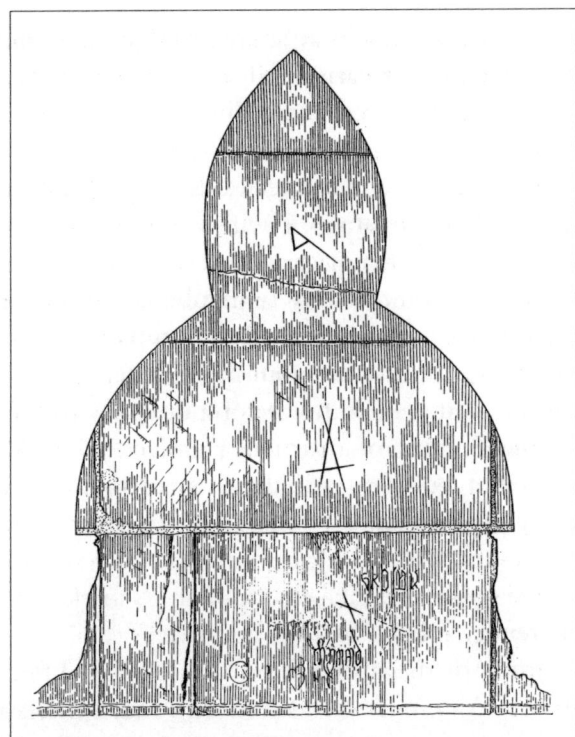

Figure 1.4 Detail of plain walling behind one arch of the blank arcade in the chapter house at Southwell Minster. Three masons' marks can be seen (triangle with tail, A-shape and X-shape) and some later medieval graffiti.

kind of piecework system was usually only applicable for plain walling, whereas carved work was more often paid by the day, in which case there was no point in placing a masons' mark on the stone. Masons' marks, therefore, do not help us identify the carvers.

However, a generation earlier, around 1250-1260, the choir and presbytery of Southwell Minster had been rebuilt by a workforce which consistently used masons' marks throughout the project, and an impressive study of these by Jennifer Alexander has enabled the sequence of construction of the choir and other eastern parts of the church to be better understood.[17] The study shows that an eastern chapel attached to the north transept was built as part of the same project – several masons' marks found in this chapel match marks in the rebuilt choir. Hence, Alexander concludes, the chapel must have been built before the choir workforce was dispersed. This chapel adjoins the vestibule of the chapter house, which was built against it in such a way that buttresses to the north transept are seen in the vestibule where some of the masons' marks may be noted.

The masons' marks at Southwell, Alexander notes, 'were cut freehand using a punch or narrow-edged chisel struck decisively' and were made before the stone was laid in the walls, as can be seen from a few marks which are set in positions 'where it would be physically impossible for them to have been cut afterwards'.[18] While occasionally there are marks that are like miniature drawings, in one case at Southwell representing a door-key, the majority are based on three or four intersecting straight lines formed into easily remembered patterns. What is important to understand is that nearly all the simpler marks reappear frequently in different places at different dates, where they were used by different masons, and they do not belong uniquely to individual masons, except for the duration of a particular project. When Alexander identified 150 different types of mark in the choir, presbytery and north transept chapel at Southwell, that could mean that 150 masons had been employed over the several years it took to complete these works, except that a son would sometimes take over his father's mark when the father died, or an apprentice might take over his master's.[19]

Study of the distribution of marks in different parts of the choir showed Alexander that, for much of the time, masons worked together in teams of between 9 and 13 men in one part of the building, with larger teams of up to 22 elsewhere. Needless to say, the number of people employed could be smaller for a project that proceeded more slowly, but all these findings show that the four or six men thought to have been working on carvings for the chapter house were probably quite a small fraction of all those employed. It should be remembered that as well as banker masons (or freemasons) who cut the stone, there were also layers, who spread mortar and placed the stones in position, and in a building with significant areas of rubble walling this would be built by rough masons. The men who carved foliage and head stops were usually banker masons who had proved to be good at carving and were not the specialist sculptors or 'imagers' who will be encountered later.

While the masons' marks in the chapter house at Southwell occur mainly on plain walling and do not help with the question of how many carvers worked on the foliage (or on the head stops) an instance of masons' marks that may shed more light on how the work of stone cutting and carving was organised is to be seen in the north aisle of the nave at Beverley Minster where, instead of head stops of the modest size seen at Southwell, there is a series of much larger carvings depicting musicians.[20] These date from the 1330s – perhaps 40 years after the work at Southwell – and belong to a phase in the history of Beverley when it was the scene of some of the best sculpture to be seen anywhere in England, much of it concentrated on a monument known as the Percy tomb.[21] An impressive analysis by Nicholas Dawton has identified sculpture on the tomb as the work of five distinct hands.[22]

The carvings of musicians, which seem to reflect the work of just one hand, could be by one of these five sculptors. Each musician is supported by a block of stone approximately 610mm (2ft) wide, with the upper corners cut back to the more oblique shape required for the blank arches in the wall arcade (*Figure 1.5*). Towards one of the bottom corners of each block is a mason's mark, and on the several blocks that support sculptures of musicians, there are five different marks. That could mean that five different banker masons prepared the stone for the carver, cutting the springing of the arches to shape but leaving an empty V-shape where the sculpted musicians were to be fitted. There was probably a division of labour between the banker masons who prepared the stone in the workshop, and the masons who finished the sculpture after the stone had been built into the wall, at which point there would be no risk of damage to delicate parts of the carving while it was being moved.

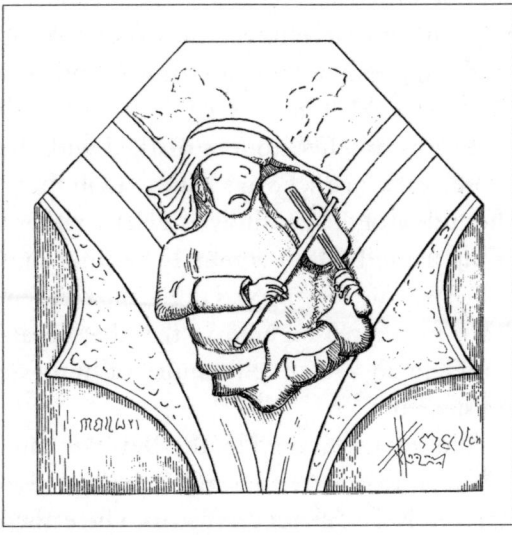

Figure 1.5 Beverley Minster, East Riding of Yorkshire: schematic representation of a carving in the north aisle of the nave. The carving is supported by a block of stone 610mm (2ft) wide. On this particular stone there is a mason's mark on the lower right corner with the name Malton scratched alongside it. The same name, written rather differently, occurs again on the left.

Thus even if we are right in thinking that the finished carvings represent the work of one craftsman, probably with an assistant or apprentice who might begin the carving of each roughed-out blank, the five banker masons whose marks can be seen also made a considerable contribution. Similarly at Southwell, where we see work by four principal carvers, there would always be other masons involved. The rough finish of some of the less prominent heads suggests that assistants and banker masons were all allowed to have a go at some carvings.

It is worth adding that the carvings of musicians at Beverley are thought to have been completed in the 1330s, and that in 1335, a mason named William de Malton (from Huggate) was appointed master mason by the chapter of Beverley Minster.[23] It is thought that William had been working at the Minster for some time before gaining this appointment, so it is possible that he was one of the banker masons whose marks are associated with the carvings of musicians. Alternatively, it is possible that William de Malton was more concerned with overall design and with window tracery.

One point that may be relevant is that some words are scratched on the stonework (*Figure 1.5*), rather like the graffiti at Southwell (*Figure 1.4*). They are within easy reach of anybody walking in the north aisle and therefore could have been written at any time during the next seven centuries. However, it is striking that the name Malton appears twice, apparently in two different medieval hands, on the block of stone which supports the carving of a fiddler (*Figure 1.5*). In one place, 'Malton' is written very close to the mason's mark on this piece of stone, leading to the suggestion that the name identifies this as the personal mark of William de Malton.[24]

Nearby, another stone is marked with the name Myllyngton, written more neatly in a scholar's hand, and in that case it seems more likely that the author of the graffito was a cleric rather than a mason. However, even if the name Malton is merely another graffito, written a considerable time after the carving was done, the fact remains that William de Malton was a master mason here, so that the repeated name on this block could represent an authentic memory of him even if, quite probably, it is not his signature.

Another issue raised by the Beverley musician carvings, especially the fiddler, is that there are similar carvings elsewhere in the region, though apparently by different sculptors. The earliest is at St Mary's Abbey, York, perhaps carved just before 1300 (*Plate 4*). Another fiddler is located on the back of the reredos at Beverley, and a fourth, considerably later in date, is in the gatehouse of Bridlington Priory. It may be that similarities in pose between these four carvings of fiddlers arise from the posture necessary to play a violin combined with the necessity, on a boss or corbel, of producing a greatly shortened figure. However one might again wonder whether there was a drawing in circulation among local carvers which they modified with regard to headgear, beard and other details, according to their own individual taste. However, the best evidence for use of drawings by Beverley craftsmen is in the stained glass. Some glass formerly in nave aisle windows dating from *c.*1330-40 is closely related to York Minster glass. Some is so similar it must be based on the same cartoon as was used for two aisle windows at the west end of York by Thomas de Bouesdun.[25]

The carving of the fiddler from St Mary's Abbey was on a boss looking down from a vault. It is now detached from the building, and can be seen in the Yorkshire Museum (which occupies part of the abbey site). In this location parts of the boss that would have been hidden within joints are visible and display another kind of mason's mark – not a banker mark identifying a workman for payment purposes, but an assembly mark or position mark in the form of a cross showing which way round the boss should go when fitted into the vault (*Plate 4*). Also visible is a straight line, scribed on the stone as a centre line, to guide the cutting of the moulding on the vaulting rib. Whether or not carvers had drawings on parchment, they certainly drew guidelines and outlines on the stones they were working. On other faces, where a critical joint was to be made, the stonework of this boss was quite deeply grooved to enable molten lead to be poured in to secure the bond.[26]

TYPES, PORTRAITS AND CRAFTSMEN IN PERSON

The fiddlers and other musicians represented in the north aisle at Beverley Minster are quite obviously meant to represent musicians as 'types'. The emphasis is not on the facial features that would now be regarded as important in a portrait, but on the odd poses they adopted in their energetic playing and on the flamboyant headgear some of them wore, often suggesting turbans.

Similarly, the head stops at Southwell Minster represent types rather than individual people. There are kings, queens and bishops, easily recognisable by their headgear; there are women wearing the fashionable hats of the time (one, with damaged chin, in *Plate 2*), and there are also men wearing skull-caps and bonnet-like hoods such as were worn by artisans of many kinds, but particularly by stone masons. However certain heads here and in many churches are persistently identified as personal likenesses of individuals. One head at Southwell with a flat-topped hat is often said to represent the master mason in charge of building the chapter house,[27] even though his headgear makes it more likely that he was intended as some other type, perhaps a clerk or priest. If he was connected with the building project, he might have been the clerk-of-works.

The chapter house at Salisbury Cathedral contains clearer examples, including some 'very life-like head corbels', but again, they are probably not portraits.[28] One has already been mentioned as perhaps based on a drawing made at Reims. Others have the caps worn by masons and if we compare heads of this kind in the chapter houses at Salisbury and Southwell with other carvings in the cathedrals at Wells, Bristol and Lincoln, it seems clear that there was a mason 'type' which is always recognisable despite variations with regard to beard (or lack of it) or with regard to the nature of the cap (either sewn leather or cloth, or else knitted). However, this does not mean that all masons wore such headgear all the time. When actually on the job, some wore tunics with hoods that could be pulled over the head when required for more protection than a cap afforded.[29]

It can be argued that an interest in facial expression of the kind that is necessary to produce real portraits was first seen in England at Westminster Abbey in the middle of the thirteenth century, particularly in a series of heads that are rarely seen because they are high up in the south transept and choir. The majority are still types, or 'idealised heads', including a dreaming youth, a laughing man and an African, but some are more individual and expressive.[30]

Despite the evident lack of real portraiture in thirteenth-century carving, the biographical dictionary of medieval craftsmen and 'architects' by John Harvey includes a select list of masons' portraits in cases where he thought there could be no doubt about the identification.[31]

One of the most memorable examples is to be found high up towards the west end of the north nave triforium in Wells Cathedral. It depicts a

Figure 1.6 Heads with stone masons' caps in buildings associated with the master mason Adam Lock (died 1229): in Bristol (left) and Wells (right).

bearded man with flowing hair and a mason's cap and is often identified as Adam Lock, the master mason responsible for building the west end of the nave. In a recent study, Warwick Rodwell does not dissent from this identification,[32] but he does point to other sculptures at Wells which show more signs of real portraiture.

Adam Lock's career has been reconstructed from documents, as well as from the evidence of buildings, by Colchester and Harvey,[33] and by Sampson.[34] The latter believes that Lock may have been employed at Wells from the 1180s, and may have worked as a carver in the western arcades of the transepts, where perhaps he executed some of the human and animal figures that enliven the capitals. It is then thought that he became master mason in charge of work on the nave at Wells, perhaps from *c.*1205.

About 1219 or 1220, a letter from the abbot of St Augustine's Abbey at Bristol to the dean of Wells referred to a craftsman only by the initial L. The abbot was asking for his help in building a lady chapel at Bristol (now the Elder Lady Chapel in Bristol Cathedral). Lock probably spent some time working on that project, but he continued to live in Wells and work on the cathedral there, and on his death in 1229 a reference was found in his will to his wife and the house they occupied.[35]

Colchester and Harvey show that mouldings at Bristol were so similar to some mouldings at Wells that the same templates may have been used, making it seem that Lock took templates with him when he worked at Bristol.[36] Further evidence of his presence has been seen in carved heads of stone masons just below the springing of the (later) vault in the chapel he is thought to have built.[37] Situated in singularly badly-lit locations, these heads are hard to assess, but the fact that there are two masons' heads indicates that they represent the mason as a type rather than any particular individual. The head stop located toward the west end at Wells is similar in outline, with beard and close-fitting cap (*Figure 1.6*), but the face is less expressive and the beard more formally trimmed. This must be work of a different carver and Sampson estimates that it was carved at about the time of Adam Lock's death in 1229, and could be a memorial to him, but not a portrait.[38] Even more than the heads at Bristol, the carving appears to represent the type of a senior mason rather than the likeness of one specific man. Even so, in its context high up in the nave at Wells, this is an effective and moving sculpture which one senses must commemorate Adam Lock in some way.

TRACES OF DRAWING

Lock may have supervised the laying of foundations for the west front of Wells Cathedral, but he died before construction had proceeded very far, and was succeeded as master mason by Thomas Norreys. Work proceeded through the 1230s, and was completed in 1245.

The west front was conceived as a screen with niches for the display of sculpture and today has the largest surviving collection of medieval figure sculpture in Britain. Subjects include people mentioned in the New Testament on the southern half of the elevation and characters from the Old Testament on the northern half, with some later saints, English kings and other notables worked into the scheme. Christ is seated in majesty (now as a modern sculpture) in the highest niche at the centre of the elevation.

While the minor sculpture considered earlier, at Southwell as at Wells, was integral to the structure and was carved by masons on the regular

Stone-carvers: identities and drawings

workforce, the statues on the west front at Wells are likely to be the work of specialist sculptors or imagers, perhaps from Bristol and Glastonbury. From tool marks on the stone, Jerry Sampson has shown that they used a three-inch (76mm) axe for roughing-out the general shape of a statue, then flat chisels (10 and 16mm in size) and gouges. There was also occasional use of a drill for under-cutting.[39]

Work on a statue began with an outline drawn on the stone surface that was going to be carved. Preliminary drawing might be in chalk or leadpoint, but what can still sometimes be seen are scribed lines, cut into the surface of the stone with a hard metal point. Examining the statues from scaffolding, Sampson found scribed lines on the backs of some of them, representing fragments of the original drawing. He noted, though, that there is still uncertainty about what drawings may have existed in other forms, perhaps on parchment.[40]

This example can be paralleled by many others in later chapters, where the identities of individuals are unknown, but where detailed observation of tooling and other kinds of mark can tell us a lot about the craftsmen and how they organised their work. At Southwell and Beverley, masons' marks give an indication of the size of the workforce and suggest ideas about division of labour between banker masons, layers and carvers. Despite the anonymity of many craftsmen, two have been mentioned who are relatively well documented: Adam Lock at Wells and William de Malton at Beverley. There are also instances where carving was so distinctive in style that the carver can be identified by his work even when his name is not known, as with the Hands Master at Southwell, who was probably the mason Pevsner identified as the 'master of the entrance arch'.

In many instances, it is clear that carving was done by masons who also worked on the structural stonework of buildings. This is sometimes claimed for both Adam Lock and William de Malton. Hence study of minor sculpture may sometimes be relevant to understanding the careers of master masons who designed buildings.

However, the questions that have been asked about the drawings used by craftsmen have not been satisfactorily answered. There is the evidence from the mirror-image carvings at Southwell, which seems to imply that outlines of leaves were pricked through from a parchment drawing. There are scribed centre lines on carved bosses at St Mary's Abbey, York (*Plate 4*), and scribed outlines remaining on some sculpture at Wells, but little more than that survives. The greater naturalism of carved foliage and of some carved heads at Southwell and other places in the 1280s and 1290s may suggest sketching or modelling from life, but no sketches remain.

Although this evidence for drawing is frustratingly vague, it is worth noting the indication that some masons kept small collections of their own drawings and patterns. Not long after the musicians were carved at Beverley, there are documentary references to 'patterns' in the possession of carpenters (Chapter 4), and when a London 'imager' or sculptor named John de Mymmes died in 1349 his widow, Maud, inherited his stock of tools and 'patterns' with instructions to give some of them to an apprentice for whom she was now responsible.[41] However, the reference is vague, and it is not clear whether the 'patterns' were sketches, full-size cartoons for sculpture, or perhaps templates. Later chapters will show some real, surviving drawings by craftsmen and will discuss evidence from other marks and numbers, and from setting-out lines.

CHAPTER 2

EARLY ARCHITECTURAL DRAWING

(masons' drawings on walls and tracing floors to *c.*1360)

VARIETIES OF DRAWING

One reason for believing that the carvers and sculptors discussed in the previous chapter must have made drawings, despite the lack of surviving examples, is that the majority of carvers were stone masons, and among masons, drawing was a well-established practice. Their architectural drawings, where they remain from the thirteenth or fourteenth centuries, consist largely of lines marked out with compasses whose metal points scored or sometimes quite deeply cut the surface on which the mason was working.

Figure 2.1, for example, is a copy of a drawing on a wall at Ely Cathedral dating from the 1250s. The wall was covered with a thin skim of plaster which has mostly flaked away, but the main lines of the drawing were so emphatically scribed with a compass point that they incised the stone as well as the plaster. Another example of a drawing on a plastered wall once existed at Castle Acre Priory, Norfolk. In 1881, according to G.G. Coulton, severe frosts peeled a layer of plaster from one of the niches in the south transept and revealed an earlier plaster surface, on which 'an elaborate decorated window had been sketched'. The drawing appeared to have been done soon after the plaster had been applied, while it was still wet. A few years later, 'other frosts destroyed this also; and in 1913 only a few strokes were yet visible'.[1]

Medieval drawings that survive on stone or plaster surfaces like this are of several types, some being small sketches, while others are large formal drawings. Neither meets the expectations of historians accustomed to

Figure 2.1 Ely Cathedral, Cambridgeshire: Drawing of a window inscribed on the interior of the south wall of the Galilee Porch, c.1250. The small drawing to the right showing two circles touching (with some other arcs) appears to be related to the design within the large circle at the top of the window, which was itself developed from pairs of touching circles. Measured copy, July 2002; scale bar is 200mm.

seeing drawings on parchment or paper who, until recently, assumed that early medieval builders did not make drawings as part of the process of design.

Pictorial drawings of buildings were made before this, of course, and later became common in manuscript illumination and stained glass windows, but there are said to have been no drawings of any practical use to a working mason. Buildings were designed on site it is claimed, without drawing as an 'intermediary stage'. So J.S. Ackerman in 1998 stated that documentation 'of the origins of ... architectural drawing begins with the graphic records of the workshop of Reims in the second decade of the thirteenth century'.[2]

Branner also cited drawings on parchment from Reims Cathedral and mentioned the sketches of Villard de Honnecourt, many of which were also done at Reims.[3] In addition, Branner noted the significance of drawings made on the stonework of buildings and on tracing floors. Examples he mentioned include 'stencils' for the springing of a vault inscribed on stone at Southwark Cathedral, London, discovered in the nineteenth century. These turn out to be setting-out lines and curves marked on stone to guide the cutting and placing of stone components of the vault, and are not design drawings. He also cited quite extensive drawings on stone floors in French cathedrals, notably Soissons (c. 1235) and Clermont (or Clermont-Ferrand).[4]

The present book is concerned specifically with English architecture and, rather than illustrating French examples (even from Villard's justly famous sketchbook) the aim is to study such drawings as exist in England. Apart from a handful of rather late drawings on parchment, several earlier drawings have been found on the fabric of medieval buildings, notably at Lincoln by Jenny Alexander[5] and in Yorkshire by Stuart Harrison.[6] Important sixteenth-century examples which show the persistence of medieval forms of drawing have also been documented, in Gloucestershire by Kirsty Rodwell[7] and in Hampshire by John Crook.[8]

One of the earliest examples is at Byland Abbey in the North Riding of Yorkshire, probably dating from soon after 1200. Here, Harrison and Barker have shown that a fragment of drawing on a floor slab is part of an accurate, full-size representation of the rose window in the west front of the abbey church and another drawing, on a wall rather than a floor, is a detail of the centre of the window. Plate 19 shows the interior of the ruined nave looking towards the west end, with the remains of the large rose window clearly visible. The site of the mural drawing, just inside the west front, is to the right of the main doorway, where the stonework is quite weathered. Even so, fragments of the drawing can still be seen (Plate 20), and are drawn out in Figure 2.2. Harrison and Barker used these drawings together with the remaining stonework to reconstruct the design of the window.[9] Not far away at Gisborough Priory there are full-size profiles of shafts and piers inscribed on a stone floor in the Priory Church.[10]

Some full-size drawings such as these were used to make templates, that is, flat wooden patterns which gave the mason a set of outlines for the shape he was cutting in stone. Templates were often made of beech or imported oak from the Baltic region, but there are also occasional references to templates cut from lead sheet.[11] It was an advantage to do the drawings on a floor (referred to as a 'tracing floor' if set aside for drawing) because templates could be laid out on it, and a table would usually be too small for the design of a large window.

When drawings were made on a wall, they could be useful to work out design ideas, check detail or guide assembly, but were less useful for working directly with templates. At Byland Abbey, it is assumed that the detail of the rose window drawn on the wall also appeared on the

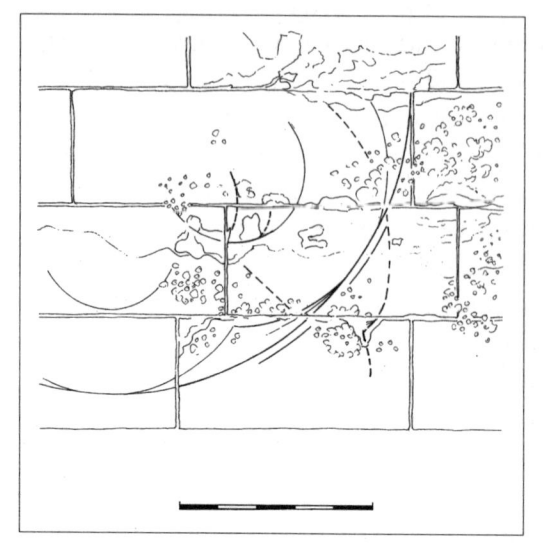

Figure 2.2 Byland Abbey, North Riding. Fragment of drawing inscribed inside the west wall of the church, including the same detail as seen in Plate 20, for which this illustration provides a key. Dashed lines are marks on the stone that are not part of the original drawing. The scale bar is approximately 500mm.

tracing floor, which is where the templates would have been made. The evidence for the Byland tracing floor is important as it represents what seems to be the earliest surviving example in England of such a floor. However other Cistercian abbeys in Yorkshire, notably Kirkstall and Fountains, had rose windows dating from *c.*1155-60 which were almost certainly constructed in the same way as the later one at Byland, using similar tracing-floor drawings.[12]

Contemporary with or a little later than the round window at Byland is a much smaller round window at the Temple Church in London with eight spokes radiating from a central roundel. The architect who uncovered it during a restoration of the church in the 1860s found lines scratched on the stones of the outer rim of the wheel which seemed to show that the shape to which each stone was to be cut was drawn on it individually without using a template.[13] This implies that the stones themselves were laid out on top of a drawing rather than the drawing being used to make a template. That would be feasible for a small window such as this one, with only eight voussoirs in its outer rim, but the method suggested might not have been so satisfactory for a window as large and elaborate as the rose window which once existed at Byland.

Even so, the evidence from the window at the Temple Church should be a warning against too readily assuming that cutting stone to shape for windows, arches, vaults and doorways always depended on a three-stage process: 1) drawing on a tracing floor 2) production of templates from the drawing 3) use of templates to guide the cutting of the stone.

An alternative method of ensuring that the stone components of a window or arch would fit together was to lay them out on top of an outline drawn on the ground (or on a paved floor). Adjustments to shapes could then be made by direct comparison of the component with the outline drawing and with other components, without a template. This is comparable to methods used by carpenters, to be described in Chapter 4, where a frame would be assembled in a horizontal position on the ground. The components of the frame would then be numbered, so that when the horizontal assembly on the ground was taken apart, the sequence in which it was to be re-erected vertically would be clear. Occasionally stonework is seen to be numbered in the same way as members of timber structures were and, in such instances, we may suspect that the stones were cut using 'carpenters' methods', that is with a drawn outline on the ground, but without using templates.

The evidence from Byland Abbey and Gisborough Priory, however fragmentary, is that tracing floors were being used several decades before 'architectural drawings' have been otherwise documented. However, Jean Bony has shown that even earlier, at Durham Cathedral, full-size drawings leading to the production of templates were probably used to achieve the precision evident in the stonework of the great piers, with their prominent spiral patterns, first in the choir, and then in the transepts and nave. Unfortunately, nothing survives of these drawings.[14]

Following this evidence regarding early tracing floors, there is no further information until after 1300, but at that time there are several references to 'tracing houses', most notably at the former St Stephen's Chapel in the Palace of Westminster, where the tracing house (*trasura* in Latin) may have been a temporary building that was specially erected for use while the chapel was being built and may have had a floor of oak boards. It was specifically mentioned in 1331 when a master mason named Thomas of Canterbury was working there on templates (or 'moulds') – or perhaps he was actually doing some drawing, for the wording is unclear. Master Thomas was probably the designer of much of the chapel, which was destroyed in the great fire at the Palace of Westminster in 1834, and he also worked on the Tower of London.[15]

Apart from drawings on tracing floors, there is a range of other drawings to consider, most of them on the fabric of buildings and scribed on stone or plaster with a metal point. Drawings on stone surfaces at Gloucester will be discussed in Chapter 5, one showing the profile of a moulding. Other such drawings more often represent window tracery and some can be recognised as small, preliminary sketches drawn by masons when they were developing designs for windows. At Lincoln Cathedral, there are several small mural drawings made with compasses, some of which are probably preliminary ideas for the large round window made in the 1220s which is known as the Bishop's Eye.[16]

At Cambridge, there is a small drawing of a late thirteenth-century window with 'geometrical' tracery on a slab of stone (or more specifically, clunch) that was found at St John's College. The drawing is quite small – it measures only 145mm x 90mm – and is on a slab about 190mm square.[17] On a plastered wall at Christchurch Priory, Hampshire, also dating from the late thirteenth century, is a drawing of a similar window with geometrical tracery, but this time the drawing is likely to be full size.[18] These two drawings are similar to, but more elaborate than, the drawing in the Galilee porch at Ely Cathedral previously mentioned (*Figure 2.1*). This seems to be a preliminary design for windows inserted into the older walls of the south transept around 1250. Among various circle patterns inscribed nearby on the same wall, one appears to be a trial for the design of the cusps in the upper part of the window, built up from circles that touched at the centre of the large circular light.

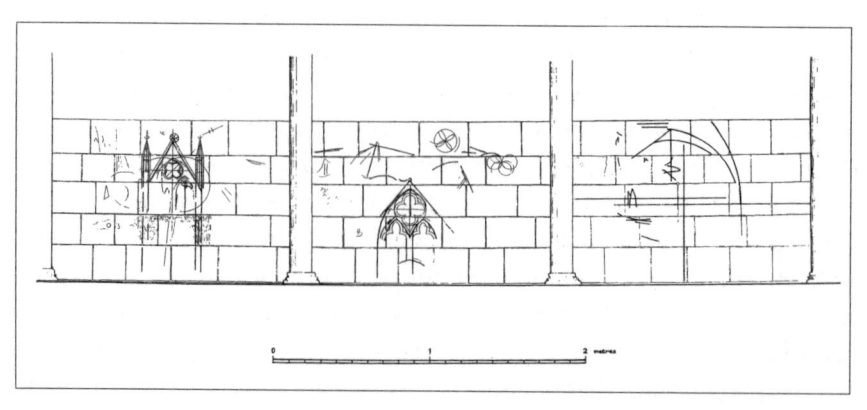

Figure 2.3 Ely Cathedral, Cambridgeshire: Overall view of a group of drawings on the interior of the south wall of the Galilee Porch. The drawings are divided into three sections by detached shafts in front of the wall, and the window design shown in Figure 2.1 is in the central bay. An elevation is drawn on the left, and there are longer radius curves on the right. Measured copy, July 2002; scale bar is 2m.

Figure 2.4 St Mary's Church, Gamlingay, Cambridgeshire. Rubbing of a small drawing amongst graffiti on the third pier in the north arcade of the nave showing a fourteenth-century window. The broad white line across the rubbing is a mortared joint in the stonework. Scale bar is 100mm.

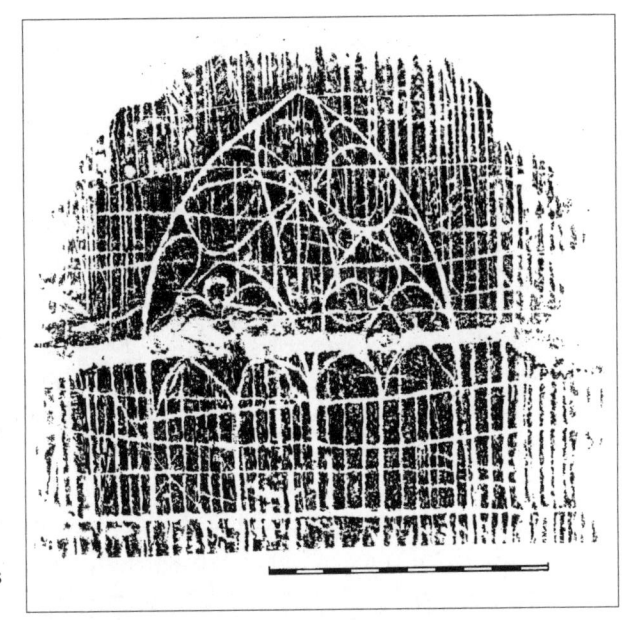

Maddison interprets the whole group of drawings as evidence that the Galilee Porch at Ely was temporarily used as a tracing house around 1250. This is more than a century earlier than the documentary evidence for a stone-paved tracing house at Ely,[19] but it is relevant to note that some curves on the wall of the Galilee Porch were made using large compasses such as were needed for work on tracing floors. These curves are not part of any identifiable drawing on the wall (*Figure 2.3*) and may be simply the result of the compasses being tried out. They do, however, suggest a tracing floor in the vicinity, which could have been in a temporary building nearby, or it could be that the porch itself was temporarily closed and its main ground-floor surface used. Least likely in this instance, the tracing floor could have been in the roof space about the porch vault.

Other sketches of window tracery may still be seen in churches at Leighton Buzzard (Bedfordshire)[20] and at several places in Cambridgeshire and Hertfordshire.[21] Most belong to the next century, that is, after 1300, and most are just sketches, made without drawing instruments. Many sketches of this kind can be regarded as casual graffiti, but where drawings appear to be serious representations of windows (*Figure 2.4*), and particularly where compasses were used in drawing them, they can sometimes be understood as preliminary ideas for window designs.

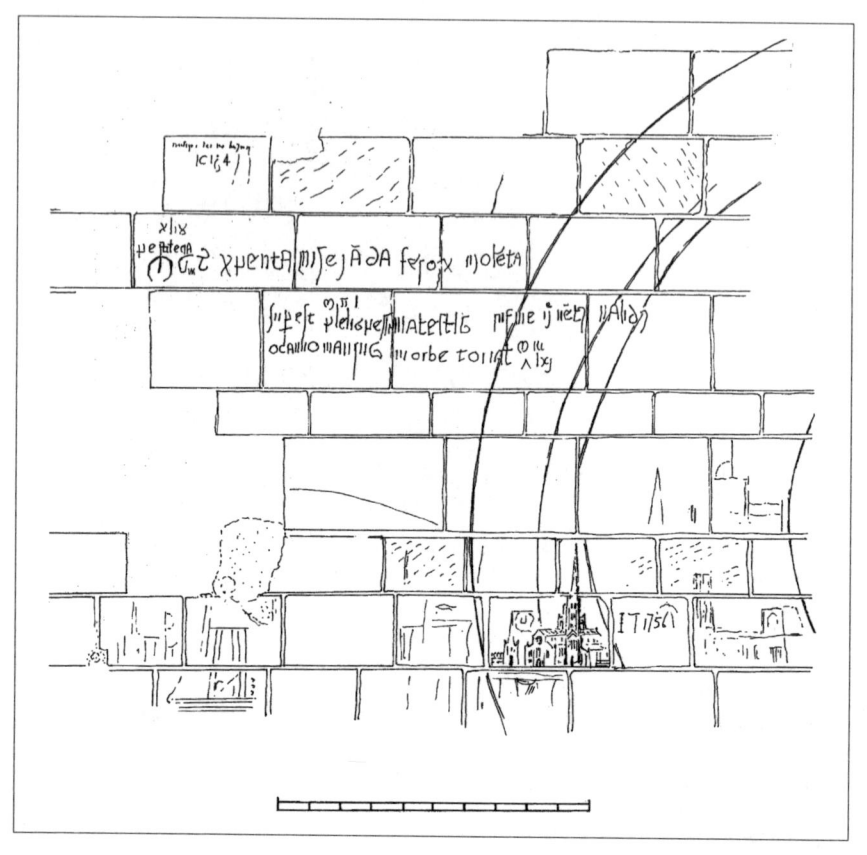

Figure 2.5 St Mary's Church, Ashwell, Hertfordshire; graffiti on an internal elevation of the north wall of the tower with arcs of three or four large circles and small drawings of buildings. The incised wording refers to the Black Death and other outbreaks of plague. The last line ends with the date 1361 written as $^{mccc}\Lambda$ lxj. A tree-ring date on beams above thought to be original to the tower is 1365–76. Copied and measured July 2000; scale bar is 1m.

St Mary's Church at Ashwell in Hertfordshire has a great variety of fourteenth- and fifteenth-century drawings on its walls,[22] some of which can be dismissed as casual graffiti, and others of which may be exercises in geometry. However, there are also serious architectural drawings dating from the time in the 1360s when the church tower was being built and there are curves on a wall which appear to have been made using large compasses such as were required for work on a tracing floor (*Figure 2.5*). The latter may indicate that a tracing floor existed in or near the base of the tower when this part of the church was under construction.

Figure 2.6 St Mary's Church, Ashwell, Hertfordshire; drawing on a wall at the west end of the south aisle showing the pointed and cusped head of a narrow lancet window. The plan of the window opening is also indicated, with the oblique line at A representing the external face of the splayed window jamb, and the three lines at B showing variant designs for the inner face. The scale bar is 100mm. Tracing, April 2001.

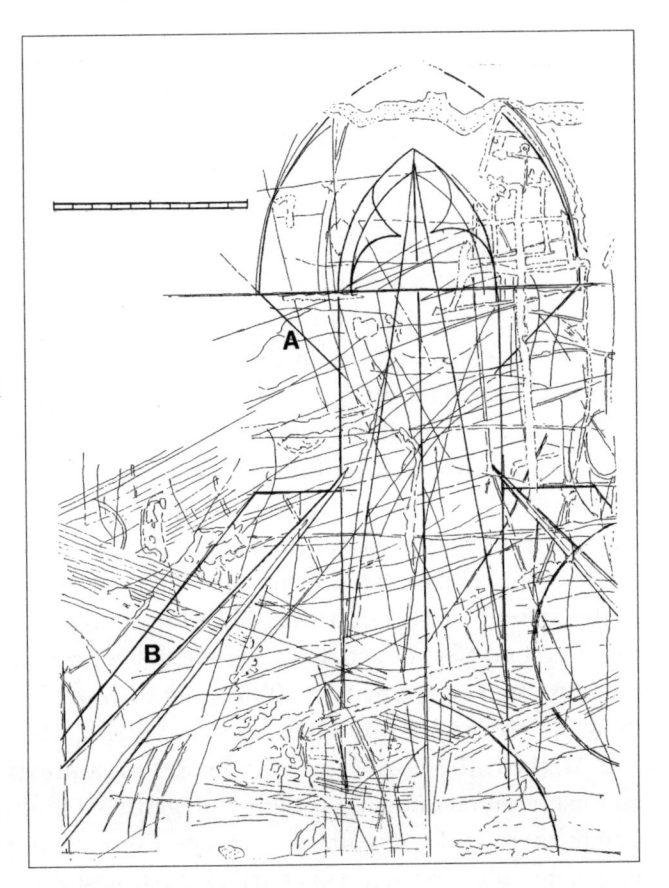

On another wall is a simple but precise drawing of a lancet window or perhaps one of the narrow slit windows used in the tower (*Figure 2.6*). The window head is set out with compasses and a plan of the window opening is superimposed on the elevation. The wall on which the drawing appears is actually a buttress to the tower, although now within the south aisle of the church. The drawing is not easy to see among a confusion of later graffiti that surrounds it.

TRACING FLOORS AND DRAWING INSTRUMENTS

It will be clear from these examples that there are several kinds of drawing to be found on the fabric of thirteenth and fourteenth-century buildings, including large drawings on tracing floors, sketches of window detail and geometrical drawings made for practice or for instructional purposes, or sometimes just to check the adjustment of compasses, which may explain the circles that appear in Figure 2.3. There are also, of course, many graffiti that have nothing to do with architectural drawing at all.

Some discrimination between different kinds of drawing can be made by taking note of what instruments were used: freehand sketches drawn without instruments will often be graffiti unrelated to architectural design. Drawings made with a small pair of compasses and a straight-edge are often preliminary design sketches or practice drawings.

However, curves drawn with very large, long-radius compasses, such as were used for making full-size drawings of window tracery, may be clues to the existence of tracing floors in the vicinity. Examples of such long-radius curves on walls at Ely Cathedral and at Ashwell (Hertfordshire) have been mentioned, and these two sites are included in the present analysis of tracing-floor locations. On this basis, evidence for several possible or actual tracing floors has been mentioned and two are illustrated (see especially *Plate 5*). Four have – or had – surviving drawings (Byland, Gisborough, York and Wells) while at two sites (Ely and Ashwell) the use of large compasses in contexts where there are also many mural drawings is highly suggestive, and there are also places where there is documentary evidence for a tracing floor or tracing house, notably at St Stephen's Chapel, Westminster. Other documentary records will be mentioned later.

The discussion so far is inevitably biased towards drawings made on bare stone walls or on plastered surfaces, simply because of their durability. However, in 1377, when a well-known mason from Gloucester, Master Robert Lesyngham, went to Exeter to design new cloisters, parchment was purchased on which he was to draw the plan (*forma*). In 1390, another 'skin of parchment' was bought for two pence so that the same Master Robert could 'paint a design for the new east window'.[23] Neither of these drawings now exists.

There is also documentary evidence that some drawings were set out on wooden boards. In one Scottish instance drawings were being made on the actual boards from which templates or moulds were to be made.[24] If similar practices were common in England the problem of transferring lines from a drawing on the tracing floor to the wooden surface from which the template was cut would be avoided.

Alternatively, if complete drawings were made on the tracing floor, details could be transferred from the floor to a board by going over the relevant part of the drawing with a moist lampblack mixture, then placing the board on top of the drawing. The impression made on the board where the lampblack had adhered would, of course, be a mirror image of the drawing on the floor, but when the template was cut to shape and then turned over, it would fit the drawing. Building accounts sometimes include purchase of lampblack in contexts which suggest some procedure of this sort.[25]

Most drawings began with a base line on which the mason placed his compass point to mark the first and most prominent curves in his drawing. Often, too, he marked a centre line for the drawing, at right angles to the base line. One clue to the nature of drawings that have disappeared from tracing floors is the occasional survival of a line along which metal compass points have left a series of holes. One such line examined on the tracing floor at York shows so many compass points that it was quite clearly the base line of an intricate drawing, but the rest of the drawing is missing, perhaps because it was set out on template boards that were laid out on the floor, or else because it was in chalk and has long since been wiped away.[26]

Alongside documentary references to tracing floors there are also references to small drawing-boards made of wood. Oak boards imported from Baltic ports were often bought for this purpose and at the Palace of Westminster in 1323 were referred to as 'Estrich boards' (East Reich boards). However when 50 Estrich boards were purchased in 1332 to make the tracing house (*trasura*) larger, it sounds very much as if the tracing floor itself was made from such boards.[27] When drawing-boards or tracing floors were of wood, they could well have been employed in the same way as the trestle tables on which makers of stained glass drew out full-size cartoons for their window designs. The surface of the trestle table was usually whitewashed, and charcoal was then used for drawing on it.[28]

Much later, it should be noted, floors of mould lofts used by shipbuilders were usually of wood, with the drawings either scribed with metal points or done in chalk. It is conceivable that there were more timber-boarded tracing floors than we are now aware of and it could be that, instead of being whitened with whitewash like glazier's tables, wooden tracing floors were given a thin skim of plaster to produce a smoother surface for drawing.

One final way in which drawings may possibly have been done is on 'dust boards' such as were used for calculations and for geometry. A table or tray was sprinkled evenly with moist sand and a stylus (often referred to as a 'radius') was used to write or draw in the sand. In one version of his translation of Euclid's geometry, Adelard of Bath, in the 1120s, described a demonstration in geometry by a master who drew with a stick on a table covered with sand.[29]

It is most unlikely that this last method was used for architectural drawing, except that a thin sprinkling of dust on a tracing floor could have served to obscure scribed lines remaining from earlier drawings. However, reference to dust boards can serve as reminder of the unexpected and wide range of surfaces used for drawing around 1200. The few surviving tracing floors and mural drawings give the false impression that plaster or stone were the only surfaces used. There are examples of stone tracing floors in French cathedrals and there is the evidence from Byland Abbey and Gisborough Priory. At Ely Cathedral, although the nature of the tracing floor related to the drawings in the Galilee Porch is unknown, there is reference to a later tracing floor that had a paved stone surface. It was constructed in 1387 next to a masons' lodge whose members seem to have had typical occupational names: stones for the floor were dressed smooth ('scappled') by Peter Mason, and the paving was laid by John Leyer.[30]

So far, apart from drawings on parchment, three other kinds of surface have been identified as being used for drawing: wooden boards, stone walls (and paving) and plaster. It is thought that beaten earth and clay floors were sometimes used as well. Colchester and Harvey noted that plaster is mentioned very frequently[31] and many of their references may indicate a drawing surface improvised by laying a thin layer of plaster over an existing floor to give a smoother, more even finish. However, 'plaster' could indicate all kinds of mixtures in which lime was used with sifted ashes, dung and clay, all of which could provide hard, smooth surfaces suitable for drawing.

Although improvised tracing floors laid over ordinary floor surfaces do not survive in England, simply because the floors of most buildings have been replaced more than once, we get an indication of where they may have been by noting the locations of architectural sketches on walls. Assuming that masons most often made their sketches close to where they were drawing more formally, then at Ashwell and other

Hertfordshire and Cambridgeshire churches it seems likely that floors in the western parts of aisles or naves may have been used for the small number of drawings needed in building an ordinary parish church. In other instances, stonework for windows was bought in ready-made from the quarry, in which case no tracing-floor drawings would be needed at the church itself. If it is true that the ground floor of the Galilee Porch at Ely was briefly used as a tracing house in the 1250s, it is worth nothing that the main role of the porch may have been its use in the important Palm Sunday and Easter processions, and that during other seasons access to it could be restricted so that the floor could be used for drawing.[32]

At Vale Royal Abbey in Cheshire, there is reference in 1359 to the north transept of the church being used as a tracing house,[33] which would probably mean the floor of the transept itself, not an upper room. In many large churches the north transept would have been a part of the building that could be roped off without much inconvenience and in several places may have been used for drawing. For Vale Royal, there are contracts with the master mason who was working there in 1359, William de Helpeston. They mention the transept tracing house, and also refer to templates, using the old word for them and saying that William could 'change and ordain his moulds' at his discretion.[34]

The choice of what floor space to use for drawing would often have been dictated by the large size of the drawing required. For example, Tatton-Brown suggests that when the spire of Salisbury Cathedral was under construction, it would probably have been necessary to have a full-size drawing of the whole thing. The only place where such an enormous drawing could be set out under cover was on the floor of the cathedral nave.[35]

It should be borne in mind also that tracing houses were sometimes constructed as temporary buildings quite separate from the building being erected. In contrast, the stone floor at Byland was at first-floor level, above the abbey warming house,[36] and the tracing floors at York and Wells are both on an upper level.

GYPSUM PLASTER FLOORS

The surviving tracing floors at York and Wells were probably untypical of most working floors used by masons. They were of restricted area and could not have accommodated the largest drawings. They were both on upper floors with access via stone staircases up which it would have been difficult to carry the materials needed for making templates and in contrast to the tracing floor in the transept at Vale Royal, they were located in secluded, perhaps private parts of the buildings they served. They also differed from many tracing floors mentioned in documents as being permanent structures, used for two centuries or more, rather than being used only when a particular project was under way.

This means that we need to distinguish between different kinds of floor on which drawings were made. Firstly, there would have been places where the stone components of an arch or window were laid out in instances where templates were not used for every detail, as in the making of the round window for the Temple Church in London. Floors used in this way would be comparable to the framing grounds used by carpenters (Chapter 4), and like the latter, may sometimes have been in the open, perhaps at the quarry where the stone was produced.

Next there are the tracing houses and tracing floors mentioned in the documents referenced above, where templates (moulds) are often mentioned as well and where it seems that drawings were set out for the express purpose of making templates. Working floors such as these would usually be at ground level, as the examples cited at Vale Royal and Ely probably were.

A third type of floor is then represented by the examples at Wells (*Plate 5*) and York located in upper rooms which, as Alexander Holton puts it, have the character of 'design spaces' where the master masons could 'experiment with new concepts' in relative privacy.[37]

At York, the tracing house, usually referred to as the 'masons' loft' is a room above the vestibule which links the north transept of the minster to the chapter house. The vestibule and chapter house were built together in a continuous programme of work, but with a complicated history of changes in design. However, it is now accepted that the chapter house was being completed in 1288 and the vestibule was finished soon after. The extra storey built to accommodate the masons' loft was clearly a late modification to the design, since it cuts across the cornice of the chapter house, obscuring carving that had been finished only a year or two earlier.[38] However, there is no evidence of a break in construction, hence the masons' loft is also assumed to have been constructed and roofed in the 1290s. The roof structure above the loft is related in its carpentry design to the roof of the chapter house (as will be seen in

Chapter 4) for which timber was felled in 1288, and it is likely that the loft roof itself was built soon after that.

Key to the permanence and effectiveness of the York and Wells tracing floors was their hard gypsum plaster surfaces, which could be repeatedly used, like a blackboard, with redundant drawings in chalk or charcoal easily wiped off, and with lines incised by metal points fine enough to ignore or obscure with dust (as on a dust board) when a new drawing was made.[39] But while the more familiar lime plaster had long been used on walls, gypsum plaster was something of an innovation in thirteenth-century England, introduced after it had been seen in France. Hence it was referred to as 'French plaster' or 'plaster-of-Paris'.[40]

Natural gypsum is a mineral which can be described as a hydrated calcium sulphate ($CaSO_4.2H_2O$) and to make the plaster it was heated to drive off water. This produced a white, powdery substance which, when again mixed with water, could be spread and shaped as a plaster, but which set hard as soon as chemical recombination with the water was complete. One advantage was that it set much faster than lime plaster and with a harder surface.

Sources of gypsum used in the Middle Ages included 'plaster of Corfe', found near the Purbeck marble beds at Corfe in Dorset, and deposits near Ripon and Knaresborough, 18 miles north-west of York. There were also deposits near Nottingham, where alabaster was recognised as the same material as gypsum, and waste from quarrying and carving alabaster could be used to make plaster. In Nottinghamshire later in the fourteenth century, 'figures in the arcading of the White Hart at Newark' were made of moulded plaster, and perhaps at this time the use of gypsum plaster for making hard, smooth floors in houses (including upstairs floors) began to develop, although dated examples are later.[41]

The use of gypsum plaster for tracing floors is not likely to have developed from experience of house floors, though. One possibility is that information was reaching York about tracing floors on the continent, where gypsum was used near Strasbourg[42] and plaster of an unspecified kind was used at Troyes.[43] But while the *concept* of a plaster tracing floor could well have come from either place, there is also the question of how local expertise in the use of gypsum developed. One point here is that men employed by the 'king's works' seem to have had more experience of this material than most craftsmen. Thus one of the earliest documented uses of gypsum plaster in England was in 1252, when

Henry III was staying at Nottingham Castle and was taking a personal interest in repairs and improvements to the building. Referring to the residential accommodation, he ordered his workmen 'to make a great louvre in the hall roof; to finish off the wooden dais with French plaster ... to plaster [the queen's] chamber, wardrobe and chapel, and draw lines in the plaster'.[44] The drawn lines were to be part of a decorative scheme, probably intended to simulate masonry joints, but there is some doubt as to whether the scheme was ever completed.

It is of interest that there are references to gypsum plaster being used at the sites of other royal castles, notably in the queen's chamber at Scarborough Castle (in 1284, when a York plasterer may have been involved) and at Knaresborough (in 1303).[45] After that, the material was more widely used and a regular market had developed in London by 1340, with white plaster-of-Paris sold at 1s 5d the bushel, but with the coarser 'black' plaster selling for only 1s 0d.[46]

Knaresborough and Nottingham were particularly significant centres because they were close to natural sources of gypsum. Knaresborough is also near York and most plaster-of-Paris used in the city would probably come from that area. A particularly important project at this time was the rebuilding of a tower at Knaresborough Castle, begun in 1307 on orders from Edward II soon after his accession. He appointed Gilbert de Stapleton as clerk-of-works for the project and Hugh de Tichemers (or Titchmarsh) of London as master mason, with five other skilled masons to assist. A lodge and tracing house (*domus tracer*) were constructed for their use by the master carpenter William de Bocton (or Bokton).[47]

The building of this lodge reflects a practice common at major construction sites of erecting a timber-framed shed or lodge to shelter the benches at which the banker-masons worked, with a tracing house adjoining. Another example, mentioned earlier, is the lodge and tracing house at Ely built in 1387. That had a paved stone tracing floor, but there is no information from Knaresborough about the surface used for drawing. The building work it served included quite elaborate vaults in the lower storeys of the tower (which survive largely complete)[48] and detail of these as well as windows would need to have been drawn out on the tracing floor.

Work on the tower at Knaresborough was periodically delayed by shortages of funds and uncertainty about the intended design, and Master Hugh de Tichemers then had to leave the job and travel to wherever the king was at the time, to find out his 'express wishes' for the building and obtain warrants for more cash. During these absences, perhaps in 1309 and again in 1311-12, another mason, Master Hugh of Boudon (or Bowden) was seconded from York Minster to supervise work on the castle.[49]

Hugh de Boudon's periods of work at Knaresborough made a significant link between York craftsmen and the king's works, which has been used to account for the appearance of ballflower ornament on a window at Knaresborough and then above the west doorway at York. Ideas picked up from craftsmen at Knaresborough could also be associated with improvements to the gypsum plaster tracing floor in the masons' loft. Although some sources confidently present Hugh de Boudon as 'the master mason of York Minster', there is much uncertainty about his precise role until 1322. After that it seems that he was principal master mason with a particular responsibility for construction of the west front.[50]

Whatever part Hugh de Boudon may have played, it is evident that a certain amount of experimentation was necessary before the existing tracing floor was available for use. So although the structure of the masons' loft may have been completed during the 1290s and experience was gained at Knaresborough prior to 1312, the existing drawing surface may not have been laid until later.

The masons' loft is located above the chapter house vestibule. Plate 21 shows the exterior of the vestibule with the chapter house behind and the small rectangular windows of the loft high up in the structure. These windows at first sight seem hardly adequate to light a drawing office. The room has an L-shaped plan, with the floor in one arm of the L made of wooden boards (see the schematic plan, *Figure 2.7*). The plaster floor in the other arm ends at an irregular edge, as if it once extended over the area which now has the boarded surface, and it is tempting to think that it once extended to the point where two steps in the wooden floor now go down to a lower level. It should also perhaps be stressed that the present floor-boards are not old.

The structure below the floor was the stone vault that formed the ceiling of the chapter house vestibule. The procedure adopted for laying a flat plaster floor above this was first to fill the voids above the vault with rubble, some of which consists of small chippings produced by masons as they were working stone, probably for the nave of the minster.[51] This fill was brought to a level and the plaster was laid directly over it. In one or two places, particularly where there are holes in the floor, it can be observed that the first plaster to be laid was a white layer which laboratory examination shows was nearly pure plaster-of-Paris.[52] If this was intended to provide a surface on which drawings could be made, it would soon have been found that it was too soft and friable for heavy compasses with metal points to be used for drawing. Such instruments would tend to plough up the surface of the plaster rather than leaving a neat incised line. However, it would have made a reasonable surface on which to draw in charcoal or crayon.

It is possible that this surface was laid over at least part of the available floor area as soon as the masons' loft was completed in 1290s, perhaps by the York plasterer who had used gypsum plaster at Scarborough Castle a few years earlier. However, it is also possible that experiments were made with other types of tracing floor, such as wooden boards of the kind used at Westminster (and in later shipyard drawing lofts). Either way, it seems clear that the white plaster layer which underlies the present floor was an experiment which proved unsatisfactory, so to complete the floor, a harder surface was laid with a coarser form of gypsum plaster. Perhaps this was 'black plaster', such as was available later in London,[53] or perhaps it was specially formulated by mixing in a little fine ash with some clay. When this was laid, it brought the total thickness of plaster to around 50mm. The additional layer has a much harder surface than pure plaster-of-Paris and is dark grey in colour. It is tempting to think that Hugh de Boudon's experiences in Knaresborough played a part in arriving at this solution since, at Knaresborough, he was close to the major local source of gypsum and in contact with men from the king's works who probably had other experience of the material.

When the plaster was laid, but before it had set, the final finish was produced by gently moulding and puddling the surface with bare feet (distinct human footprints can be seen in two places) a process which expelled bubbles entrained in the plaster mix, and pushed down any lumps, leaving a smooth but slightly undulating surface. The floor was not laid all at once but in distinct sections, the demarcations of which now show as cracks and it can be seen that the puddling process was not equally successful on all sections of the floor. At the north end, in particular, the plaster seems to have set without being puddled at all,

Early Architectural Drawing

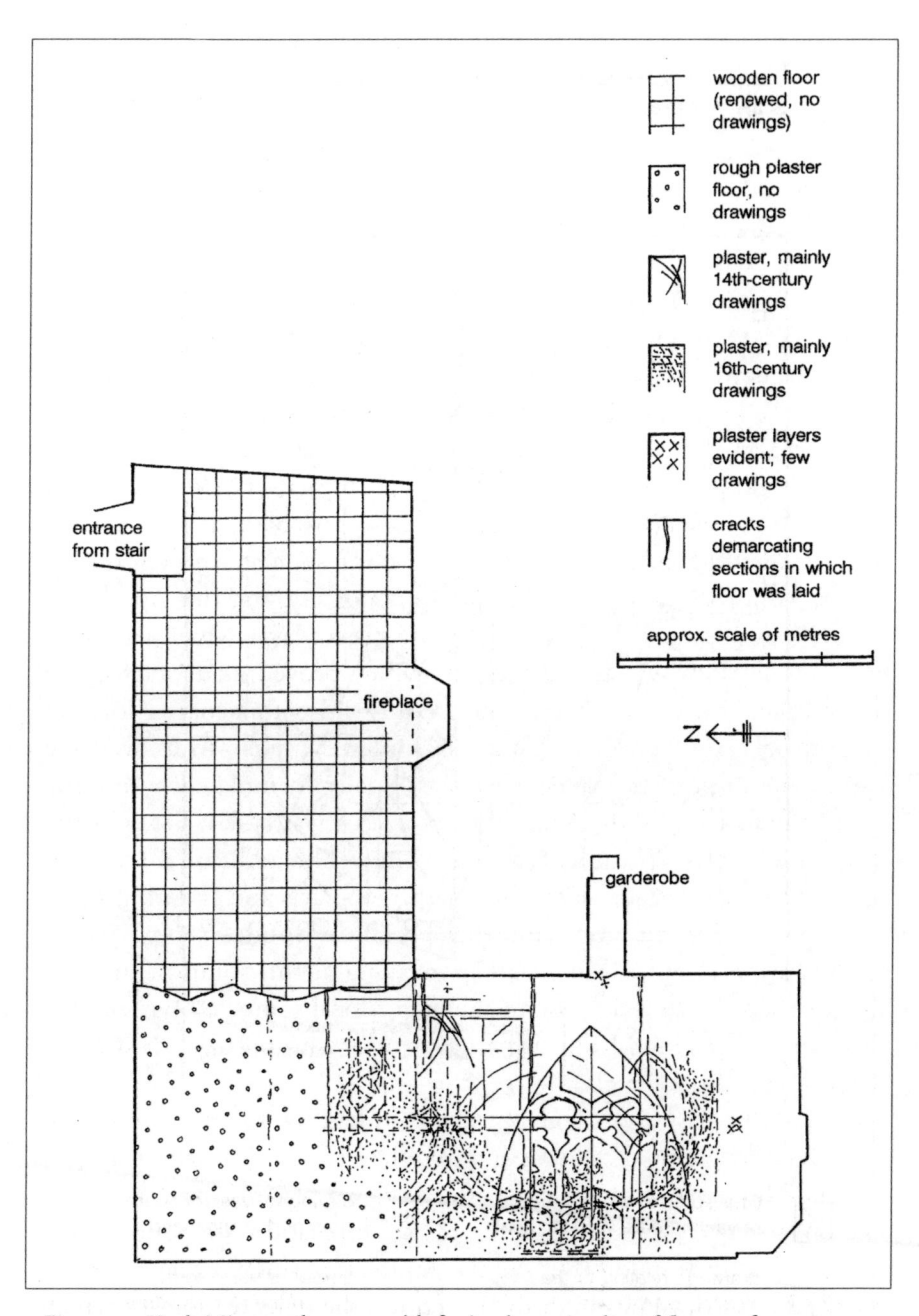

Figure 2.7 York Minster: the masons' loft. A schematic plan of floor surfaces. Copyright © *Dean & Chapter of York*

Medieval Architectural Drawing

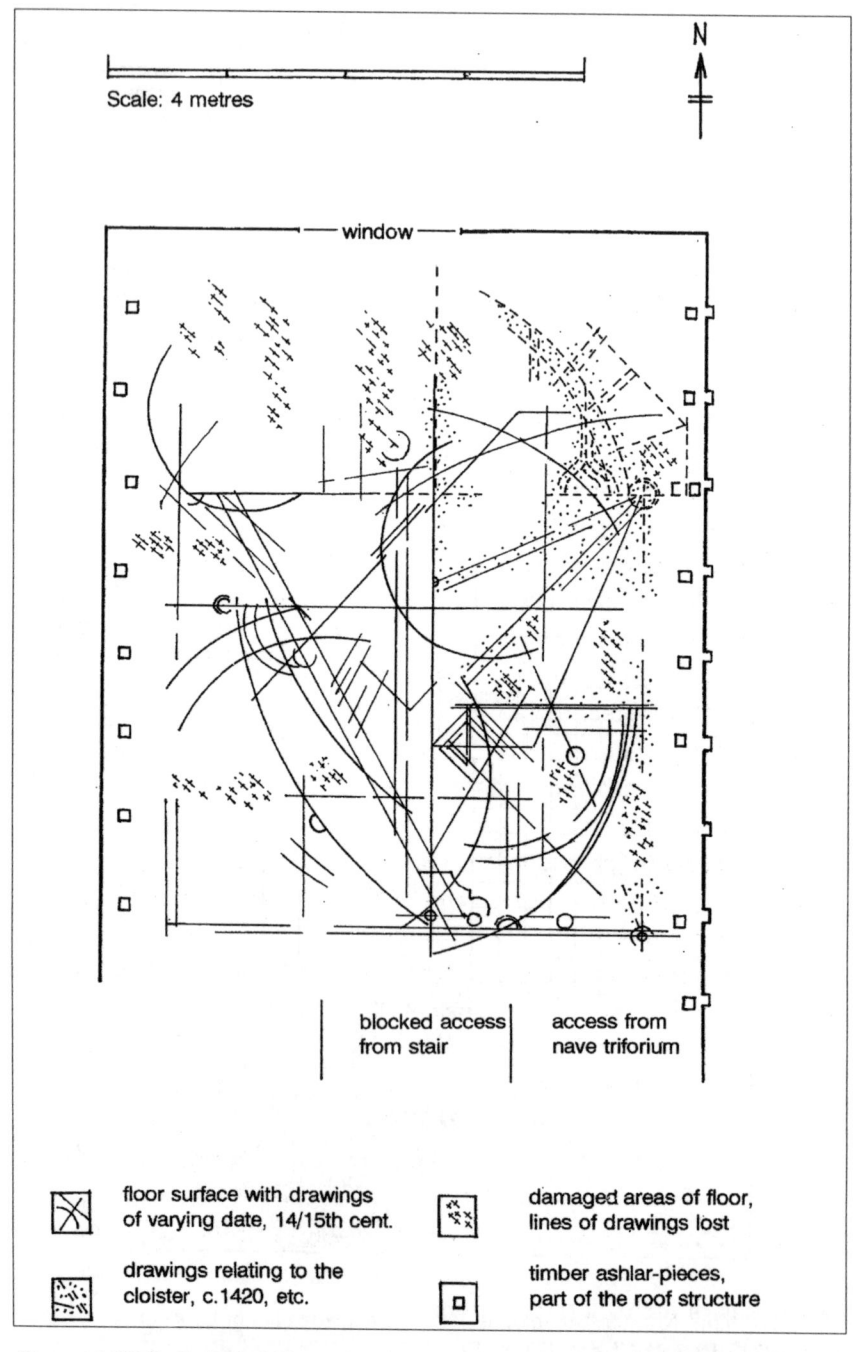

Scale: 4 metres

N

— window —

blocked access from stair

access from nave triforium

floor surface with drawings of varying date, 14/15th cent.

damaged areas of floor, lines of drawings lost

drawings relating to the cloister, c.1420, etc.

timber ashlar-pieces, part of the roof structure

Figure 2.8 Wells Cathedral: floor plan of the room above the north porch with overall view of the most prominent drawings on the tracing floor, the whole surface of which is of gypsum plaster.

leaving a rough surface that would have been difficult to draw on (*Figure 2.7*), though it could still be used for laying out templates.

DRAWINGS AT WELLS AND YORK

Although the tracing floor at Wells Cathedral, Somerset, has not been studied in as much detail, it appears to be very similar.[54] We cannot be sure whether gypsum tracing floors were widely used, but it seems more likely that they were relatively uncommon. Hence the Wells floor may have been laid with direct knowledge of what had been done at York. Like the York masons' loft, it is located on an upper floor level, above the stone vault of the north porch. The porch was probably built between 1205 and 1215, but was altered shortly before 1320 when a parapet was added.[55] The tracing floor was laid only after this alteration was completed and an overall plan of the floor shows a row of square timbers along both sides (*Figure 2.8*). The latter are ashlar pieces in the roof structure whose feet were submerged in the plaster when it was laid (*Plate 5*).

During the nineteenth century, this attic room was used as a school room, resulting in considerable damage to the floor. There are holes in the surface where table legs and benches were once placed and abraded areas where furniture was dragged across the floor. There is hardly a single drawing that is not interrupted by damage to the surface at some point.

Some surviving drawings on the Wells floor can be dated to *c.*1420, and will be discussed in a later chapter on fifteenth-century drawings. However, the floor was probably laid a century before that, and it is worth commenting that the master mason at Wells Cathedral from 1329 until 1347 was William Joy, the inventive designer responsible for the vault of the retrochoir and the strainer arches under the central tower.[56] It could be that the earliest drawings on the Wells tracing floor are connected with Joy's work on the retrochoir, though much more research would be necessary to confirm this. Moreover, if the Wells floor were to date from the 1330s or 1340s, consistent with the idea that Joy was responsible for it, that would also be consistent with the idea that it was made with knowledge of the York tracing floor.

A preliminary study of the fragmentary drawings incised on the tracing floor at York indicates that the different masons who worked here had very varied styles of drawing. Some drew heavily with their compasses,

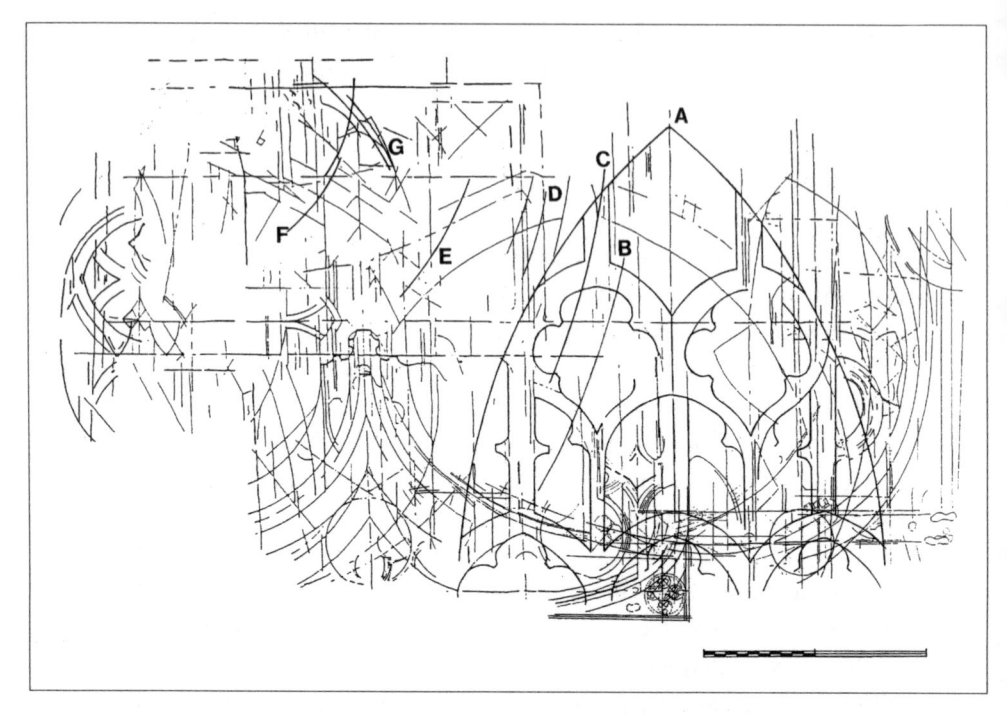

Figure 2.9 Overview of drawings on the tracing floor at York Minster, with the tracery design for the south choir aisle windows labelled A at its apex. Other curves are lettered as explained in the text, and the scale bar is 2m. *Developed from a copy made for John Harvey; Copyright © Dean and Chapter of York*

leaving clear, firm incised lines, while others drew more lightly. One man, when drawing long curves, applied intermittent pressure so that each curve appears as a series of long dashes. Others may have drawn mainly in chalk or charcoal and their lines will have long since been wiped away.

The majority of recognisable drawings at York fall into two groups, those probably made in the fourteenth century, perhaps within 50 years of the floor being laid, and those made after 1520 by the master mason John Forman, whose emphatic style of drawing tends to dominate parts of the floor, indicated in Figure 2.7 as having 'mainly sixteenth-century drawings'. Forman's drawings will be discussed in a subsequent chapter and what we need to look at here are the earlier ones. No doubt there were also drawings made in the fifteenth century, but they are not now as clear as the others.

John Harvey made the pioneer study of this tracing floor in the 1960s and published a plan of the floor surface showing the drawings.[57] On those parts of the floor that have been studied afresh during research for the present book, mainly by taking rubbings and making tracings, the general accuracy of Harvey's plan has been confirmed, but some additional curves and other details have been found. Thus Figure 2.9 is based on Harvey's plan, but with the newly discovered curves added. There is obvious potential for an even more accurate and comprehensive survey, possibly using photogrammetry.

Harvey identified one of the drawings at York as an unambiguous representation of the design for tracery used for windows in the aisles of the eastern arm of the Minster. It is the drawing marked A in Figure 2.9 and study of windows in the eastern arm shows that although the same basic design is repeated several times, there are variations in proportion and detail, especially between windows in the lady chapel aisle and in the choir aisle, and between the north and south sides of the building. The window illustrated in Plate 22 is from the south choir aisle and is slightly wider than the drawing (which, of course, is full size). The extra width is allowed for with small extensions to the tracery. It is likely that changes to a design such as this were made by altering or replacing templates without making a new drawing.

This part of the building was begun in 1361 when William le Hoton the younger was master mason, having succeeded his father in the job. Hence, William Hoton is assumed to have made the drawing.[58] The completeness of this drawing (*Figure 2.9* at A) is unusual since nearly all the other drawings to be seen here or on the tracing floor at Wells are fragmentary. The drawing is also untypical in showing a complete window where many show only half of a symmetrical design. Whereas some other drawings give the impression of having been completed in chalk or on the boards from which templates were cut, in this case the whole outline of the window is incised on the floor. And while some drawings have tentatively drawn or duplicated lines such as one might expect in an abandoned design experiment, this drawing has every line present, clearly and firmly drawn.

It may be that the unusual completeness of this window drawing of *c.* 1361 was due to a need to give some sort of presentation to show the minster clergy what kind of window was proposed. Hence this was neither a design sketch nor a working drawing, but more probably marks a key stage in construction of the eastern arm of the minster where the master mason needed a drawing he could show the church authorities to gain approval for the design he proposed.

Beyond these general considerations, if we are to understand the tracing floor more adequately, it is important to examine the many fragmentary curves. Each can be catalogued according to its radius and length, and whether it appears to be related to any particular base line or centre line. An impression may also be gained as to whether a particular curve was likely to form the relatively sharply pointed shapes used for windows and arches in the fourteenth century, or the flatter shape that became more common later. After that, the more systematic cataloguing of such data as radius and length led to the identification of a series of related curves that are labelled B to F in Figure 2.9.

As already mentioned, the curves meeting at A in this figure belong to the large window drawing, but close to this are curves B and C and a group of three curves at D, all of which are inverted relative to A. Options for the interpretation of these curves are, firstly, to think that that they are part of a large and elaborate drawing partly done in chalk and now largely erased or, secondly, to consider that the curves might be position marks, showing where a set of templates were to be laid out. A third option might be to think that they were related to preliminary design work and were never part of a completed drawing. To some degree the curves are reminiscent of some of the curves seen in mural drawings, notably at Ely (*Figure 2.3*) and Ashwell (*Figure 2.5*) which seemed to indicate that the masons were just checking the adjustment of their compasses.

If these curves were interpreted as related to design experiments that were never completed, perhaps the only worthwhile question to ask about them is: where, in the architecture of York Minster, are there features incorporating curves of the radii seen here on the tracing floor?

The five curves, B to D, have radii varying from about 16ft (about 5m) for D to 23ft (7m) for B, and are commensurate in radius and length to the curves that would be needed to make full-size drawings of arches in the nave or choir, or to draw the larger windows in many parts of the building.

The group of curves at G is inverted relative to the rather similar curves marked F, and seems to include more detail. These shorter-radius curves, assuming they are part of a full-size drawing, are commensurate with the

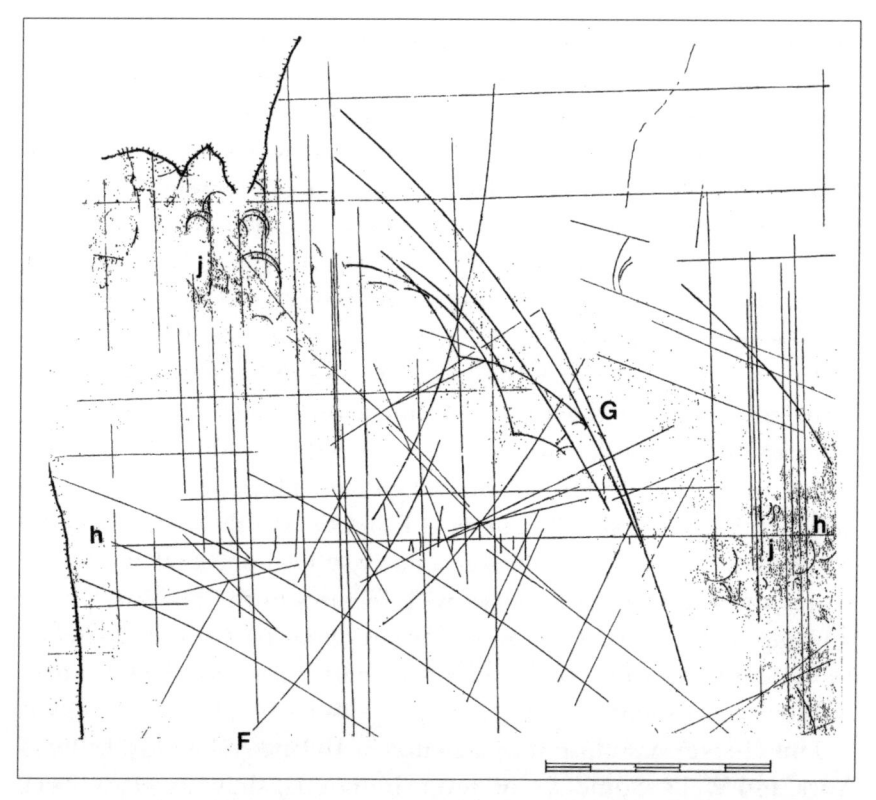

Figure 2.10 Lines and curves on the tracing floor at York Minster. This is a new, more detailed, copy of the curves shown in Figure 2.9 at F and G. Barbed lines show cracks and breaks in the floor surface; h-h is a base line for other drawings, now missing. The scale bar is 500mm. *Copyright © Dean and Chapter of York*

curves used in the smaller windows in the church and in some of the doorways, and are illustrated in more detail in Figure 2.10. This detail may suggest that the drawing was made to try out designs for the cusping of an arched opening. There is no sign that there was tracery within the opening, in which case the drawing may represent either a doorway or a tomb recess. They could even be related to either of the two openings of the main west doorway. This might be credible if it were thought that the master mason was merely exploring possibilities for the design of the west doorway, but there is no close match and the purpose of the drawing remains uncertain. It is worth adding, though, that to the left of the curves in question, and less clearly to the right, are a number of small circles and arcs (at locations marked **j** in Figure 2.10). These do not make a complete drawing but seem to be randomly placed. However, the smallest circles are about the right size to represent ballflower ornament, a detail which (as previously noted) is also to be seen in the region of the west doorway.

Another noteworthy feature of Figure 2.10 is the line at **h - h** on which many intercepts are marked, suggesting that there was once a drawing here for which this was a base line with some dimensions marked on it with a compass point, but with everything else then drawn out in chalk. Once the chalk drawing was wiped away, all that remained was the marked-out base line.

A review of all the curves B-G illustrates the difficulty of interpreting some tracing-floor drawings. The most probable location in York Minster where a collection of curves with this combination of radii forms an important part of the design (including both long-radius curves at B and the sharper curves at F and G) is at the west end of the nave and the west front. However, a purely statistical correlation of the radius and length of each curve with features in the building proves nothing, since there is no architectural detail that can be matched to the curves in the actual stonework apart from, just possibly, some ballflower ornament.

This chapter has illustrated drawings at Byland Abbey, Ely, Ashwell, York and Wells. Some six or seven individual drawings have been examined, dating from *c.*1200 to the 1360s. Other thirteenth-century drawings mentioned, but not illustrated, are at Cambridge and Christchurch Priory. This is not a large number of drawings, but it is considerably more than were thought to exist by the architectural historians quoted earlier. The problem now is to explain how the drawings were used. Were they as important for making templates as commonly assumed? Does the fragmentary nature of surviving drawings on tracing floors reflect the disappearance of many lines and curves drawn in chalk or charcoal? Is it the case that the surviving tracing floors at York and Wells were not working floors used for making templates, but were mainly used for experimental design work, with many drawings left incomplete?

CHAPTER 3

GEOMETRY IN MEDIEVAL DRAWING

(drawings and wall paintings, *c*.1200-1420)

CONCEPTUALISING PLANS

It can sometimes seem that the geometry used by medieval masons when they made their drawings was entirely a matter of circles and curves if they were designing window tracery, but became concerned exclusively with squares when they were working on plans. Thus architectural historians interested in how plans developed write about *ad quadratum* design – that is, design according to the square (and its diagonal) – while some who write about windows see the rose window as a fundamental form and study how compasses were used in setting out tracery.[1]

However, it is window tracery that seems most often to have been drawn on the tracing floors at Wells and York and the drawings include many circles and curves. There is a grid of straight lines on both floors as well, but it is hard to pick out more than one or two deliberately-drawn squares and it is also hard to find evidence for work on the plans of buildings.

The absence of plans (and elevations) among surviving drawings becomes less surprising when we recall that all the formal drawings on tracing floors were full-size representations of architectural detail. There were no scale drawings in this period and the small mural drawings often seen on walls rather than floors were more in the nature of sketches or geometrical diagrams. A plan or elevation could be sketched, or could be shown in a pictorial way, but if a plan was drawn full size, in the way drawings on tracing floors were, it would occupy as much space on the ground as the actual building. So while indeed there was a 'drawing process' for working out details of plans it took place on site, when the lines of the building were being staked out. Before considering that, however, we should note an example of a plan drawn out quite differently, in a remarkable representation on parchment of Canterbury Cathedral and the associated monastic buildings.[2] This dates from some time between 1153 and 1167 and shows an elaborate system of canals, conduits, lead pipes and cisterns devised by a monk, Prior Wibert, 'to water and drain the monastery'.[3]

The cathedral, seen at the top of the drawing in Plate 23, is on the south side of the complex of monastic buildings and is depicted with its east end to the left. At this date the cathedral was a wholly Romanesque building, but in 1174 the choir was gutted by fire. Its shell survived, but the interior was rebuilt by the French master mason, William of Sens, in 1175-78 and was extended a short distance eastwards by his successor, William the Englishman, in 1179-84 to accommodate the shrine of Thomas Becket (murdered in 1170). Some details and mouldings are so similar to work in Sens Cathedral (south-west of Paris) that it has been suggested that the first William brought templates from there, but the design differs from Sens in its proportions and in the use of black polished Purbeck marble shafts as a decorative feature.[4]

The story of how William of Sens fell from the scaffolding at Canterbury and was badly injured, recorded by the monk Gervaise, is well-known. William continued for a while to direct work on the building from a stretcher and one interpretation of why he had to stay on the job despite his injuries is that there were no design drawings that other masons could follow in his absence.[5] The only complete version of the design, it is suggested, was in William's head. This is perhaps only partly true, but even so, one theme in the history of drawing concerns the question of how designs were communicated and shared within the group of craftsmen working on a building. Drawing is a way of expressing thoughts about a building for purposes of both communication and design. The Canterbury drawing shows a group of buildings 'conceptualised' in this way with great clarity, but the representation is essentially pictorial.

On a tracing floor, designs were conceptualised in a different way, using geometry, and were certainly not pictorial. A detailed study of French practice in the time of William of Sens implies a challenge to the view that designs for a major project existed mainly in the master mason's head. This study, by John James, indicates that drawings were made mainly in the process of constructing templates for mouldings and tracery.

The limitations of these drawings were, firstly, that they were mostly of details, with few representations of the building as a whole, and secondly, that they were always based on geometry, but the geometry was not fully explicit. When a mason looked at a colleague's drawing of a window or moulding, John James suggests, he could not easily deduce what sequence of geometrical constructions had been used. Geometrical procedures were not standardised and, in copying details of a drawing, a second mason would inevitably introduce variations into the design. For that reason, a new man taking over when the previous master had retired or died could continue the overall design, but would not know how to repeat the details of the original master's drawings and might prefer to make new templates.[6] Hence mouldings would differ slightly in shape after he took charge. In any case, if it is true that at Canterbury the first Master William brought templates with him from Sens, some of the relevant tracing-floor drawings may have been in France rather than at Canterbury.

However, all this refers to the design of detail and does not illuminate the question about what overall plans were drawn. Turning back to the waterworks drawing as a possible example of such a plan, several buildings it shows survive and are recognisable, including what is now called the lavatory tower. It is shown on the drawing as linked to the cathedral by two arches. This semi-octagonal tower, built by Prior Wibert *c.*1150-60, contained a cistern and washing place for the monks on its upper floor, the cistern being supplied with rainwater from the roofs of the cathedral via pipes that are coloured yellow-brown on the plan (*Plate 23*). Since the roofs were covered with lead sheet, it is not surprising that the plumbers who did the roofing work were also able to contrive lead pipes. Coming down to ground level from the upper floor of the lavatory tower, there were two pipes connecting with the rest of the water system and here we see that other colours used on the plan are red for the main water supply to the site via a conduit from a source on high ground some distance away and blue-green for drainage. Priority uses for the incoming water were in the infirmary and the *lavatorium* outside the refectory, where water and cleanliness had ritual meaning. From there water went to the kitchens and after that to the latrines (*necessaria*) and fishponds. The drainage system took waste water away to irrigate apple trees, vines and cereals (bottom left).

As a plan of a complex of buildings, this drawing is remarkable for its detail, but the representation of buildings is not precise, and this is in no sense a design drawing. In fact, the plan may be a record made after the buildings and water system had been constructed.

There is, of course, a great deal of difference between representing a building in a pictorial manner, as shown here, and the accurate, full-size drawings of window detail illustrated in the previous chapter. While elevations of a pictorial kind are common in thirteenth- and fourteenth-century manuscript illuminations and stained glass, elevations drawn with anything like the accuracy of the window details are hard to find. The best example is one at Ely (on the left in *Figure 2.3*) which may be a design for rebuilding the south transept of the cathedral.

As to drawings showing ground plans rather than elevations, Villard de Honnecourt in France made five sketch plans showing the eastern parts of churches, perhaps in the 1230s, so it would seem likely that his English contemporaries may have done the same. However, drawing plans and sections in a precise way was understandably slower to emerge than accurate drawings of elevations because the elevation of a building can be seen, whereas the plan or section has to be imagined. Ackerman points out that Villard de Honnecourt not only sketched plans and elevations, but also drew some of the earliest sections surviving in continental Europe.[7] They show cross-sections through walls with buttresses at Reims Cathedral. A little less than a century later, sections of the cathedral at Prague were being drawn with great assurance in the workshop of the master mason, Peter Parler.[8]

It is hard to point to any comparable drawings in England, but one thing that was being done there from the mid-fourteenth century was to combine the plan of some small part of a building with its elevation in one drawing, as will be shown later in this chapter. This combination represents another way of thinking about design and conceptualising a building. Needless to say the principles and methods of scale drawing took longer to emerge.

In the light of this slow evolution of drawing conventions and concepts, we need to consider the claim sometimes made that medieval buildings were constructed without any drawn plans. Could it be true that the plans of buildings were usually laid out on the ground without preliminary drawings? With regard to Wells Cathedral, for example, Jerry Sampson suggests that the plan of the nave was set out on the ground without any drawing, but that the elevation of the west front would have been drawn.[9]

The indications that plans of major buildings were not drawn out on parchment, nor on a tracing floor, does not mean, of course, that there was no design or planning. There were systematic procedures for staking out the plan of a new building on the site. After this had been done, the layout of stakes, pegs and cords on the ground would constitute a full-size 'drawing' that could be discussed and modified before the foundations were dug. In that sense, the process modern designers go through when they draw a plan and discuss it with those commissioning the building could be followed even without a drawing on parchment. The difference was that this would all be done on site and revisions to plans would entail moving stakes and cords on the ground, not erasing lines on a drawing.

A standard geometrical procedure was followed in surveying and setting out the lines of a building on site, and the 'drawing process' by which the plan of a church was laid out on the ground was then somewhat as follows:[10] to begin with, the ground was cleared, then the outlines of the plan were pegged out as a series of squares. Each square was checked by stretching a cord across the diagonals to see that both diagonals were the same length, so ensuring that the square was not skewed. In a large church with nave, choir and transepts, the crossing of the transepts and the main axis of the building would usually be the starting point, where an initial square was marked out on the ground.

The plans of a number of early medieval buildings have now been analysed by several authorities on geometry and proportion and the results are so consistent (in principle if not in detail) that there can be little doubt that plans of major Romanesque and early Gothic buildings were worked out in this way, as a series of squares, with the diagonals of the squares also used to determine certain proportions. Norwich Cathedral, begun 1096 on a site where it was possible to clear the few earlier structures,[11] is a particularly clear example of the geometrical setting out of a plan and is at the centre of debate among scholars on this subject.[12] The plan at Norwich is thought to have been related to the design of other major churches, notably those at Ely, Bury St Edmunds and, earlier, Winchester.[13] At York, beginning in 1088, the Romanesque church of St Mary's Abbey, has been seen as another example of *ad quadratum* design,[14] that is, of a plan based on the geometry of squares.[15]

When precise measurements of these buildings are taken to check that their plans are really based on squares in the manner proposed, it becomes clear that most were designed using measurements based on English feet. This generally refers to a foot of about 305mm, but standards could vary, even within England. In France, a Roman foot of about 295mm was often used (although at Notre Dame in Paris, measurement was based on a foot of 325mm).[16] When a longer measure was needed, this was often a perch of 16½ft (5m) and dimensions of two perches (33ft or 10m) recur in several places, for example St Mary's Abbey, York.[17] In this book, dimensions are quoted in feet whenever it is relevant to consider what measurements may have been used by the people who constructed particular buildings.

Among later buildings evidently designed using the geometry of the square and its diagonal as a basis for proportions is Wells Cathedral, where the plan was laid out about 1180. Here, the internal floor area of the transepts comprises two squares of side 75ft (24m), and the nave can be represented as two more 75ft squares.[18] Later still, after 1220, the design of Beverley Minster owes its 'visual clarity' to a very coherent system of proportions regarding heights as well as widths and floor areas.[19]

Thus, historians of architecture seem to be agreed that systems of design based on the square and its diagonal were widely used in developing the plans of buildings. However, this conclusion arises from measurement and study of the buildings themselves, not from the evidence of medieval drawings. That is understandable since plans are not well represented in the available drawings, so the geometry of planning is not well shown either.

What is seen more often on tracing floors, on walls, and even on parchment drawings, is principally the detail of window tracery or mouldings. When drawings of these subjects are examined, it is found that most have ruled centre lines, usually with base lines set out at right angles. The repeated use of the tracing floors at Wells and York for many drawings means that there are a great number of such lines forming an irregular grid covering much of both floors, but only occasionally is a deliberately-drawn square discernible. However, it is also noticeable that there are numerous compass-drawn curves, some representing window shapes, and there are a number of small circles which at first sight are less easy to understand. Thus it is easy to gain the impression that the circle was more important than the square in the design of architectural detail, whatever was the case with plans.

A DRAWN PLAN AT WELLS

One of the few instances of a drawing incorporating a square is on the tracing floor at Wells and raises different issues from any considered so far. That is because one side of the square also serves as the base line for a drawing of window tracery. To illustrate this as part of a general problem of interpreting tracing-floor drawings, it is best to begin with the window design. Then, with the help of a series of illustrations (*Figures 3.1 to 3.5*), it is possible to show how understanding of the drawing as a whole can expand from one detail of the window to a much larger design.

When first seen on the actual floor, this example at Wells is not easy to follow, partly because other drawings are superimposed on it, and partly also because some lines are interrupted by damage to the floor surface. Plate 6 is a photograph of a small area of the tracing floor in which the curves outlining a window can be picked out on the right. This is one of a set of photographs used by John Harvey in making his own record of drawings on the floor.[20] However, comparison of Harvey's record with lines on the floor revealed a number of small distortions arising from his use of overlapping photographs, so new tracings were made of selected areas of the floor (*Figure 3.1*).

The detail recorded in this way seemed to represent an ogee shape, so all windows in the cathedral and its precincts containing ogees were examined. Included in this were windows in the Vicars' Close which L.S. Colchester thought were represented in the drawing, but after careful measurement it was concluded that the dimensions of the Close windows did not match.[21] When measured drawings based on these and other windows were superimposed on copies of what is on the tracing floor, a good fit was obtained only for tracery detail from the eastern walk of the cloisters (*Figure 3.2*). In order to work out how this drawn detail was related to other curves on the tracing floor, a centre line to which it seemed to relate was identified on the floor. This gave a sense of the original extent of the drawing, which, like others on the tracing floors at Wells and York, only represents half of a symmetrical design.

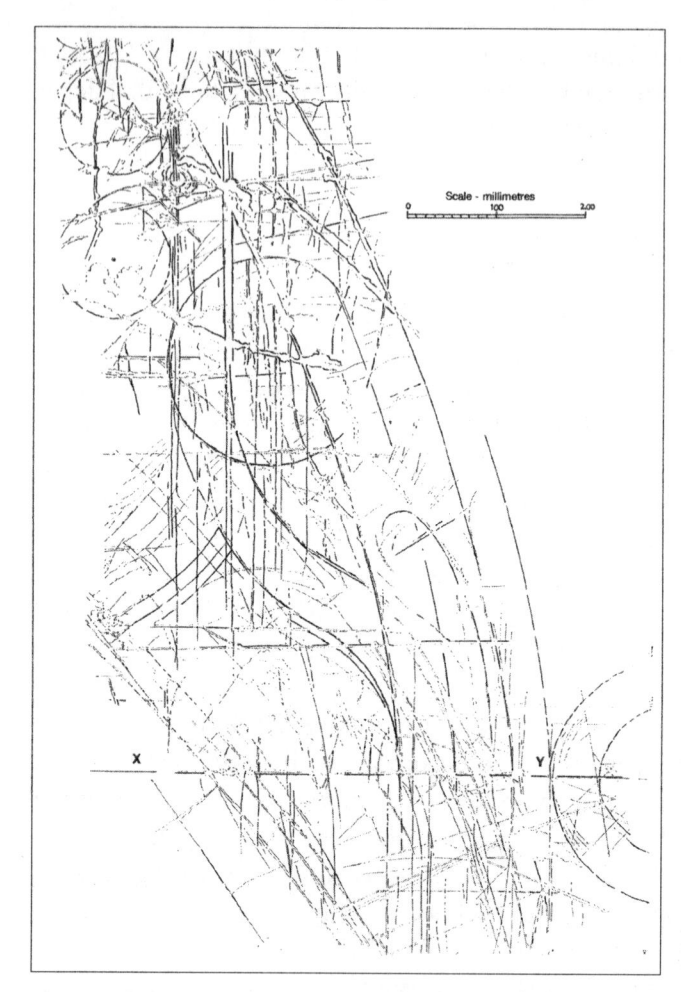

Figure 3.1 Detail of drawing on a small area of the Wells tracing floor (letters **X** and **Y** have been added to define the base line). Scale bar shows 200mm.

Much of the drawing is missing, but the distance from the centre line to the long curve nearest the ogee detail was found to measure 1.63m (5ft 4in), so the internal width of the window represented here was 3.26m (10ft 8in). On measuring the relevant cloister windows, their width was found to match closely. This seems to confirm the identification of the tracing-floor drawing with the cloister windows.

The next step was to make a scale drawing of a window from the east cloister accurate enough to discover whether other lines on the tracing floor might fit. Each of the cloister windows has six ogee-headed lights that seem to explain the ogee curves on the drawing and Figure 3.3 shows how some of the circles that appear on the drawing seem to be

Geometry in medieval drawing

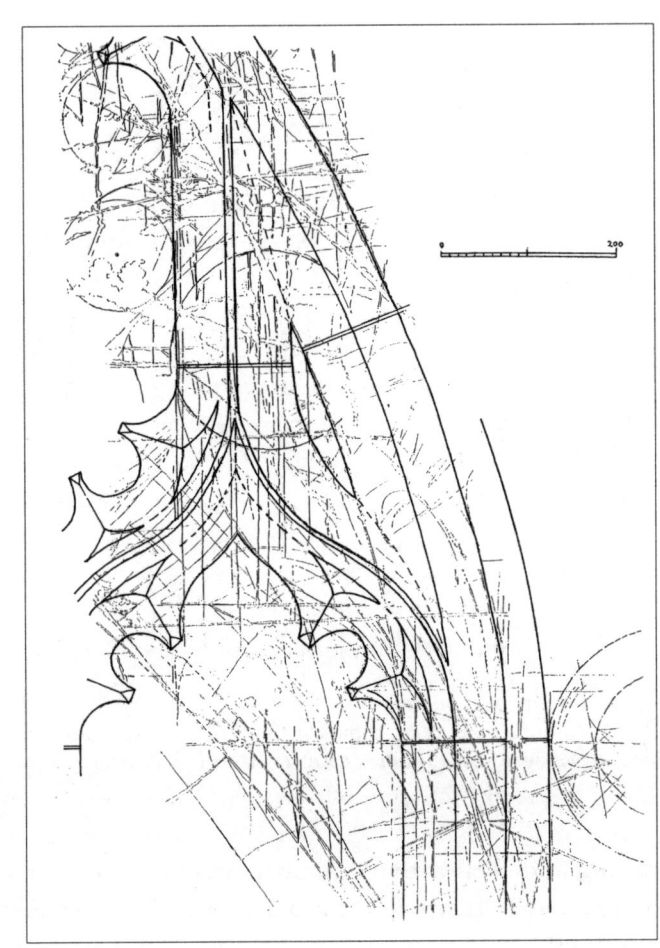

Figure 3.2 The same fragment of drawing from Wells as in Figure 3.1, but now with detail from a cloister window, drawn to the same scale and superimposed. Scale bar shows 200mm.

related to cusping in the smaller lights at the head of the window. The figure shows part of the tracery of this window design and emphasises how much of the drawing is missing. It raises again the question about whether drawings were sometimes completed in chalk, which was wiped off soon after.

With the drawing of the window reconstructed in this way, what then called for explanation was a circle on the base line of the drawing (on the extreme right in *Figures 3.1* and *3.2*). This did not make sense as part of the window drawing, but is set out as if related in some manner. Moreover, there were lines radiating from the circle extending across the

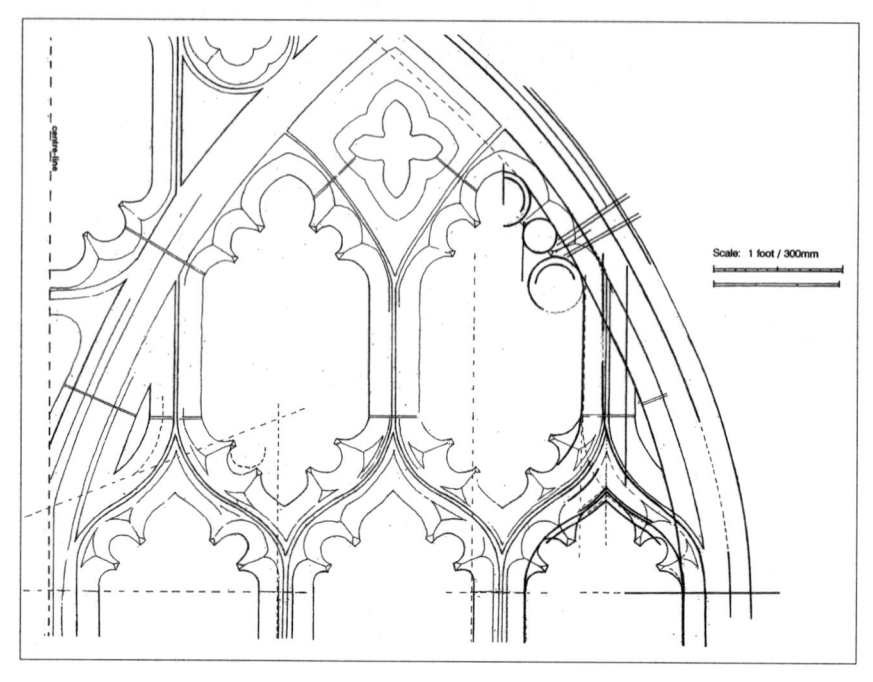

Figure 3.3 Part of a window from the east cloister at Wells Cathedral with selected lines from the tracing floor, copied at the same scale and superimposed in bold around the ogee shape on the right, and as dashed lines elsewhere. Scale: 1ft/300mm.

tracing floor below the window drawing. Figure 3.4 was drawn as an outline plane of the whole tracing floor with the window drawing at the top and the lines which radiate from the circle on the right. One of the latter appears to form the diagonal of a square which itself is a quarter of a larger square. Rather than being only an exercise in geometry, there are indications that this diagram is a plan in which the circle on the right represents a vertical shaft alongside the window. The diagonal might then indicate the rib of a vault springing from the shaft.

Since the window in the drawing belongs to the cathedral cloister, it seemed worth considering what else from that part of the cathedral might be represented. The cloister walks extend along three sides of a rectangular courtyard and were built in stages over a considerable time.[22] The east walk, comprising 13 nearly identical bays, was built first (or rather, rebuilt incorporating fabric from an earlier cloister). It was part of a scheme to re-house the cathedral library, which is accommodated in a first-floor room above. Money was left for the

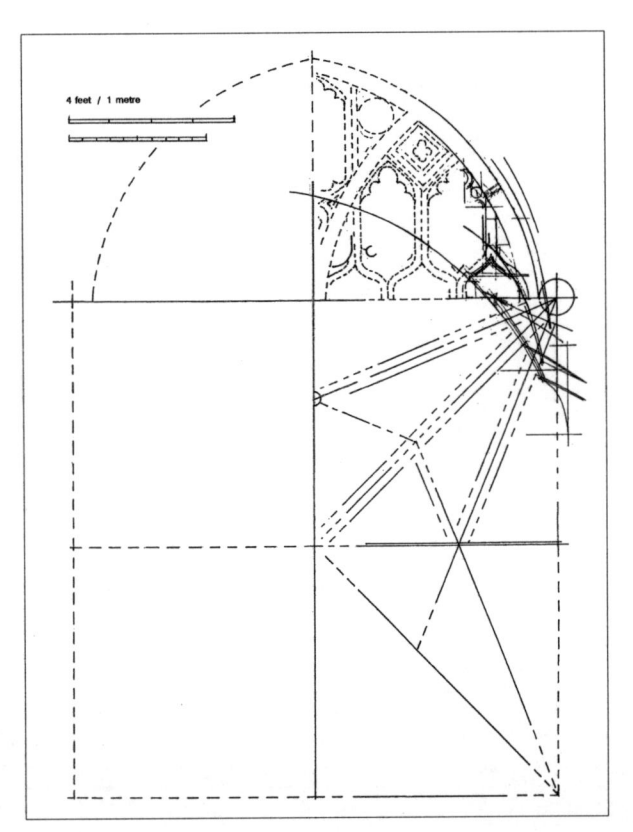

Figure 3.4 Lines on the tracing floor at Wells surviving from a drawing of one bay in the cathedral cloister. An elevation of the window in that bay is at the top and a plan of the vault below. Dashed lines represent a reconstruction of parts of the tracing-floor design that are now missing or unclear. The original drawing included only half of the symmetrical design (on the right) and the rest is shown in outline.

library by Bishop Bubwith when he died in 1424, but Colchester and Harvey believed that work may have begun around 1420, while Bubwith was still alive to supervise it.[23] The drawing on the tracing floor may therefore have been made as early as this. The name of the mason responsible is unknown, although there are suggestions of a connection with Gloucester (where cloisters were begun in 1381) and also with Exeter (where Robert Lesyngham,[24] a mason already encountered, drew a plan for the cloister in 1377).

Each of the 13 bays of the east walk of the cloister is about 3.6m or 12ft square and vaulted. The basic plan of one bay appears to be represented on the tracing floor by the large square in Figure 3.4 that has one side coinciding with the base line of the window drawing. The square is wider than the window to allow for the width of the buttress placed between the windows, and on the drawing measures rather less than 3.6m along each side. Hence the drawing roughly matches dimensions of the east

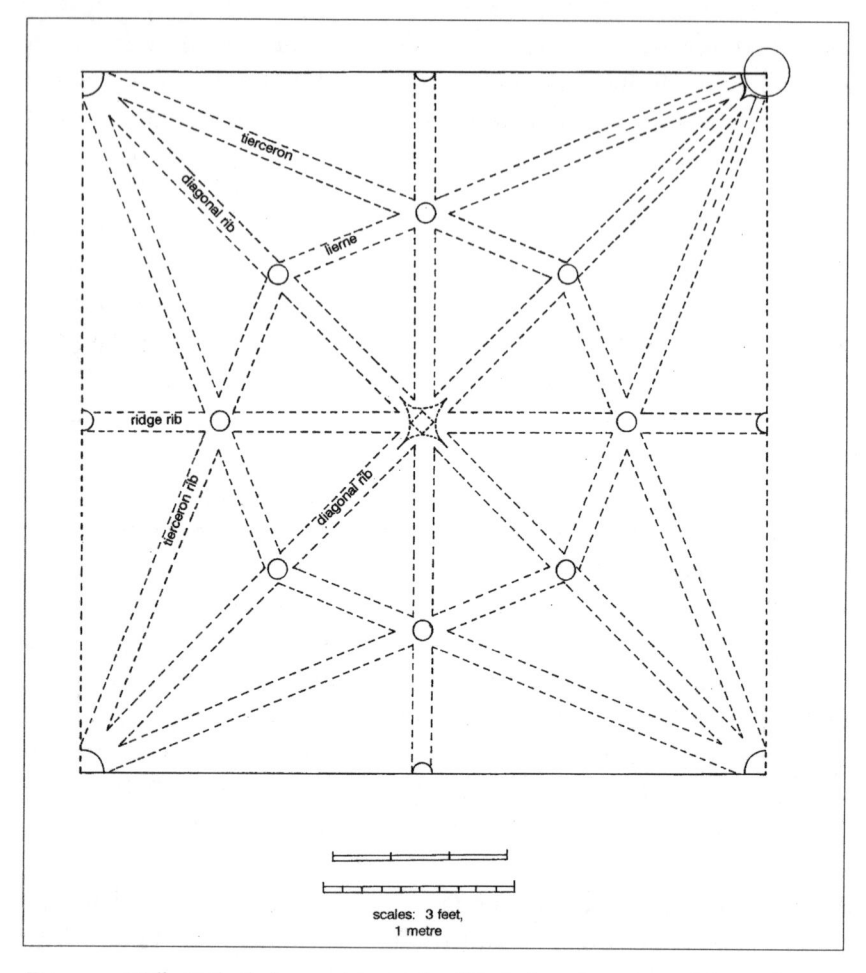

Figure 3.5 Wells Cathedral, east cloister: simplified plan of one bay of the vault.

cloister. This is shown in Figure 3.4 with full black lines representing lines visible on the floor (but only such lines as are relevant to the cloister drawing). The diagonal ribs are clear only in one corner, radiating from the small circle mentioned previously, even more certainly a wall shaft at the springing of the vault.

To confirm this apparent match between the tracing-floor diagram and one bay in the cloister vault, it would be desirable to make a more precise copy of what is on the floor and then resurvey the actual vault. However, given the provisional stage reached in the present work, only rough outlines can be provided (*Figures 3.4* and *3.5*). Each vault rib that can be recognised on the tracing floor seems to be shown by its centre line with two parallel lines indicating its width. There is also a series of curves superimposed on the extreme right-hand side of the tracing-floor drawing which may be intended to show the curvature of each rib (although a measurement of the curvature of the actual ribs would be needed to be sure).

This exercise underlines the difficulty of making sense of drawings which are now only fragments, but it is a rewarding example because it shows elements from elevations and sections (the window and the vault rib curves) combined in one drawing with a plan. The design of a sample bay in the cloisters is thereby represented along with detail of the window that was to light that bay.

Combining plan and elevation in one drawing was a technique quite often used by medieval master masons. An example discussed in the previous chapter was the drawing of a lancet window at Ashwell where a plan view of the window opening was combined with the elevation (*Figure 2.6*). Another example where a plan view of mouldings forms part of an elevation of an arch is illustrated in Chapter 5 (*Figure 5.10*). So while the English drawings reviewed here do not include sections to compare with the examples from Reims and Prague,[25] the habit of drawing plans and elevations together seems to have been well established and provided an effective way of conceptualising a three-dimensional design.

The small, 12ft bays of the Wells cloister are a rare instance of an element from the overall plan of a building that was small enough to be drawn full size on a tracing floor. The absence of other examples does not mean that they were not drawn out like this, but areas of flooring much larger than the confined space of a tracing floor must have been used. In some instances, where a vault was being designed, the building had already been roofed and it is likely that the floor below or near the intended vault would be used for the drawing.

The other general point about the way plans were laid out is that the geometry used was more practical than the deductive Greek geometry that was taught in the (new) universities. There has been considerable debate about who had the necessary expertise in geometry and in setting out buildings, going back to the design of Romanesque cathedrals such as Winchester, Ely and Norwich. What we see on tracing floors is certainly the work of master masons, but the suggestion is sometimes made that churchmen were often involved in the geometry of the basic plans of buildings. Nigel Hiscock suggests that in the 1070s and 1080s, Bishop Walkelin of Winchester and his brother Simeon took an active interest in design and that, 'it was Walkelin who made the journey to Norwich to survey the site'.[26]

Later in the Middle Ages there were other churchmen, such as Alan of Walsingham (with respect to the octagon at Ely) and William of Wykeham (at Winchester) who had undoubted expertise in the supervision of building works and may have been capable of setting out the plan of a new building. However, such work was probably done in most instances by master masons after discussion with the churchmen who were supervising the projects. Our difficulty here partly arises from the modern desire to identify a specific person as the architect of a building. The expertise of somebody like Alan of Walsingham was of a different kind from the expertise of the master masons and carpenters in charge of construction, and none of these people corresponded precisely to a modern architect. Thus Harvey is open to much criticism for describing his wonderful biographical dictionary of building craftsmen as a dictionary of 'medieval architects'. Responsibilities for design were shared quite differently from what the term 'architect' implies and from what is usual today.[27]

A notable example of confusion about this is shown by claims that Elias of Dereham was the 'architect' of Salisbury Cathedral. Master Elias was a scholar, priest and administrator, an assistant to bishops who sometimes helped with their accounts, sometimes with their political duties. For example, after King John granted Magna Carta in 1215, Elias was entrusted with circulating copies of the document.[28]

However, he became particularly well-known as an administrator of building works. He knew Adam Lock, the master mason at Wells Cathedral and, as will be explained later, he may have been consulted about the west front at Wells. More important, though, Elias was appointed 'keeper of the fabric' at the new Salisbury Cathedral in 1224-5. This was four years after the foundation stone had been laid, when construction at the east end was well advanced.[29] Thus his role may have been less concerned with design than with managing building works and keeping accounts of expenditure. The Bishop responsible for rebuilding the cathedral on an entirely new site, Richard Poore, probably had considerably more influence over the design from the start of the project, long before Elias arrived. However it would be a

Geometry in medieval drawing

mistake to think of either the Bishop or Elias as architects. The design more probably evolved through a complex dialogue between clerics such as these two, and masons such as Nicholas of Ely (who appears to have been in charge). Both groups 'in tandem' deserve to be considered as 'designers'.[30]

TRIANGLES IN DESIGN

Even though the plan of a building was usually set out as a series of squares, with proportions based on the sides and diagonals of squares, there were other options for the elevation and section. In some instances, the square was again the basis of proportions, as in the west fronts of Wells Cathedral[31] and Peterborough.[32] It is also possible that the tall proportions of the section of Westminster Abbey were based on a square of side equal to the overall width of the building.[33] Towards the west end of the nave, where the structure is not complicated by the presence of the cloister, the overall width of the building, including its buttresses, is 31.7m (104ft). The internal height of the nave, to the crown of the vault, is 30.8m (101ft). The near equality of height to width tends to confirm

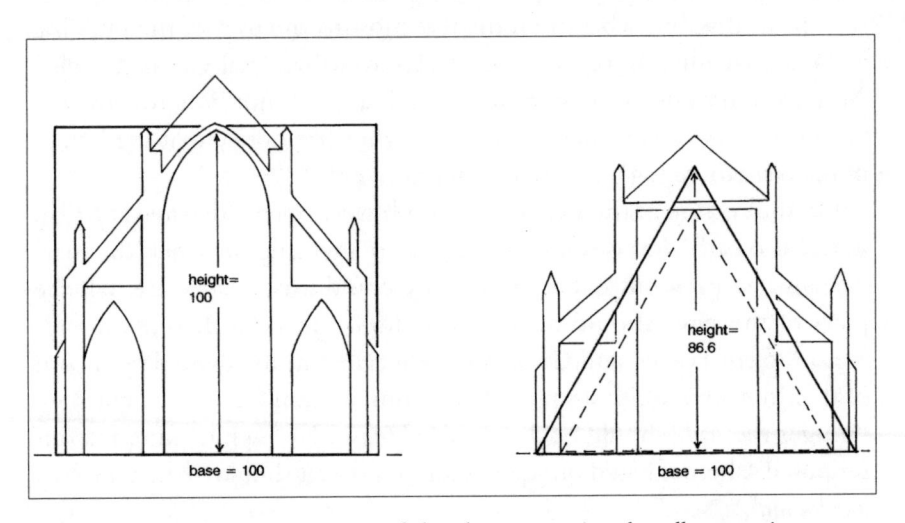

Figure 3.6 Schematic cross-sections of churches, comparing the tall proportions achieved with *ad quadratum* design in a vaulted building (left), and the lower proportions associated with *ad triangulum* design (shown for a building with a timber roof structure).

that the design was conceived as being contained within a square. The ridge of the roof, though, rises significantly higher.

In other buildings, especially those intended to have a less towering profile, another option was to use the dimensions of an equilateral triangle as a guide to design. In such a triangle, all the angles are 60 degrees, and all three sides are the same length. However the height of this triangle is less than the length of its base, and for an equilateral triangle, the height measures 86.6 per cent of the length of one side. This means that the elevation and section of a building designed *ad triangulum* will tend to be only 86.6 per cent as high as a building of the same width designed *ad quadratum* (Figure 3.6).

As an example, the internal width of the nave at Selby Abbey (West Riding of Yorkshire) is 17.78m (just over 58ft). The height of the nave is 15.54m (51ft), which is about 87 per cent of the width – close enough to the theoretical ratio for Eric Fernie to conclude that 'Selby can justifiably be described as a design *ad triangulum*'.[34]

It will be noticed that the external width measurement is quoted for Westminster, whereas the calculation at Selby refers to the internal width. The difference this might make is illustrated by the two triangles drawn for the *ad triangulum* illustration in Figure 3.6. A detailed study of how the geometry of each building was worked out would be required to explain this, but what often matters most to the user of the building is the internal height of the nave relative to its internal width. At Selby Abbey the nave is just over twice as high as it is wide, whereas the tall proportions at Westminster are evident when we notice that the height of the nave there is $3^1/_2$ times its internal width.[35]

On the continent these design methods were openly debated at Milan where the cathedral was much larger than anything of which the local masons had previous experience. They could not decide how tall the piers of the nave should be, nor how high the vault. In 1386 master masons from France and Germany were called in to advise. The record of their differing opinions provides documentation that some craftsmen thought the nave should be designed '*ad triangulum*', while other masons proposed schemes based on squares, or said that it should be designed '*ad quadratum*'.[36]

There are hardly any English medieval drawings that illustrate *ad triangulum* design but, in their absence, it is worth noting a brief period in the fourteenth century when sharply angled forms suggestive of

Figure 3.7 Fourteenth-century doorway and window openings of triangular form at Bristol, Urchfont (Wiltshire), and below, Wells Cathedral.

triangles were sometimes used for doorways or windows instead of the more usual arch shapes based on curves. When William Joy was master mason at Wells, he was responsible for a group of three windows high up in the east wall of the cathedral. This array of glass only illuminates the roof space, not the public parts of the church, and so is rarely noticed, but it consists of two triangular-headed windows with a diamond or lozenge-shaped window above (*Figure 3.7*). However, the triangles in the windows reflect the roof slope of just over 50 degrees and are not equilateral triangles. There are more triangular-headed openings in other buildings thought to have been influenced by William Joy.[37]

Contemporary with Joy's work in the 1320s and 1330s were a number of regional schools of masonry design in which the architectural forms of the Decorated style in architecture, with its intricate tracery, ogee detail and luxuriant carving, were sometimes combined with stark geometrical shapes – triangles, hexagons and octagons. Joy himself was associated with what has been called the 'Bristol school' exemplified by

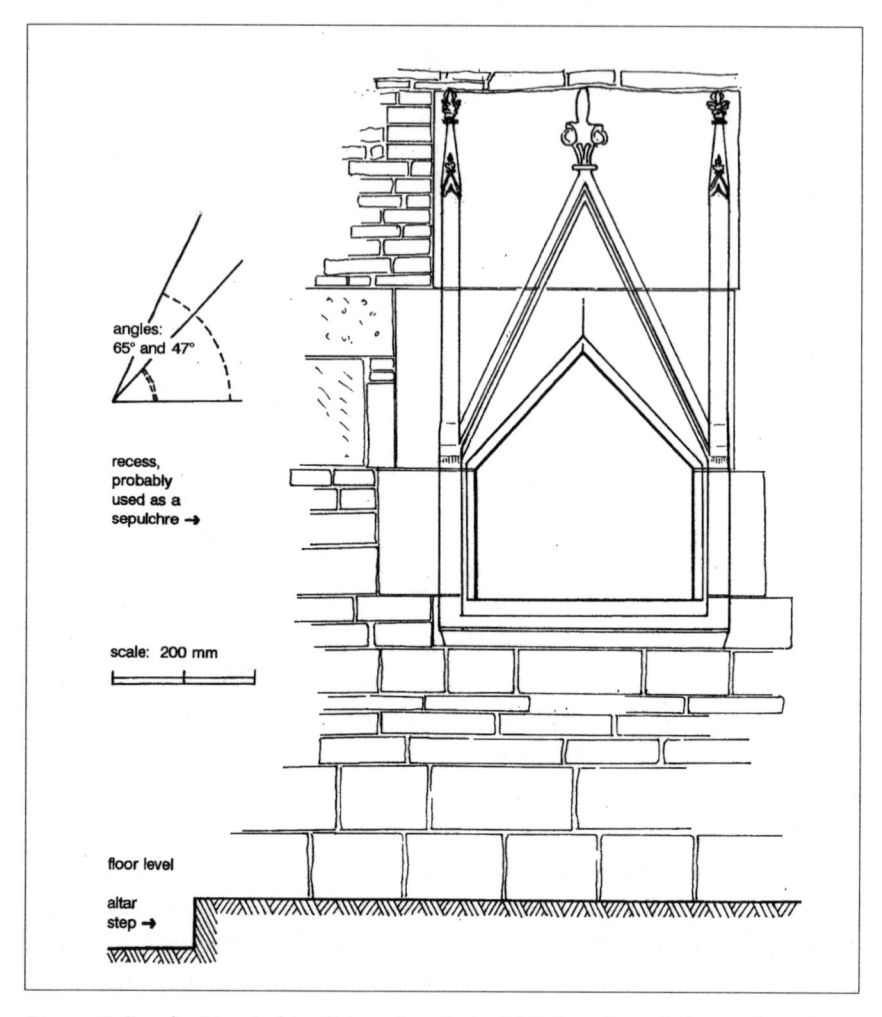

Figure 3.8 Ewerby, Lincolnshire. Recess (aumbry) with 'triangular arch' in a wall on the north side of the altar in St Andrew's Church.

what is now Bristol Cathedral, and by the great Bristol parish church of St Mary Redcliffe. One invention of the Bristol designers was an arch shape based on half an octagon (or in some cases, part of a hexagon) first used for tomb recesses, but then adapted for doorways in the Redcliffe church, at Berkeley Castle, Gloucestershire (*Plate 7*),[38] and Kingsland Church, Herefordshire.[39]

Another regional school in the fourteenth century was located in Lincolnshire and nearby parts of Nottinghamshire and the East Riding, where there is a series of churches with spectacular curvilinear window tracery and richly carved corbels and gargoyles. One special feature of these churches is that a few have an elaborately carved Easter sepulchre, that is a representation of the tomb of Christ used in the medieval liturgy for Good Friday and Easter day.[40] Elsewhere, Easter sepulchres were usually made of wood, but the innovation that appeared in Lincolnshire was a stone-carved form, made like a niche in the wall of the chancel, with an arched head, and often surmounted by a decorative gable. It is striking that in two of these sepulchres, in the churches at Heckington and Navenby, Lincolnshire, the tomb recess has a triangular-headed opening.

A third Easter sepulchre at Ewerby, near Heckington, has no sculptural adornment and is often regarded merely as an aumbry (cupboard) for communion vessels. However, the triangular-headed opening demonstrates a clear relationship with the other two sepulchres and its simplicity makes the geometry of the design even more striking. As in the sepulchres at Heckington and Navenby, the angles at the base of the triangular-headed opening at Ewerby appear to be 45 degrees, but are actually slightly steeper (*Figure 3.8*). A rather similar steepening of the expected angle also applies to the gable outline above the tomb recess. The gable looks like an equilateral triangle, but the actual angle at Ewerby is not 60 degrees but 65 degrees.

The geometry explicit in the Lincolnshire sepulchres may seem to be the kind of scheme that would be worked out first in a drawing. Although nothing of the sort survives, when Sekiles reviewed the whole group of churches associated with the Lincolnshire 'school', she argued that many details of carvings and windows recur so often and in such standardised forms that they demonstrate the regular use of drawings.[41]

CIRCLES IN DRAWING

One point made earlier in this chapter is that, although the plans of many buildings were based on the geometry of the square and although some elevations were proportioned by reference to equilateral triangles, very few drawings have been found in which squares or triangles are prominent. The geometrical figure that is seen most often on tracing floors, walls, or on any other surface where drawings survive, is the circle,

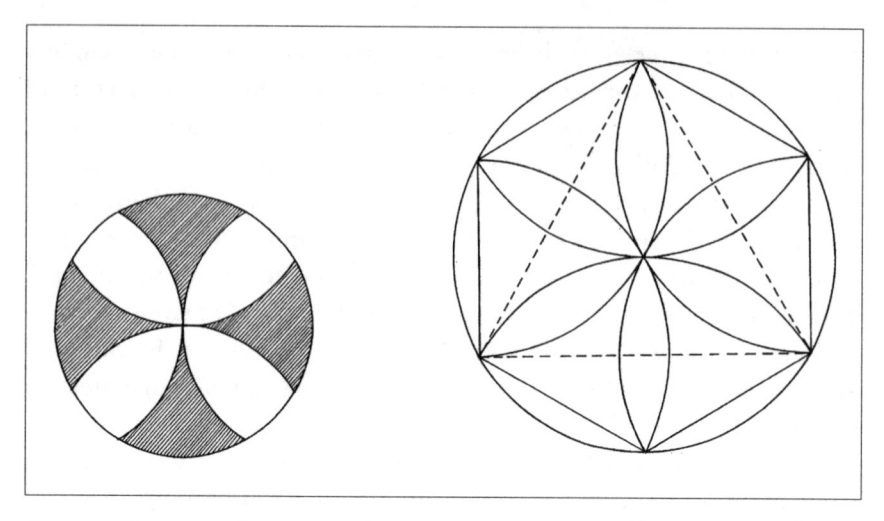

Figure 3.9 A consecration cross and a hexagon constructed with compasses and a straight-edge. The consecration cross (left) is based on examples in Nayland and Long Melford churches in Suffolk, where the hatched area was, in some cases, coloured red. The hexagon (right) was drawn by first marking out the familiar daisy-wheel pattern seen on many buildings.

with many arcs of circles also. Drawings of window tracery account for many of these circles and curves, especially on tracing floors, but even so, large numbers of circles remain unexplained.

What needs to be understood first is that compasses were the medieval masons' most important drawing instrument and were used in conjunction with an L-shaped set-square. Pictures of stone masons regularly show them with compasses and a square.[42] Whatever the mason wanted to draw, he would nearly always use his compasses at some stage. Compasses were used in setting out the lines of an equilateral triangle, or in constructing lines based on the diagonal of a square. The familiar daisy-wheel pattern, often drawn when people were merely playing with compasses, also provided a way of constructing a hexagon or for outlining a cross-shape (*Figure 3.9*).

Numerous drawings made with compasses are to be seen on the walls and woodwork of old buildings and it may be useful to distinguish five kinds of circle drawing:[43] (1) related to window design (2) used to construct other geometrical shapes such as the hexagon in Figure 3.9 (3) arising from geometrical exercises, doodling and play (4) used for scribing outlines for wall paintings; and (5) drawn for ritual purposes.

Figure 3.10 Exeter Cathedral: detail in a painting on the back of one of the sedilia. The gently curved stone back of the seat is shown as if flat to avoid distortion of the drawing. The concentric compass-drawn circles (diameters 146 and 156mm) are emphasised relative to the free-hand painted curves.

Often when circles are found on a wall it is difficult to know which of these categories they fall into. The difficulty is illustrated by drawings in the south aisle of the church at Polstead, Suffolk. On a pier towards the east end of the aisle, one pattern inscribed with a metal compass point consists of a series of concentric circles, the outer one 355mm in diameter. Another pattern, just below, is an interlocking group of smaller circles within which daisy wheels can be seen. This might appear a geometrical exercise, or might be interpreted as a ritual drawing. However, it might also be a practice drawing for a wall painting, because, at the other end of the aisle, on a flat area of wall, there are more 355mm circles, partly inscribed with compasses, but partly marked out in crayon and paint. There is sufficient colour adhering to the wall for it to be clear that this is the remnant of a wall painting whose subject is unidentifiable except that it included two wheels with spokes as may be seen in Plate 24. The first group of drawings might well be related to this in some way.

A more complete painting which incorporates many incised circles drawn with compasses is to be seen on sedilia in Exeter Cathedral. Located alongside the high altar, the sedilia form a towering, pinnacled structure with three seats whose curved stone backs are painted to suggest curtains of patterned cloth hanging in folds (*Plate 8*). Behind one seat, the pattern in the cloth is shown as a series of overlapping circles, whereas on the back of another seat, the illusion is of folds in a cloth patterned with larger circles (*Figure 3.10*).

The curve in the stonework, the illusion of folded cloth, and the delicate hand-painted lines disguise the regular geometry of the circles, but close inspection shows that they are incised with compasses. Small holes in the surface at the centre of each circle show where the compass point was placed when it was drawn. The circumference of a typical circle in fact consists of two incised circles, 146 and 156mm in diameter, with painted curves coinciding with and located in between them. The colours are subdued but harmonious – to the modern eye the circles seem to be outlined in mauve and light brown, although the pigments used were various ochres.

The sedilia were made at the same time as the bishop's throne and other carved furnishings in the region of the high altar.[44] They were probably painted in 1320. The fabric rolls (building accounts) are more detailed than for most major churches and list five painters employed by the cathedral and working by the altar in 1320-21, including Symon, Thomas and Benedict, with others referred to by the initials N and R. It is significant that 'N. Painter' was paid more than the others, in one week specifically for work on an 'image' (a picture or sculpture representing a person). His pay was sometimes as much as 1s 10d per week when others were paid 1s or 1s 4d, and one reference seems to identify him as Nicholas Chynnot.[45] So it was probably this Nicholas who had overall responsibility for the design, with its effect of hanging folds, and for laying out the circle patterns, although it is likely that some of the others did the detailed painting.

These examples should alert us to the possibility that unexplained circle patterns on walls or piers may sometimes be the setting-out lines for paintings, or perhaps the result of a painter practising some preliminary lines or checking the setting of his compasses. Although many paintings were based entirely on freehand drawing, there were several popular subjects where accurately-drawn circles were needed. For example, a moral subject which required a whole series of circles was the Wheel of Life or the Wheel of Fortune, in one case showing different stages of life from birth to death, and in the other representing the rise of a man to wealth and influence and his subsequent fall. Examples of such paintings, often fragmentary, are to be seen in Leominster Priory Church

(Herefordshire), St Mary's Church, Kempley (Gloucestershire) and St Michael's, Swaton (Lincolnshire). All involve a series of up to ten circles framing small scenes, and revolving inside a much larger circle.[46] Close examination will usually show the hard outline where circles have been incised in the wall plaster using a pair of compasses. In Plate 25 a detail of one circle is shown in close-up alongside the main picture and the deeply-incised line made by a compass point, probably before the plaster was dry, can be clearly seen.

In a domestic context, there are remarkable wall paintings dating from the 1320s decorating the main room of a manor house at Longthorpe Tower, Peterborough,[47] and they include another wheel subject, the Wheel of the Five Senses. Commenting on the techniques used in this work, Rouse and Baker note that most of the setting-out lines in these paintings are in faint red or pink, but circles 'were all set out in the plaster with a compass', as was the rim of the wheel, with its spokes also incised by 'mechanical means', namely a metal point and a straight-edge.[48]

What is of general relevance here is that incised lines on plaster made with compasses were regularly used in conjunction with other media, including chalk or charcoal as well as paint. Preliminary drawing for paintings involved use of compasses wherever a regular curve was required. In a comparable manner, architectural drawings on tracing floors or walls that now seem incomplete were almost certainly developed further than is now evident using chalk, charcoal or perhaps red ochre crayons.

Only a minority of unexplained circles incised on walls belong to wall paintings that have otherwise been lost, however, and some other circle drawings were clearly made for ritual purposes. Most obviously there were consecration crosses, marked on the fabric of every new or altered church when it was dedicated. Sometimes the crosses were incised on stonework or plaster with compasses and then painted. The example on the left in Figure 3.9 is based on consecration crosses to be seen in two Suffolk churches.

By contrast, a daisy wheel is illustrated in Figure 3.9 to show how compasses could be used in setting out a hexagon, but daisy wheels were not just a means of doing geometry – they appear very frequently in ritual drawings, often, it is said, as a charm against evil influences.

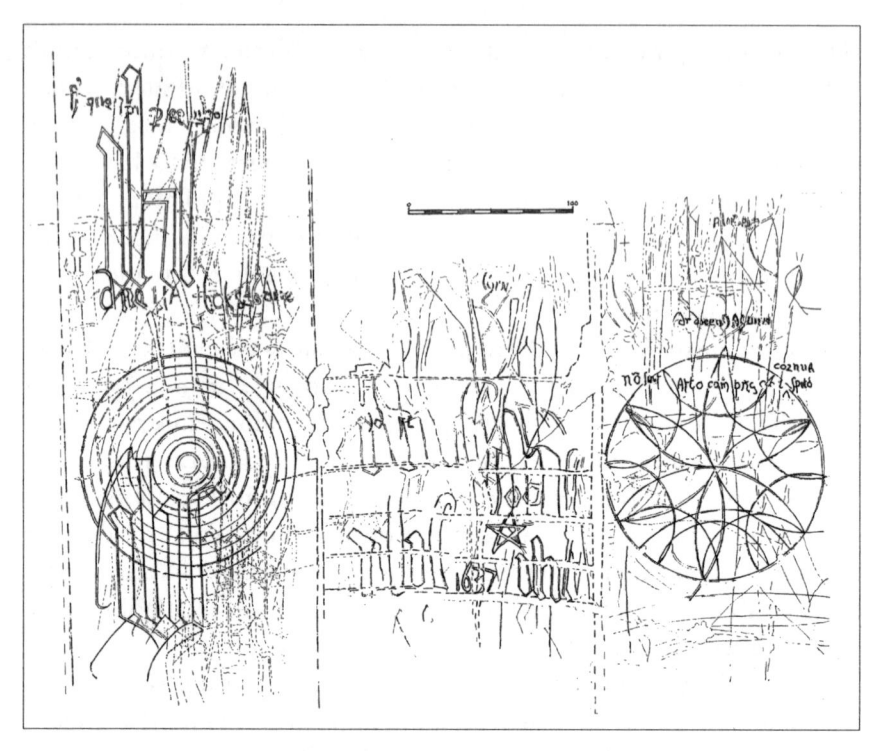

Figure 3.11 Graffiti on the west pier in the south arcade, St Mary's Church, Ashwell, Hertfordshire. The incised circles and lettering are in several medieval and later hands (note the date 1637 low down in the centre). The drawings occupy three adjacent faces of a 12-sided pier, and the paired dashed lines mark the angled corners between faces. Other dashed lines represent random scratches and (in the centre panel) deliberate defacement. Dimensions of the circles are indicated by the 100mm scale bar.

Drawings of spirals are less often seen, but they could sometimes be drawn as an exercise in geometry, or again may have had a ritual purpose. An example is a spiral inscribed on a pier in the south nave triforium at Wells Cathedral, visible only from within the triforium gallery.[49]

An unusual ritual drawing which includes a daisy wheel is to be found among the varied collection of inscribed markings in St Mary's Church, Ashwell (Hertfordshire). On a pier in the south arcade, almost the first thing seen by people as they come through the main door, is a nest of concentric circles intersected by vertical lines (*Figure 3.11*, bottom left). At first sight this can look like yet another sketch of window tracery, but then one realises that the vertical lines are not window mullions but

Figure 3.12 Female figure representing geometry, with square and compasses, redrawn from the thirteenth-century painted ceiling of Peterborough Cathedral.

the outlines of very large letters, which spell out the monogram IHC (or IHS if the last letter is read as a long S). This, of course, stands for the name of Jesus. The monogram is repeated higher up where there is more writing that begins 'dne', probably an abbreviation for 'Domine' (meaning 'O Lord') with further words to the right that have not been deciphered. This is clearly a ritual drawing of some sort, and seems to include a prayer.[50]

The pier on which this is displayed is of a complex, twelve-sided shape and there are marks on two adjacent faces which seem to continue the ritual drawing. To the right, beyond an angle in the face of the pier, the letters IHC or IHS are repeated four times, but are less well executed and smaller than previously, and may be the work of different people at a later date. These letters have been partly obliterated by deliberate gouging of the stone surface (shown by horizontal dashed lines in *Figure 3.11*). A date, 1637, may indicate when this destruction was carried out, perhaps by a puritan hostile to evidence of medieval superstition.

On the next face of the pier to the right is another pattern of circles of the same diameter and at the same height as the first one, but this time it is an ornamented daisy-wheel pattern rather than concentric circles, and it is accompanied by informal comments scribed on the stone. One line of writing points out an error in the drawing: 'non sunt arto compungente cornua', meaning, 'the corners do not join up'. And indeed, the petals of the daisy wheel do not come to a point as they should and some of the additional curves become disordered in the lower right-hand quadrant. The writer of the note adds 'sputo', or, 'I spit [on it]'.[51]

The implication may be that somebody was being instructed in basic geometry here, and if one doubts whether a mason would be literate enough to write these comments, a further note above refers to an archdeacon, so it may be that one of the clergy was playing with a mason's compasses. However, the combination of circle patterns with the repeated letters IHS has the appearance of a talisman or charm against plague and other evil, such as were sometimes illustrated in medieval books of remedies.[52] In such charms circle patterns of the kind seen here sometimes represented the sun and could well be linked to the monogram for Jesus.[53] However, there may not have been a well-considered scheme at Ashwell, as the drawings look like the work of different people spread over several generations. Some of the writing, though, could be in a fifteenth-century hand.[54]

Circle patterns, especially the kind referred to as the daisy wheel, were quite often inscribed as charms on the walls of late medieval buildings, and even more frequently in sixteenth- or seventeenth-century houses. In some regions, lozenges and saltire crosses were also used. In houses they were located on or opposite doorways or fireplaces, and were regarded as protecting the inhabitants.[55]

As further evidence of the role of circles, not only in patterns, charms and ritual marks, but in masons' drawings too, and in formal geometry, it is worth noting that compasses, along with L-shaped set-squares, were often depicted as symbols of the geometry used in construction. A well-known illustration of this is the female figure representing geometry on the painted ceiling of Peterborough Cathedral, which dates from the middle thirteenth century[56] and displays compasses and a square of exactly the kind craftsmen used (*Figure 3.12*).

The grave slab of a mason at Crowland (Lincolnshire), not far from Peterborough, similarly displays compasses and a square to represent the mason's profession. Another grave slab at Lincoln Cathedral commemorates the mason Richard of Gainsborough, but this only has the L-shaped square. It is of interest for another reason, though, for Richard may have worked the slab himself some time before his death was imminent. The date is inscribed as MCCC followed by a blank, as if he hoped that a colleague would fill in the exact year after he had passed away (which was probably nearer to 1350 than 1300).[57]

A wide-ranging survey of medieval measuring and drawing instruments depicted on monuments as well in manuscript illustrations, and embracing continental Europe as well as England, shows that compasses of many kinds were used, some very large. There were also squares, straight-edges, gauges of several kinds, levels, measuring staffs (to provide a standard of length) and the cords necessary for laying out plans on the ground.[58] But the compasses and squares appear in illustrations more regularly than the others.

CONCEPTS FOR BUILDINGS?

The preceding discussion of circle drawings and compasses has been necessary to complete a review of drawings inscribed on walls and elsewhere, but otherwise it has been a digression. The main point of the chapter has been about how different kinds of drawing may reflect different ways of conceptualising a building for the purposes of design or communication.

The contrast between drawings of architectural detail on a tracing floor and more pictorial ways of representing buildings illustrates different kinds of visual thinking about structures. The pictorial approach was quite effective for considering groups of buildings, but not for detailed design. By contrast, tracing-floor drawings show the geometry of circles and curves underlying window tracery patterns and other detail. However another sort of drawing seen on tracing floors combined elevation and plan views of small parts of buildings, and could provide a more three-dimensional concept of what was being designed.

It is widely agreed that design ideas for plans were often conceived in relation to the geometry of the square, which was used to determine the proportions of many Romanesque and Gothic buildings. However it is also worth noting how designers were sometimes attracted away from the square to use circular or polygonal forms for an apse or chapter house. Beginning with the circular plan adopted for the chapter house in Worcester Cathedral (before 1125) a theme developed that is seen again in a twelve-sided chapter house at Dore Abbey (Herefordshire) and a ten-sided one at Lincoln, and then in the classic octagonal chapter houses at Salisbury Cathedral, Westminster Abbey, York Minster and Southwell, all four built in the thirteenth century. Hexagonal plan forms were used for church porches at St Mary Redcliffe (Bristol), Ludlow (Shropshire) and Chipping Norton (Oxfordshire). Drawings in which polygons or triangles are explicit are rarely found, but triangles and segments of octagons (and hexagons) were given visual form in door-heads and above wall-recesses for tombs (including Easter sepulchres) in a few significant buildings during the fourteenth century.

With regard to plans of churches, it is possible to think that there may have been a certain tension between concepts based on combining squares and the impulse to use circular or polygonal forms. A similar tension regarding the elevations of buildings is suggested by Lawrence Hoey in trying to explain why the church at Rievaulx Abbey (North Riding) never had a rose window even when most other monastic churches in the region were building them. He wonders whether circular shapes were sometimes felt to be incompatible with the 'linear grid mentality' underlying certain designs.[59] The implication is that just as there was choice between *ad quadratum* and *ad triangulum* systems of proportion, so too there were choices about emphasising circles rather than grids.

As to surviving drawings, geometrical figures of overwhelming prominence are the circles and curves necessary to draw window tracery. Circles may also appear as part of the setting out of wall paintings. There, however, they were used in combination with other media, usually paint but sometimes charcoal or crayon, and the possibility should never be forgotten that much drawing on tracing floors may have been carried out in the latter media, and is now entirely lost.

CHAPTER 4

CARPENTERS' MARKINGS

(carpenters and joiners, *c*.1200-1400)

PATTERNS OR DRAWINGS?

It was not only masons who made full-size drawings, but so at times did the carpenters who built timber-framed houses and constructed roofs. However, evidence contemporary with the surviving tracing floors used by masons is elusive. What is clear, though, is that carpenters often needed to work closely with masons, so some similarities in working methods are to be expected. For example, the stonework of arches or arched windows had to be supported during construction by wooden formwork or centring. This not only had to follow the shape of the arch precisely, but had to be firmly supported from below by a wooden scaffold. The interior of a Gothic church might have a stone vault as its ceiling, but while the vault was being built, that also had to be supported by wooden formwork and, if it was to be kept weatherproof, it had to be sheltered by a roof with wooden rafters.[1] Small churches often had simple wooden roofs without stone vaulting, but in a few large ones, including York Minster and the transepts of Exeter Cathedral, vaults were built of timber and then were made to look like stone.[2]

Many buildings therefore depended on close collaboration between masons and carpenters, who learned a great deal about each other's trades. One man whose career illustrates this was Thomas of Witney (*c*.1270-1342) who was master mason at Winchester, Wells and Exeter, but who also had a reputation as a carpenter and seems to have designed the partly timber-framed Pilgrim's Hall at Winchester (1310) as well as being responsible for the roofs of several buildings and for designing joinery at Exeter Cathedral.[3]

Developments in the architecture of stone buildings are obvious to anybody who examines the early Gothic of Canterbury Cathedral (after 1174) Wells (*c.* 1180) and Lincoln (1190s) and compares it with what was being done at Ely or Norwich a century earlier. Developments in carpentry are not so obvious, but even before precise tree-ring dates could be determined, Fletcher and Spokes,[4] and Cecil Hewett[5] had identified a number of particularly early roofs and had noted carpentry detail associated with buildings that were generally in the Romanesque or Norman tradition, some in the monastic buildings at Ely Cathedral. These 'Romanesque roofs', dating mainly from the twelfth century, were all common-rafter roofs; that is they were made with a succession of A-frames, formed by pairs of rafters (or 'rafter couples') made of timbers cut to a uniform square section. After 1200, roofs for Gothic buildings were at first similar in construction, but tended to be significantly steeper.

It is appropriate here to mention the roofs above the two surviving plaster tracing floors, at Wells and York. Dating from the first third of the thirteenth century, the Wells roof has rafter couples each with a simple collar, as shown in Figure 4.1. About a century after it was first built, the roof was altered (along with roofs in the rest of the cathedral) when parapets were constructed where previously there had been overhanging eaves.[6] Other alterations that were necessary are indicated in Figure 4.1. On the right in this diagram is the likely original form of the roof. Only after the parapets were constructed, with consequent alterations to the feet of the rafters, was the tracing floor laid (that is after *c.* 1320). In more recent times, additional collars have been inserted and there have been many other repairs, but some original collars survive higher in the roof (*Plate 26*).

At York, the other major surviving tracing floor is sheltered by a later type of rafter roof (*Figure 4.2a*). There are over 30 couples of the type shown above the two arms of the L-shaped masons' loft in which the tracing floor is located. At the angle in the plan, a single truss of much more unusual form spans the room diagonally (*Figure 4.2b*). The central vertical post in this structure, the king post, seems to derive in concept from the central post in the roof of the nearby chapter house[7] which is made from timber felled in 1288. Other details are also comparable, including the secondary rafters, which suggests that the roof over the tracing floor dates from about the same time or a little later.

Constructed about 60 years apart, the roofs at Wells and York offer an instructive contrast in carpentry practice. In the former, collars are

Carpenters' markings

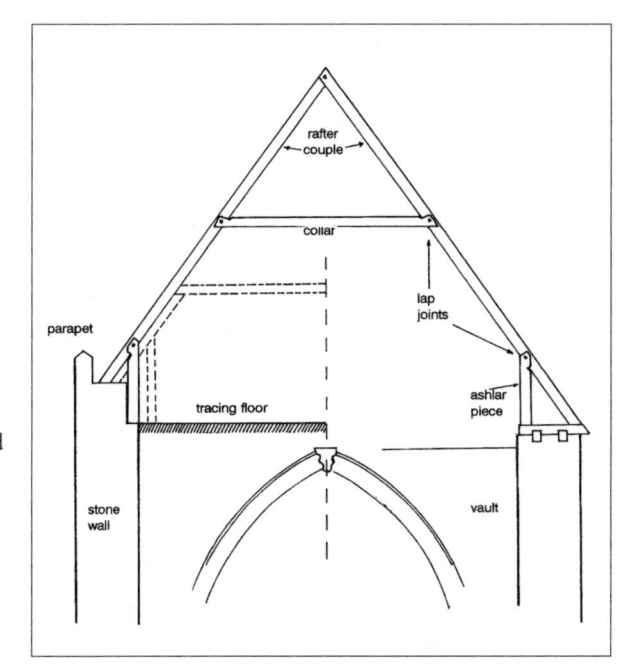

Figure 4.1 Wells Cathedral: diagrammatic view of the roof of the north porch, as it may originally have been constructed (right), and as altered later (left). Dashed lines represent a replacement ashlar piece and modern additions, including a lower collar. Not to scale.

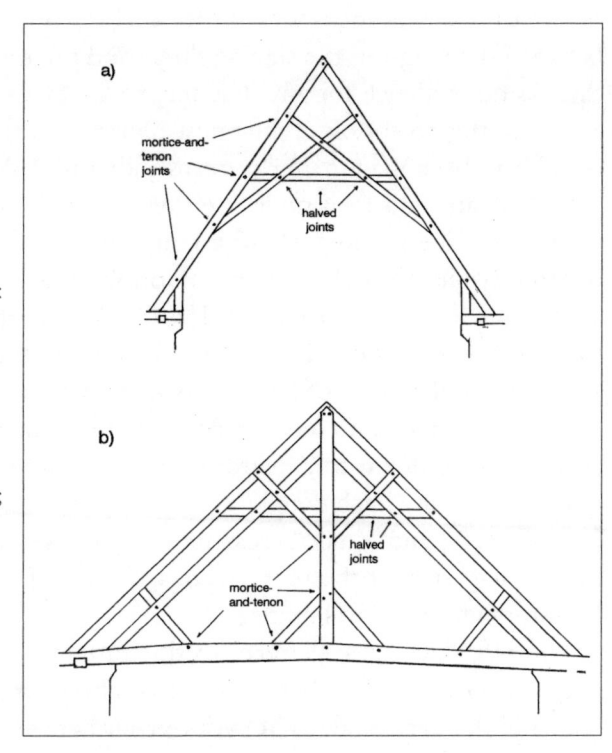

Figure 4.2 York Minster: diagrams illustrating the roof over the masons' loft
a) braced rafter couple typical of those used throughout the length of both arms of the loft;
b) truss spanning diagonally across the angled corner of the room.
Based on a drawing by Alison Armstrong. Copyright © Dean & Chapter of York

89

attached to the rafters by means of *lap joints*. In these particular examples, there is a notch in the collar close to the joint (*Plate 26*), which engages with a similar shape cut into the rafter, so a more precise term for these is to call them *notched* lap joints.

The York roof, by contrast, is made predominantly with *mortice-and-tenon* joints (although some joints with the rafters are hard to see and are left unclear in *Figure 4.2b*). Where timbers cross in this roof, however, each timber is recessed and reduced to half its thickness to accommodate the other, making a joint known as a *halving*. The increasing use of mortice-and-tenon joints was one of a number of important changes in carpentry practice that took place during the thirteenth century. In 1200, the mortice-and-tenon was used where rafters were jointed into tie beams (e.g. in St Hugh's choir, Lincoln Cathedral, *c.*1204-9)[8] but most other joints in rafter roofs were lap-joints or halvings. However by 1300, mortice-and-tenon joints had replaced the earlier types in most other parts of roofs covering stone-walled buildings.[9]

The two roofs cited from Wells and York are significant in illustrating changes in carpentry. However, in both places, the roofs were made before the tracing floors which they shelter, so there is no connection between drawings on the tracing floors and the roof carpentry. Indeed, there is no evidence for any drawings made by carpenters at this time and, with the exception of the unusual diagonal truss at York, both roofs could have been made using 'patterns' rather than drawings.

The length of a roof such as either of these could be specified by referring to the number of rafter couples it contained. When the roof of Holy Trinity Church at Caister (Norfolk) was to be replaced in 1330, a contract with the carpenters, John and Robert de Gunton, stated that they were to take down the old roof and then raise 29 'couples of clean, good timber of heart of oak'. Each couple was to be 'of the length of 25 of a man's foot' (which may mean that it was to span 25ft) and was to conform to a 'pattern' agreed between the parties, 'sealed under their seals'. Each couple was to be 'framed with tie-beams, collars [wyndbemes] and ashlars, cross-braced among the collars'.[10] The last phrase suggests that the roof was to have scissor braces rather like the York roof illustrated in Figure 4.2a.

The reference to a 'pattern' in this instance is striking. What the contract actually says is: 'a pattern agreed between the parties of a staff sealed under their seals'. The word given here as 'staff' was *fusschel* in the Norman-French original, which Harvey translated as 'stick'. It could perhaps mean a measuring rod with various dimensions marked on it, but it might indicate a sample length of rafter cut to show where joints would be made with the collars, ashlars and cross-pieces.[11]

The court rolls of Great Yarmouth which include this contract show that the same group of carpenters had worked on another Norfolk church roof in 1319. In that instance, the roof was to be 'of the width and length of the pattern', the wording here suggesting that the pattern may have been full size, perhaps even a complete rafter couple, made in advance of the rest of the roof. The leading carpenter when that contract was signed was William de Gunton, but he died later in 1319, when another contract for a different part of the church was agreed by his widow Margaret and a young son, John, with a relative, Roger. So the contract stated that 'Roger, Margaret and John shall make a roof ... of 32 rafters'. Then in 1330, with John now of age, he and Robert de Gunton, perhaps a brother, were running the business.[12]

An alternative to having a separate 'pattern', such as was used by the Gunton group of carpenters, was to use the first of the rafter couples to be made for a roof as a template, laying out the timbers of the next and subsequent couples on top of it. That this was actually done in some cases is shown by one of the transept roofs at Holy Trinity Church, Wistanstow, Shropshire, which has been dated by dendrochronology to c.1200-21. The roof has six rafter couples made of timbers about 6ins (c.150mm) square and, as Dan Miles explains, all joints are halved in a distinctly archaic manner. Several of the rafter couples not only have a set of auger holes for the pegs that hold joints together, but also a series of partly-started auger holes corresponding with the positions of pegs in the next rafter couple to the south. This shows that the timbers on which the carpenters were working were lying flat on top of the last rafter couple to be completed when the auger holes were made and that the auger passed right through one rafter to mark the timber lying below. Occasionally, even the pegs in the couple underneath were bored into, confirming that before being used as a template, it had been fully assembled and pegged together.[13]

An alternative to laying timbers on top of one another was to mark the basic shape of the rafter couples on the surface of the ground where the timbers were being laid out, often referred to as the 'framing ground'. The shape could be outlined using taut cords stretched between pegs, or it could be scribed on the ground with a pointed tool, or drawn with chalk. Then each successive set of timbers could be laid out over the outline in the same way as templates for stonework were laid out on a masons' tracing floor. The evidence from Wistanstow that the actual rafter couples were used as patterns or templates for one another suggests that no lines were marked out on the ground in this instance.

The roof of a small church or other stone building was a relatively simple structure and it would not be surprising if designs were worked out in the form of a pattern without making separate drawings, as these examples from Norfolk and Shropshire seem to imply. However, the frame for a complete house or barn, including walls and aisle posts, could not be designed or constructed so easily, and studies of the two thirteenth-century barns constructed for the Knights Templar at Cressing Temple, Essex, seem to show that they were designed by the same kind of geometrical methods as were used for establishing the proportions of churches (mentioned in the previous chapter).

Thus Adrian Gibson has shown that the cross-section of the Wheat Barn at Cressing Temple has proportions which could have been arrived at using the same principles of *ad triangulum* design as are said to have been used for designing the cross-sectional proportions of churches. Moreover, just as churches were often planned using the perch or rod of 16½ft (5.03m) as a unit of length, so too were the Cressing Temple barns. The older barn, the Barley Barn, was originally 3 perches wide and 9 perches long. By contrast, the Wheat Barn at Cressing Temple is precisely 2½ perches in total width and its height corresponds to the height of an equilateral triangle with sides of that length.[14]

These conclusions about the use of triangles in design arise entirely from modern measurements of the existing buildings, not from any medieval records or drawings showing how carpenters worked. Hence, although the proportions of the Cressing Temple barns are fully consistent with the use of *ad triangulum* design, it is open to Laurie Smith to argue that the proportions of the buildings were derived by drawing circles rather than triangles. Since equilateral triangles can be fitted neatly within circles, Smith's theory about how circles were used leads to the same results as Gibson's triangles. Figure 4.3, which is more basic than either authors' diagrams, shows how a notional aisled barn can be proportioned by these geometrical figures. Smith claims more generally that there is 'considerable evidence for circle-based design in

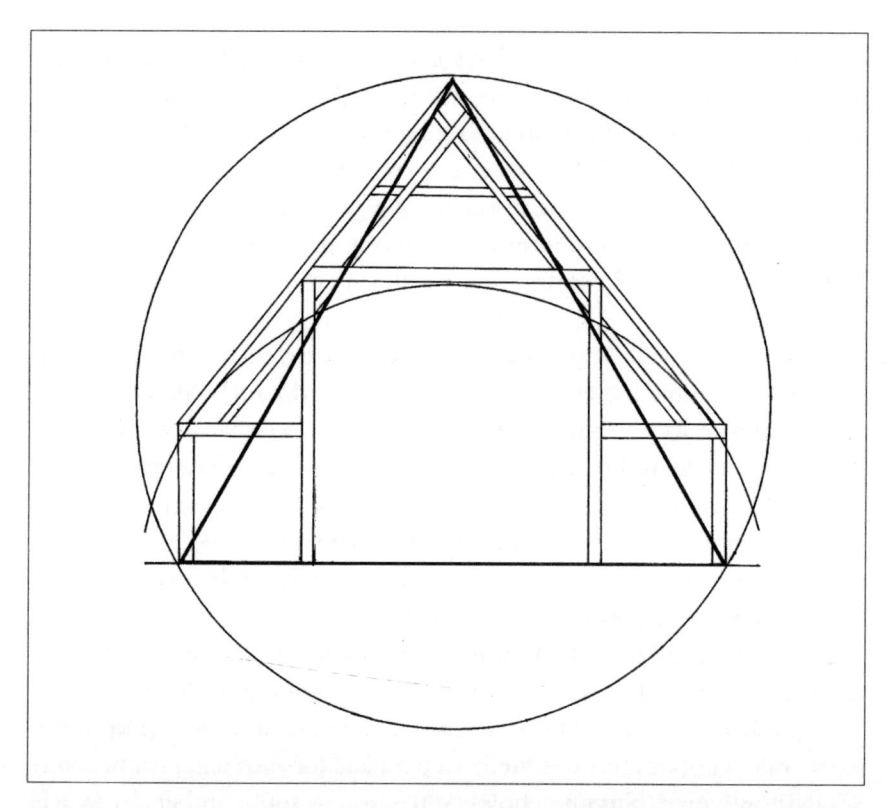

Figure 4.3 Typical cross-section of a medieval aisled barn showing how, in principle, its proportions might be related to the height of an equilateral triangle (as in *ad triangulum* design) and how the proportions may also be represented by intersecting circles.

the medieval period'.[15] This accords with the experience mentioned in previous chapters that craftsmen frequently drew circles (rather than squares or triangles) on walls and tracing floors.

EVIDENCE FOR FRAMING GROUNDS

Although we cannot really be certain about the systems of geometrical design used by carpenters, the fact that the dimensions of the Cressing Temple barns fit a consistent scheme demonstrates that they were designed according to precise criteria of some sort. For example, plans and sections are coordinated so that the height of each barn corresponds exactly to the length of two bays on plan. Such consistency would not arise from an improvised design procedure and suggests that the design of the section was worked out by means of some sort of drawing on a horizontal ground surface, referred to as the framing ground. Popularising this idea for the purposes of a guide book, Andrews and his colleague illustrate a carpenter marking out circles on the site where a barn was to be built. The carpenter is using a cord as radius to mark out a series of circles.[16]

While these deductions about the geometrical design procedure used at Cressing Temple are eminently plausible – and Laurie Smith extends the conclusion to other major medieval barns in south-east England[17] – the evidence is all indirect. No framing grounds survive in a recognisable state and there are no carpenters' drawings from before 1450. Hence, a search for more tangible evidence of how carpenters worked out designs on framing grounds and then carried them out in timber must look at other aspects of carpenters' working methods.

In fact, there are four kinds of lines and marks to be seen on structural timbers in medieval buildings which show something of the work done while timbers were laid out on the ground. The first, already mentioned, is where one set of timbers was used as a template for another as happened at Wistanstow, where blind peg holes were cut into some timbers by augers working on other material laid over them. This seems to reflect a situation where no outline or drawing had been marked out on the floor.

The second kind of evidence for work done on the framing ground is where setting-out lines have been drawn on the timbers themselves with a metal point (the point of a knife or of a pair of compasses) to show the alignment of a mortice hole, or to establish the positions of peg holes. Such setting-out lines may sometimes be extensions of lines drawn on the floor.

The third type of mark is what Miles and Russell call a plumb-and-level mark and was made in situations where the cutting of joints required that a plumb bob or level be used frequently to check alignments.[18] In such cases, the timber would be carefully levelled before work began and, where the surface of the timber had been checked and was known to be accurately horizontal (or vertical) a mark comprising crossed diagonals or some related sign would be scribed on that surface so that the carpenter could come back to it for reference when further checks on level and alignment were needed. Water Hall, Little Baddow, Essex,

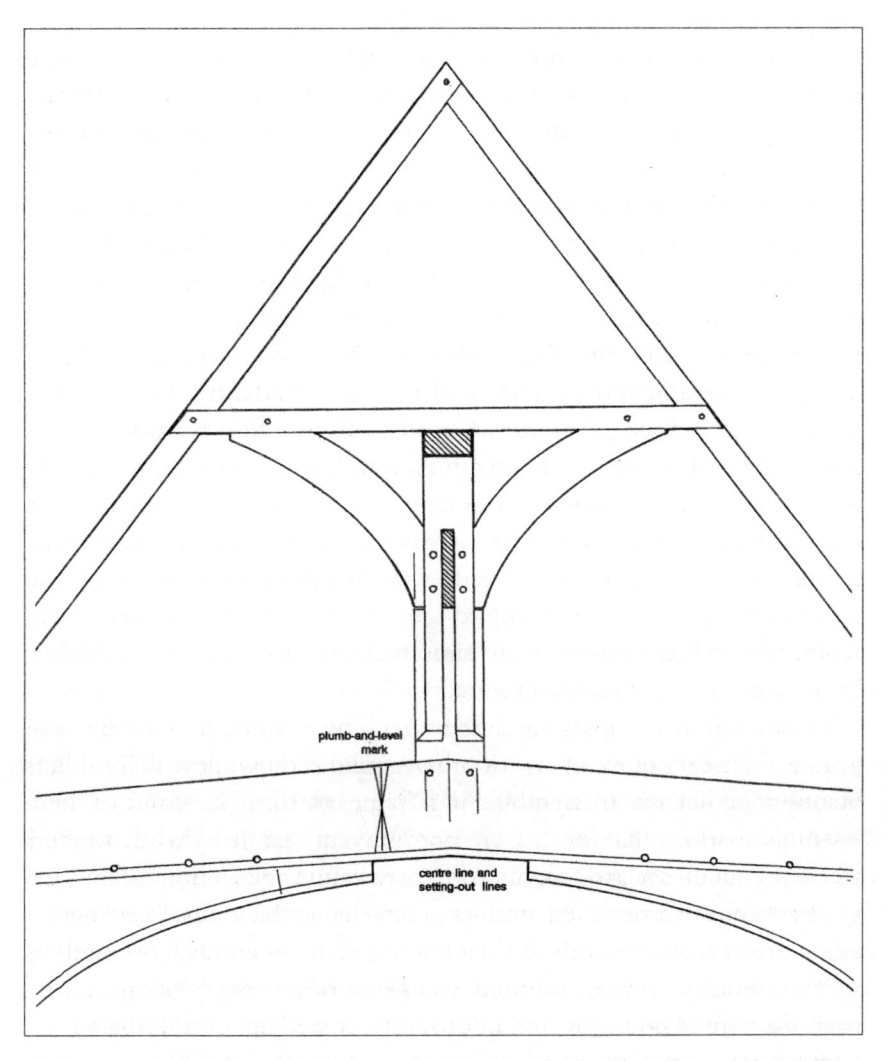

Figure 4.4 Water Hall, Little Baddow, Essex: the tie beam and crown post above the hall. Not to scale.

is a much later timber-framed structure than others considered so far, perhaps dating from *c.*1500, but it conveniently illustrates a plumb-and-level mark of this kind on the tie-beam of a truss spanning its open hall (*Figure 4.4*). Also visible are examples of setting-out lines, such as were mentioned above. These lines show where the mortice was to be cut and where peg holes were to be drilled, at the point where the base of the crown post is jointed into the tie-beam.[19]

As previously emphasised, masons and carpenters often worked closely together and tended to borrow each others' working methods. This applies also to plumb-and-level marks, although the use of these by masons has rarely been systematically recorded. Those that have again tend to be later than the period mainly dealt with in this chapter. The example illustrated (*Figure 4.5*) is in the church at Great Budworth, Cheshire, where there are centre lines scribed on some of the piers against which a plumb bob would be dropped during construction, and the centre lines are sometimes indicated with two or three cross marks. The south arcade and clerestory of this church, dating from the late fifteenth century, give an impression that this may be a masonry design heavily influenced by a carpenter. Roll mouldings running horizontally above the arches combine with vertical mouldings running up from the piers into the clerestory to make a visual frame on which plumb-and-level marks have been cut on some of the horizontal mouldings as well as on verticals. There is nothing to identify the craftsmen who did this work, although the tower of the church, dating from *c.*1500, is probably by a mason named Thomas Hunter.[20]

The fourth way of marking timber that reflects work done on framing grounds is the set of numbers (or other symbols) showing which timbers belong together when assembled in a frame or truss. The point of these assembly marks is that joints were not only cut and fitted while timbers were laid out on the ground, but roof trusses and large sections of framing were completely assembled, with pegs inserted at the joints. Then, before being taken apart, lifted onto the building and reassembled, the timbers were numbered so that components of one rafter couple (or from one wall of a framed house) would not become mixed up with timbers from another part of the structure.

A roof might consist of 20 rafter couples, all similar in appearance, but with the joints individually fitted. It was essential when timbers were lifted into position on the building that the components of each rafter couple were kept together, because the tenons on the collar for, say, the sixth couple from the east end would not fit the mortices in the seventh pair of rafters without extra cutting and shaping and the peg holes would not coincide. The obvious solution was to assign a number to each rafter couple and to mark this number on all the components of the couple.

Roman numerals were commonly used, but with various adaptations to allow for the fact that carpenters were often illiterate and would

Plate 1 Chapter house entrance, Southwell Minster (Notts.). *Copyright © English Heritage. NMR*

Plate 4 Boss from the vault of the warming house, St Mary's Abbey, York.
Photo: *J.D. Pacey*

Plate 5 Wells Cathedral, Somerset: room above the north porch with tracing floor.
Copyright © Crown copyright. NMR

Plate 8 Exeter Cathedral: the sedilia, with painting to simulate curtains on the backs of seats. *Copyright © English Heritage. NMR*

Plate 9 Hereford Cathedral: detail of choir stalls. *From Charles Tracy,* English Gothic Choir Stalls, 1200-1400, *by courtesy of the Boydell Press*

Plate 10 All Saints' Church, Hereford: back of the choir stalls showing the contrast between sawn and axe-dressed planks. *From Charles Tracy,* English Gothic Choir Stalls, 1200-1400, *by courtesy of the Boydell Press*

Plate 11 Page from William Worcestre's itinerary with profile of moulding for a doorway at St Stephen's Church, Bristol. *By permission of Corpus Christi College, Cambridge*

Plate 12 Detail of the south porch, St Stephen's Church, Bristol. *Copyright © English Heritage. NMR*

Plate 13 Doorway at St Michael-le-Belfrey Church, York. *Photo: J.D. Pacey*

Plate 14 North arcade in St Michael-le-Belfrey Church, York. *Copyright © Crown copyright. NMR*

Plate 15 The Abbot's House, Shrewsbury. *Copyright © English Heritage. NMR*

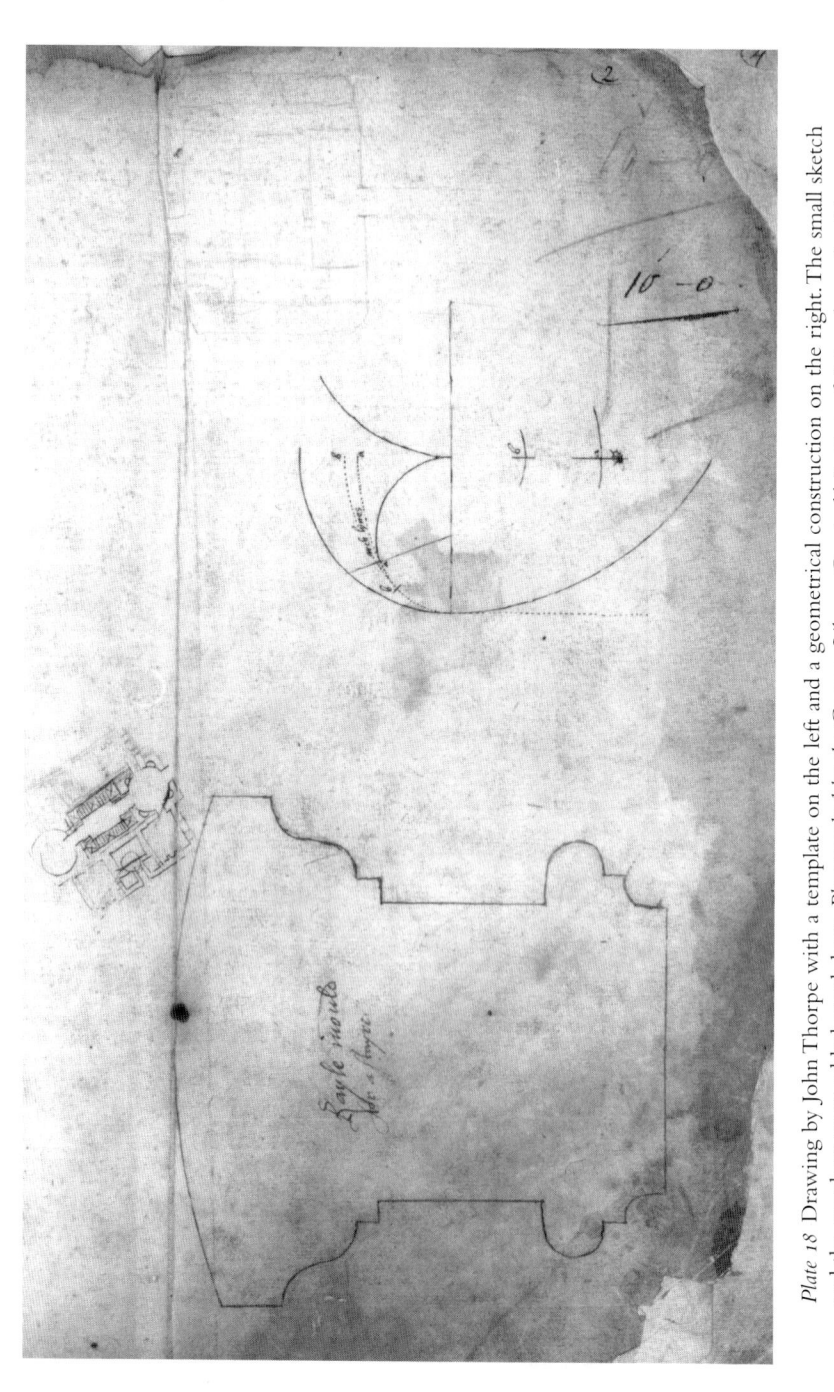

Plate 18 Drawing by John Thorpe with a template on the left and a geometrical construction on the right. The small sketch and the numbers were added much later. *Photographed by the Conway Library, Courtauld Institute of Art, and reproduced by courtesy of the Trustees of Sir John Soane's Museum*

Figure 4.5 St Mary's Church, Great Budworth, Cheshire. Pier in the south arcade of the nave, sketched from the south aisle, with a centre line identified by plumb-and-level marks scribed in the stonework.

sometimes see a timber upside down. On both counts, they could easily confuse IV and VI. Hence the convention they adopted was that four was always written IIII, whereas six could be written either VI or IV. Then nine was written VIIII, or sometimes Z (or N on its side) although, confusingly, Z could sometimes stand for ten. After ten, eleven could be written either as XI or IX. There were also several ways of conflating two or three Xs to mark 20 or 30 on a timber and various tags or loops could be added to numbers to specify in more detail where in a building a particular timber belonged. However, not all carpenters' assembly marks were derived from Roman numerals and symbols of other kinds that were occasionally used will be considered later.

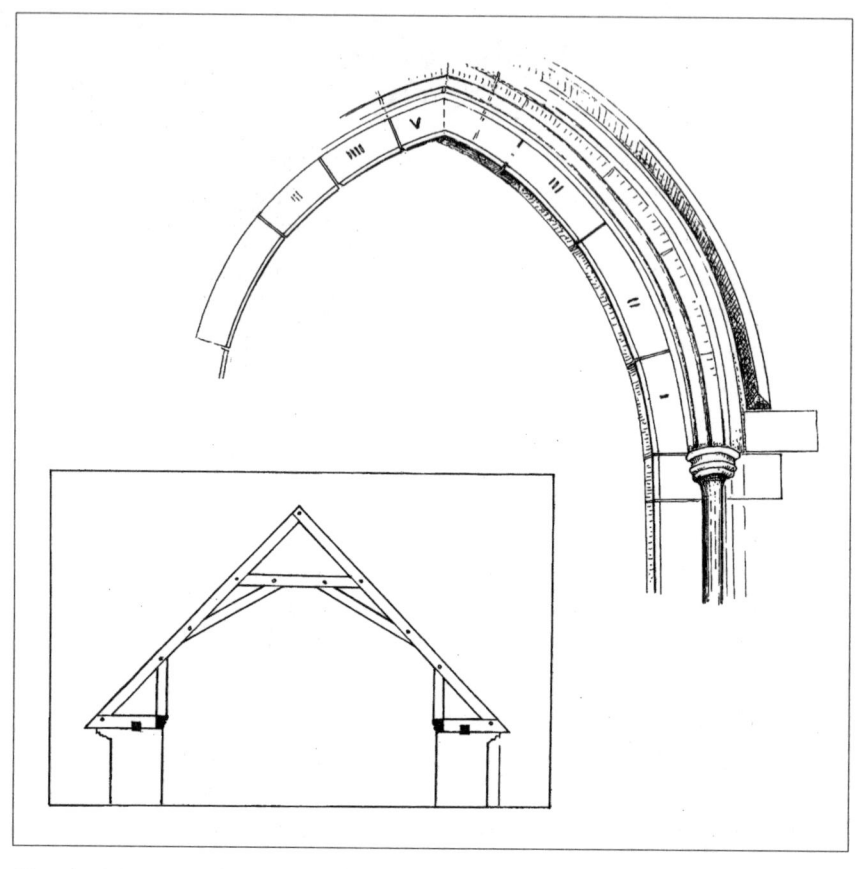

Figure 4.6 Doorway from the south porch into the church at Heckington, Lincolnshire, sketched to show masons' numbers. Inset is the roof of the porch itself in which the carpenters exclusively used mortice-and-tenon joints.

Again there are similarities between the work of carpenters and masons, since the latter sometimes used assembly marks in the form of numbers to show how the stones of an arch or vault should fit together.[21] Figure 4.6 includes a sketch of the fourteenth-century arched doorway leading from the south porch into the church at Heckington, Lincolnshire, and it will be seen that the voussoirs of the arch are numbered. Assembly marks on arches were often hidden in the mortared joints and then are only seen when a building is in ruins. Sometimes there were no numbers on stones, but a cross or other symbol might be cut on one face of a voussoir to show which way round it should go (*Plate 4*). When stones were numbered in this way, it was usually because the components of the doorway or arch were laid out flat on the ground while they were being cut and fitted in the same way as the components of timber-framed buildings. That would often mean that an outline drawing of the doorway or arch had been marked out on the ground. By placing the stones on top of the drawing and adjusting their shapes until there was a good fit, the design could be executed without using templates.

The four ways in which carpenters marked timber all provide evidence of work done before the building was erected, but the occasional setting-out lines are the only direct evidence of any sort of drawing. Other types of mark sometimes encountered include consignment marks (especially on imported timber, but usually much later) and personal marks identifying an individual craftsman. The latter are rarely found on woodwork, but examples include misericords at Exeter dating from c.1250 and later at Ludlow, Shropshire.[22] The marks at Exeter take the form of concentric circles and serve as a reminder that 'carpenters' circles' were made for many different reasons and interpretation can be difficult. Sometimes practice circles were drawn to check that a pair of compasses would maintain a set radius and sometimes circles were used as assembly marks. Ritual (apotropaic) marks or charms also sometimes appear on timber, often in the form of daisy-wheel patterns (as explained in the previous chapter). These other forms of marking can usually be distinguished from assembly marks and plumb-and-level marks by position and context, apotropaic marks often being close to doorways[23] and assembly marks related to joints.

JOINERY AND WOOD CARVING

Carpenters' assembly marks are clear evidence of how timber structures were made and put together on a framing ground and then taken apart for reassembly on the building itself. Yet they provide no evidence for how the structure was designed and whether the carpenter made any drawings in the process.

It may be worth enquiring whether there is any evidence for how medieval craftsmen approached design with regard to the smaller-scale woodwork that would have been made on a bench in a workshop rather than on a framing ground in the open. This includes joinery and carving, and seems quite distinct from what was done by the carpenters responsible for roofs and other major structures, although where building accounts survive, they sometimes show that the master carpenter responsible for the main roofs of a church also supervised the production of joinery work for screens and furnishings. For example, at Exeter Cathedral choir stalls had already been constructed before Thomas of Witney began to work there in 1313, but he designed other furnishings, including the bishops' throne, which was made by a carpenter named Robert de Galmeton.[24]

At Wells Cathedral, the master carpenter during the 1330s was John Strode and his assistant in 1341 was Bartholomew Quarter. Important large-scale construction work in progress was the roof of the retrochoir, but as well as supervising that, it is thought that John Strode was also responsible for a new set of choir stalls and may himself have contributed to their carving. The total spent on them was £75, of which £15 was for materials and, given the general level of wage rates at the time, it is deduced that the 90 stalls were probably made by three craftsmen over a period of three years,[25] beginning in 1335 or 1336 and completed by 1340. Two styles of carving have been recognised in the misericords, implying that two individuals did most of the work, so the third man employed was possibly an assistant, or responsible only for joinery and not carving. The style of one carver indicates that he had previously worked at Winchester and his carvings of animals (including a cat, owl and bat) are especially memorable.

Thus, at Exeter and Wells there are accounts that tell us a little about how work was organised and who held responsibility for making choir stalls and other furnishings, but there is very little detail about the working methods of carpenters and carvers. It is not very clear whether master craftsmen such as Witney or Strode made precise drawings for others to follow, or just gave outline instructions. However, we do gain some clues about the role drawings may have played by following a link between the choir stalls at Wells, completed by 1340, and stalls in Hereford Cathedral, probably made later in the 1340s. Many of the carvings on misericords at Hereford represent the same subjects as at Wells, notably a bat and a dragon, and they are depicted in a way which shows a close familiarity with the work at Wells, but in a markedly different personal style. The suggestion is that the carver of dragons at Hereford must have spent a considerable time at Wells. It also seems that he must have sketched carvings that he saw there, since his work at Hereford is too close to what had been done at Wells to be accounted for simply by a good visual memory.[26]

Another suggestion, though, is that the third craftsman at Wells, who worked only as an assistant, may have moved to Hereford in a more senior role. So although his style does not emerge at Wells because he was given little opportunity to work as a carver, we do see his work at Hereford.

Whoever the carvers and joiners were in Hereford Cathedral, it is of interest that some drawing by one of them (the carver of dragons) appears on a panel at the west end of the stalls, on the north side, in the form of setting-out lines. Here, the moulding which should run horizontally along the top of the panel is unfinished and remains as a flat surface on which can be seen several scribed lines, some ruled, but some continuing the curves of the blank tracery below. When the tracery itself is examined, some of the scribed curves can be followed along the tops of the mouldings (*Plate 9*). This allows part of the setting-out drawing which the carpenter or joiner incised on the timber at the start of his work to be reconstructed (*Figure 4.7*). In order to draw the curves shown, he would have needed to place his compass point at the four locations shown by small crosses, which are aligned on what was effectively the base line of the drawing.

The dragon in the spandrel may not have been part of the initial inscribed drawing on the panel, even though it is included in Figure 4.7. This is one of the details which seems to have been copied from misericords at Wells Cathedral, so perhaps the craftsman had a sketch with him that he had made at Wells. However, the unfinished state of this work is one of several discontinuities which leads Tracy to suggest that construction of these choir stalls during the 1340s was seriously interrupted at some point, perhaps by the Black Death.[27] The setting-out drawing that appears on this panel would have been entirely cut away if the mouldings had been completed.

There are more choir stalls in Hereford, at All Saints' Church, and they consist of two groups of five seats with canopies like those in the cathedral. They are later in date, however, and perhaps belong to the 1370s rather than the 1340s. Not surprisingly, in view of the lapse of time, they show the work of different carvers.[28] However, their design is closely based on the choir stalls in the cathedral and it is possible that one of the joiners who had worked there was still active, for some of the joinery looks like work by the same hand.

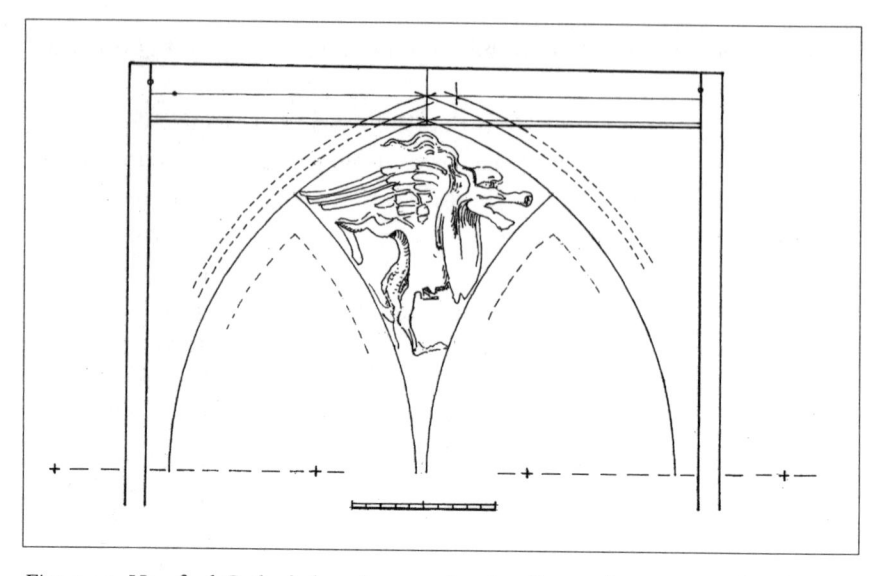

Figure 4.7 Hereford Cathedral: setting-out drawing for carving on a panel at the west end of the choir stalls.
Heavy lines indicate the edges of the panel and structural members. Other full lines show curves and lines scribed on the surface of the wood, with dashed lines for curves that are implied but no longer visible. The dashed horizontal line is the base line for the drawing, with crosses where compass points were placed in setting out the curves. The scale bar is 100mm.

The backs of the stalls at All Saints are formed of a series of planks set in a frame on which are carpenters' assembly marks in the form of Roman numerals. On the northern set of stalls, I to V appear from left to right on vertical members of the frame, while the panels have numbers VI to X, running this time from right to left. Some of the planks at the left-hand end have been replaced, but two panels at the right-hand end show the system of numbering clearly.

The lower panels, behind the actual seats, are numbered differently, however. On one is what appears to be the numeral IV (which probably means six). On the next plank is a mark consisting of a circle with a smaller circle inside it (*Figure 4.8*). Small marks enclosed by these circles may indicate a Roman numeral, but are too indistinct for one to be sure. Some other planks are similarly marked to show where individual pieces should butt against one another, so the circles appear to be a form of assembly mark showing how the three planks forming the lower part of panel VI should fit together.

Figure 4.8 All Saints, Hereford: rubbing of carpenters' marks on the back of the choir stalls on the north side of the chancel. The edges of two of the three planks which make up a panel numbered VI are shown with a slight gap in between them. The plank on the left has a sawn surface with the saw-marks showing clearly, whereas the other plank has an axe-hewn surface. The scale bar is 50mm.

The prominent saw marks on certain of these planks contrast sharply with the slightly undulating surface of others which were trimmed with an axe. These differences are evidence of the way in which tree trunks were converted into planks. The process began when a trunk was laid out on the ground and squared up with an axe. A skilled carpenter, occasionally using a plumb bob to check that he was cutting a vertical face, could trim and cut the sides of a log to remarkably smooth, parallel vertical surfaces. The finish achieved after a little further work can be seen on the smoother planks on these choir stalls.[29]

When all four sides of the log had been squared up, a taut line or cord was used to mark lines along the length of the trunk showing how it was to be cut into planks.[30] The squared tree trunk was then supported on a trestle with one end raised and was sawn into planks by two men using a long, two-handled saw. The sawyers would start at one end of the log and cut their way to somewhere near its mid-point. Then the trestle supporting the log was moved along and the log was tipped in the other direction, like a see-saw, and sawing began at the opposite end. This method of supporting the log at first one angle and then another for the purpose of sawing meant that the saw marks were always at an

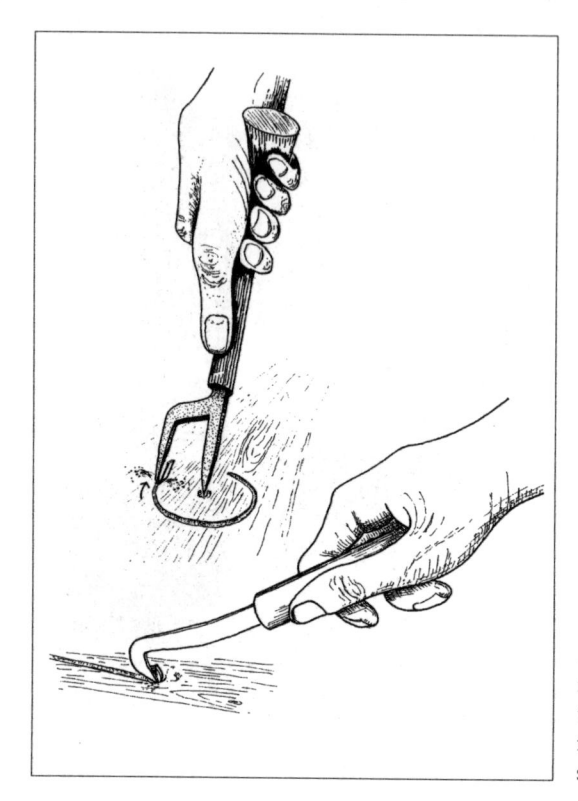

Figure 4.9 Rase-knife for marking small circles on timber (top) and a different form of the tool for scribing straight lines (below).

angle and, near the middle of the log, formed a V shape (clearly seen in *Plate 10*). This pattern is characteristic of timber sawn on a trestle, whereas pit-sawn planks have the saw marks less steeply inclined at the centre but more so at the ends.

The saw marks on choir stalls at All Saints, Hereford, are a particularly clear illustration and contrast nicely with the axe-trimmed surfaces. Sawn surfaces were preferred for the front of the stalls, but were planed down so that the saw marks no longer show.

CARPENTERS' ASSEMBLY MARKS IN DETAIL

The contrast between the Roman numerals on the All Saints choir stalls and the concentric circles that were also used to guide assembly of the planked panels, raises questions about the tools used to inscribe these marks. Numbers could be scratched onto timber with the point of a

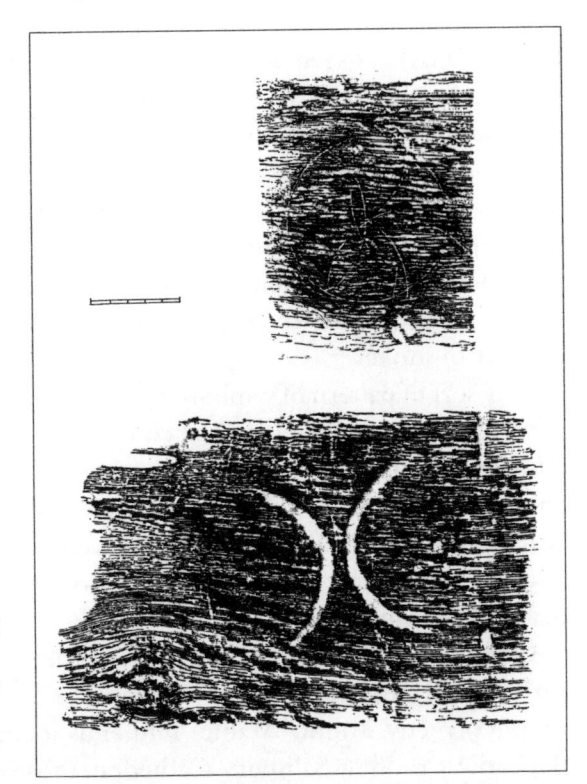

Figure 4.10 Rubbings showing arcs of circles on timbers in the chapter house roof at York Minster, comparing fine curves drawn with compasses (top) with the much broader curves cut with a rase-knife (below). The scale bar is 50mm. *Copyright © Dean & Chapter of York*

knife, cut with a chisel or stamped with a gouge. The concentric circles were made with two rase-knives, one for the large circle and another for the smaller one, each of which would have a cutting edge shaped like a hook, with one side sharpened (*Figure 4.9*).

The name of the tool comes from the same root as 'erase' and 'razor', so the alternative spelling, 'race-knife' is not used here. In its most characteristic form, as used at Hereford, this cutting tool was fitted to a handle alongside a metal prong that served as a compass point, allowing the rase-knife to be used for cutting small circles of fixed diameter.[31] A similar tool without the compass point was also sometimes used for straight lines (also seen in *Figure 4.9*). A rase-knife produces a broad, channel-section line or curve in the surface of the timber, which was much easier to see than the fine lines produced by a compass point (*Figure 4.10*).

Although the majority of carpenters' marks were Roman numerals, or were derived from them, the rase-knife provided options for different kinds of mark, as seen at Hereford. Among other systems of marking timber in which Roman numerals were not used, one is a series of tally marks on planks forming the revetment of a wharf beside the Thames at Billingsgate, London, part of which is now in the Museum of London. The revetment consists of horizontal planks pegged to a series of closely-spaced posts. The planks are numbered in sequence from bottom to top, but whereas the lower numerals might be taken for the Roman I, II and III, the numbers five to seven are marked simply as the corresponding number of strokes.[32]

Any sort of pattern of symbols that enabled all the components of one particular frame to be recognised could serve just as well as numbers for ensuring that timbers were not mixed up. When the roof of St Hugh's choir at Lincoln Cathedral was being erected, at some time during the years 1204-9, individual rafter couples were identified by a sequence of angular marks, some shaped like crosses or arrows, others suggestive of match-stick animals.[33]

One system of numbering timbers that was introduced rather earlier than might have been expected is the version of Arabic (or more correctly, Hindu-Arabic) numerals identified by Dan Miles in the earliest roofs at Salisbury Cathedral, those over the chapels at the east end, with rafter couples erected in 1224 and 1225. Similar numbers were used 20 or 30 years later in the roof of the north aisle, particularly where there is a junction with the roof of the north porch.[34] It has to be said that in the thirteenth century, Arabic numerals were still relatively unfamiliar in England and one plausible suggestion is that carpenters from France were employed at Salisbury.[35]

However, it is also important to remember that Arabic numerals were used at Wells Cathedral in the 1230s to identify niches high on the west front, at the level of the carved figures associated with the resurrection, where particular sculptures were to be located.[36] One person with connections at Wells as well as Salisbury was the cleric and administrator Elias of Dereham,[37] and the most plausible explanation of the appearance of Arabic numerals at both places within 10 or 12 years of each other is that it was he who introduced them. Elias had spent most of a decade in France prior to 1219 and, if French carpenters were employed at Salisbury, he may have recruited them. In England, Elias would also have known the reputation of a local mathematician, Adelard of Bath, who a century earlier had been to Syria, studied with Arabic-speaking mathematicians,

Carpenters' markings

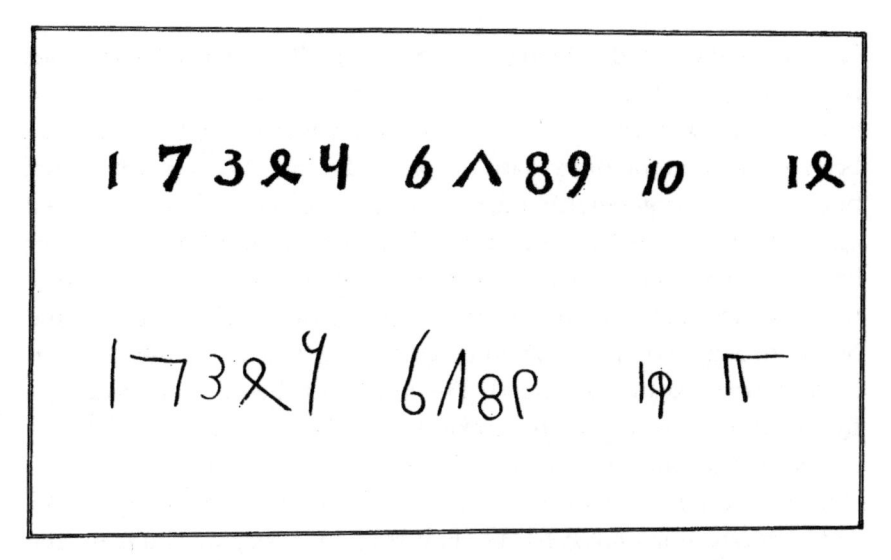

1 7 3 ᧒ 4   6 ∧ 8 9   10   1᧒

1 7 3 ᧒ Ỿ   6 ∧ 8 ρ   1φ   ⊓

Figure 4.11 Early Arabic numerals used as assembly marks with 1–5 represented in the first group of digits (the 2 written like a modern 7) and 6–9 in the second group. Then follow the numbers 10, 12 (bottom line) and 14 (top line with loop-shaped digit 4).
top: Assembly marks for sculpture at Wells Cathedral, *c.*1230 (as recorded by J.T. Irvine, *Somersetshire Archaeological & Natural History Society Proceedings* 34, 1888: 62-3).
below: Carpenters' marks at Sutton Rectory, Sussex, *c.*1330. W.D. Peckham, *Sussex Archaeological Collections* 65, 1924: 66.

and translated the most important Arabic book on arithmetic.[38] Adelard then came home and spent the latter part of his life in Wiltshire, so Salisbury and Wells would be places where his reputation lingered.

Elias of Dereham was 'keeper of the fabric' at Salisbury from 1222. He was also a friend of Adam Lock, master mason at Wells. Indeed, he witnessed Lock's will in 1229 and continued to keep in touch with developments at Wells after Lock's death.[39] The use of Arabic numerals at both places is relevant to the question of how closely involved in building were churchmen and scholars such as Elias. At Salisbury, it is possible to surmise that Elias, as keeper of the fabric, may himself have taught the workforce to mark the timbers with Arabic numerals. At Wells, Elias could have suggested the scheme whereby opposite ends of the west front were provided with sculptures representing complementary themes, with Arabic numerals marking the positions of sculptures in the northern half of the scheme, but with Roman numerals to the south. The shapes of the numerals cut in the stonework of sculptures and niches at Wells are illustrated in Figure 4.11, where the looped shape of the four is clearly seen.

No other examples of Arabic numerals used as assembly marks have been found contemporary with the examples from Wells and Salisbury, but a couple of generations later, in 1313 and 1318, they were used again by carpenters working on smaller buildings in Wells[40] and other examples have been found in southern England. In Sussex, at Sutton, north of Arundel,[41] the rectory had trusses in the hall roof numbered from 1 to 4 and wind braces numbered 1 to 12, the form of the numerals being illustrated in Figure 4.11. The shapes of the numerals four and five and the zero (with vertical stroke) should be noted. This building is described as an aisled hall and may date from the early fourteenth century although little now remains of the original structure. Outside the area, in Gloucestershire, Cleave Hall (at Bishop's Cleave) was built for the bishops of Worcester around 1300 and the surviving solar wing, with 25 rafter couples, has carpenters' marks in the form of Arabic numerals.[42]

The common factor in these and other buildings in which Arabic numerals have been recorded is that they all had ecclesiastical owners, but if we turn from southern and western counties to look at buildings of comparable date erected for ecclesiastical authorities in eastern England, we find Roman (but not Arabic) numerals as carpenters' marks and also examples of abstract circular symbols. Prime examples are the chapter house roof at York Minster and the roof of the frater at Bushmead Priory, Staploe, Bedfordshire.

The chapter house at York is an octagonal structure in which a timber vault is supported by being attached to a tall, spire-like timber roof structure, for which Cecil Hewett has provided a clear drawing (*Figure 4.12*).[43] The roof has eight arms or trusses which support a central post and it is thought that this design influenced the form of the diagonal truss above the adjacent masons' loft, illustrated earlier (*Figure 4.2b*). In that smaller truss, the central post has become a king post, a form of construction that was unusual at the time except in Hampshire.[44] The origins of the York king post is less likely to be the result of influence from Hampshire than an adaptation of the idea of the central post in the chapter house. The use of secondary rafters and struts is also similar in the masons' loft and in the chapter house roofs.

A study of the carpenters' assembly marks in the York roofs has been made as part of the research for the present book. It was found that,

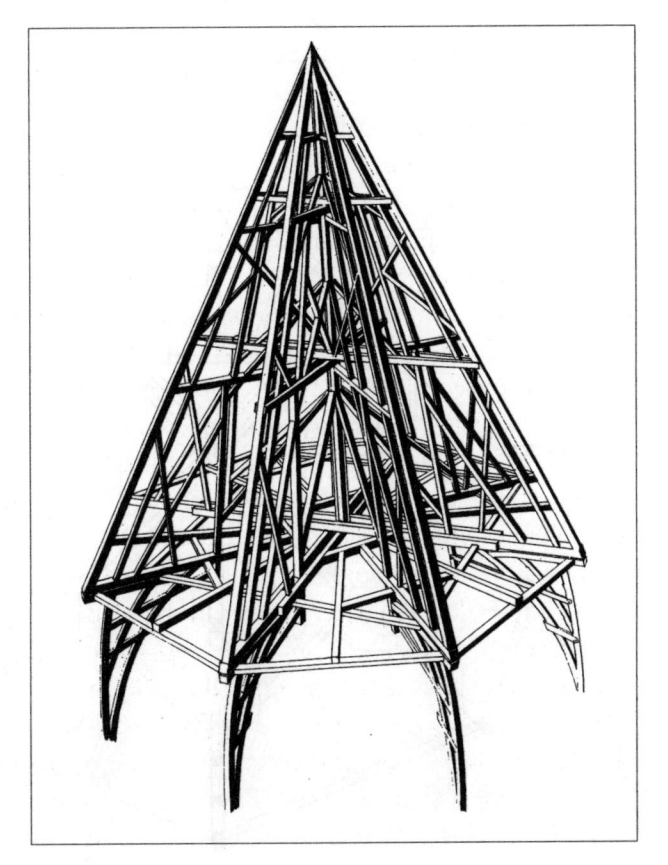

Figure 4.12 York Minster. Perspective showing framing of the chapter-house roof, as drawn by Cecil Hewett. *Reproduced by permission of the publisher from Cecil A. Hewett,* English Cathedral and Monastic Carpentry *Phillimore & Co., Chichester, 1985*

although ordinary Roman numerals were used in the roof of the masons' loft, the eight radial frames or trusses supporting the central post in the chapter house are marked with a series of symbols consisting of various combinations of circles and semicircles.[45] One mark, comprising two arcs back-to-back, has already been illustrated (*Figure 4.10*). The other marks are illustrated by Figure 4.13, which is a plan of the octagonal roof with the symbols used on each radial arm of the octagon shown within a small rectangular inset.

Very similar circle-based symbols were used in the roof at Bushmead Priory, where they were marked on the crown posts in the roof and on braces attached to the crown posts, while rafters were marked with Roman numerals.[46] Other buildings in Bedfordshire have been recorded with similar marks[47] and there have been suggestions that Bedfordshire craftsmen worked at York Minster, although the evidence for this is flimsy.[48]

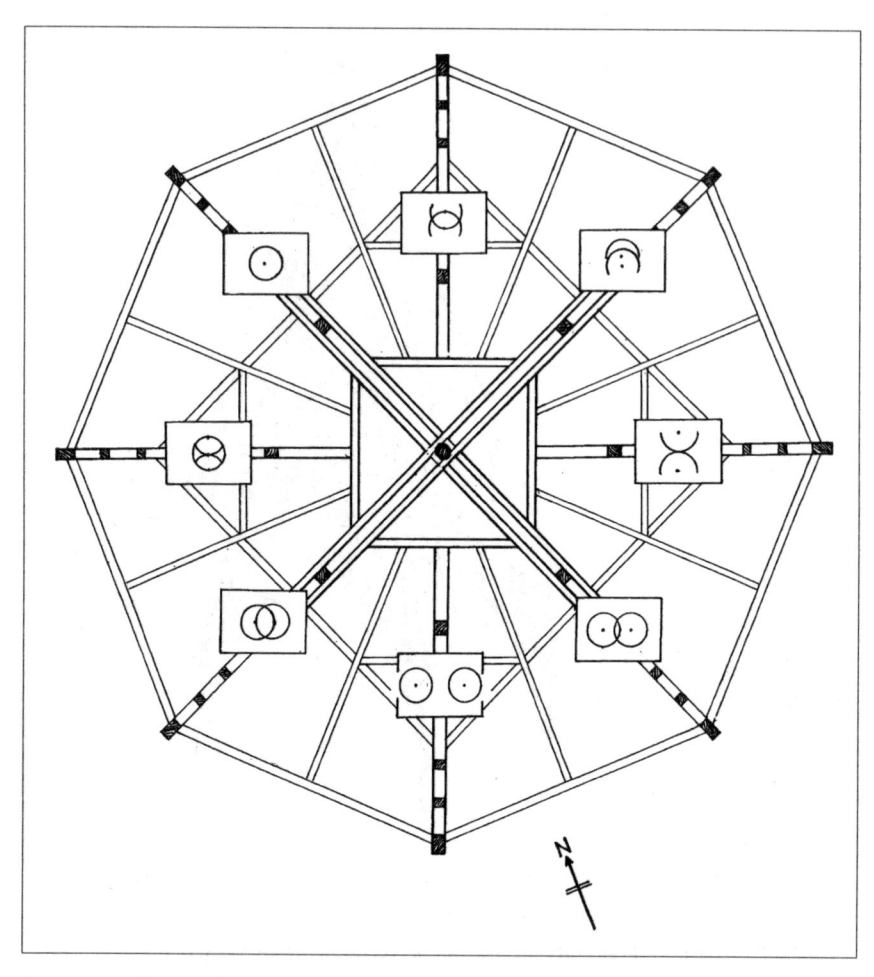

Figure 4.13 Plan of the octagonal roof of the chapter house at York Minster. Each of the main arms of the octagon consists of a complex truss in which every component timber is marked with a distinctive assembly mark comprising a pattern of circles and/or arcs. The rectangular inset shown on each arm contains a representation of the circle pattern used to mark timbers in that particular truss. Not to scale, but the overall width of the structure at this level is nearly 20m (64ft). *Copyright © Dean & Chapter of York*

Much more striking is that J.T. Smith included Bushmead Priory and one roof at York Minster as examples of a regional tradition in carpentry practice which he identified in the eastern counties of England. It was characterised by a distinctive method of bracing roofs and frames and was exemplified in aisled halls and barns as well as in church buildings.

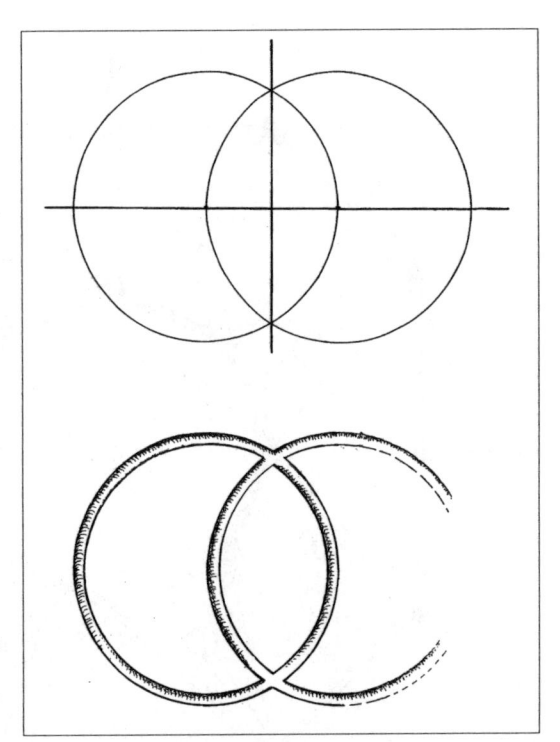

Figure 4.14 Intersecting circles drawn with the centre of one located on the circumference of the other.
Top: with the circles drawn precisely using compasses and then employed to set out two lines at right angles.
Below: drawn with a rase-knife as in carpenters' marks at Bushmead Priory (Bedfordshire) and York Minster. The Bushmead circles were often left incomplete, as shown, and are slightly smaller than the ones at York.

Smith cited the roof of the north transept in York Minster as belonging to this tradition[49] and would probably have included the chapter house roof and the truss in the masons' loft (*Figure 4.2b*) if he had seen Hewett's drawings of these structures.

If the circle marks in Bedfordshire and at York cannot be explained by movements of carpenters from one place to the other, another explanation of similarities between assembly marks in the two places could be that they were separately derived from ideas that were in widespread circulation. In discussing how very large circles may have been drawn out by carpenters when working out the proportions of barns, Laurie Smith emphasised a geometrical construction consisting of two intersecting circles of the same radius, one drawn with the compass point on the circumference of the other. Lines drawn through the centres of the circles and through the points of intersection then cross at right angles.[50] Figure 4.14 illustrates this geometry and also shows how the same pattern of intersecting circles is used as an assembly mark both at Bushmead Priory (where the outer diameter of the circles is about 50mm) and in the chapter house

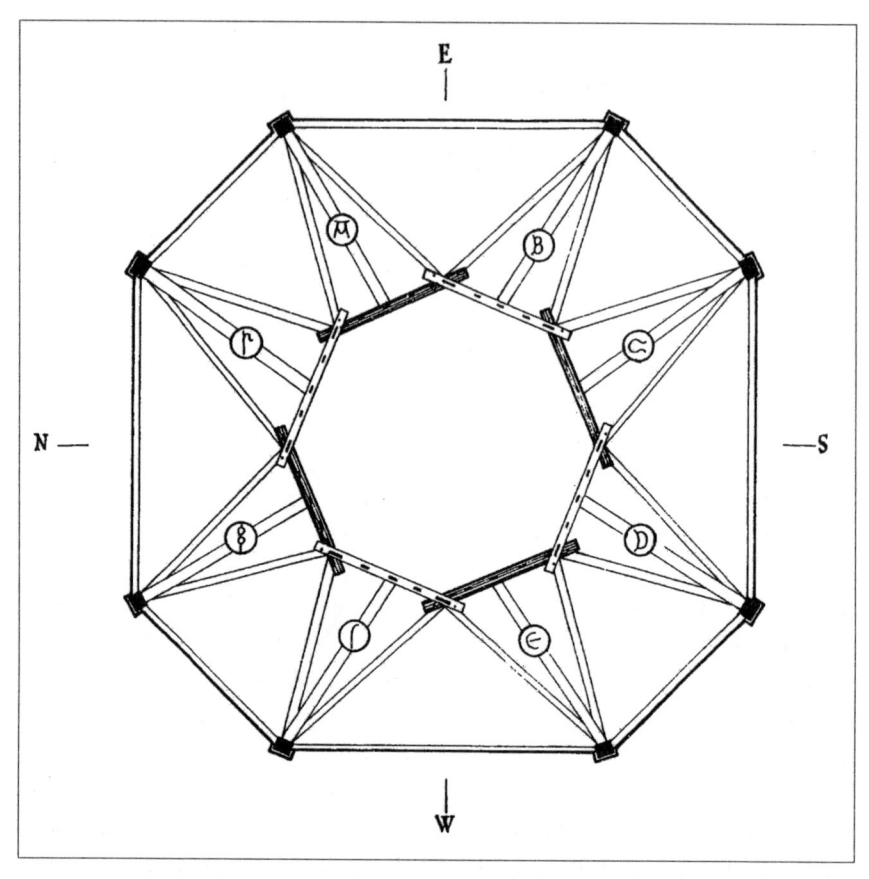

Figure 4.15 Ely Cathedral. Plan of the floor of the lantern, with letters scribed on the timbers shown in the circular insets. Drawing by Cecil Hewett. *Reproduced by permssion of the publisher from Cecil A. Hewett,* English Cathedral and Monastic Carpentery. *Phillimore & Co., Chichester, 1985*

roof at York (outer diameter 90mm). It could be, then, that the circle patterns used to identify trusses at York and at Bushmead Priory arose from experience of using comparable patterns on a larger scale in setting out designs for timber structures. However, any such view of how the assembly marks evolved must remain a matter of speculation.

It might be thought that the repertoire of different methods of identifying and marking timbers had been exhausted by these examples, but in the octagon at Ely Cathedral the timber structure supporting the roof and lantern has letters of the alphabet, from A to H, marked in Lombardic capitals on the main timbers belonging to each of the eight main arms of the structure (*Figure 4.15*).[51] Erected between 1328 and 1335, this was an extraordinarily ambitious and intricate timber structure. The account rolls of the sacrist, Alan of Walsingham survive from the second year of construction. They refer to the master mason who built the stonework of the octagon as 'Master John' (probably John Ramsey) and show that the carpenter who designed the extraordinary structure of the lantern was William Hurley, the chief carpenter in the king's Office of Works.[52]

NUMBERS AND DRAWINGS

Carpenters' assembly marks, though capable of being looked at as miniature drawings in themselves, do not answer the questions initially asked in this chapter about carpenters' design drawings and setting-out procedures. What they do provide evidence for is the way in which the carpentry of roofs and frames was executed on a separate framing ground where timbers were cut and fitted while lying flat on the ground (or supported on blocks just above the ground). They also help to demonstrate the procedure used in final assembly of the frame on site. At Ely, for example, there is clear evidence that cranes standing on the stonework of the octagon lifted timbers in a carefully planned sequence as indicated by the assembly marks. By study of joints and marks, Hewett was able to reconstruct that sequence in some detail.[53]

The largest timber structure to be erected in the fourteenth century was the roof of Westminster Hall. In this case, the framing ground was at Farnham in Surrey, from where timbers were transported by wagon to the banks of the Thames near Chertsey,[54] and thence by river. Work began in 1394, and some 450 loads of timber were carried by wagon from Farnham, mainly during 1395, with erection of the frame at Westminster accomplished by 1397. The roof was finally completed and weatherproof in 1399. The location of the framing ground near Farnham was referred to at the time as 'The Frame', a name which suggests that, not only were timbers cut and fitted there, but perhaps part of the frame was erected as a standing structure to rehearse the assembly procedure.

As with the octagon at Ely and the chapter house roof at York, the stability of the structure depended on the stone walls of the building and the way they were buttressed, and hence depended on collaboration

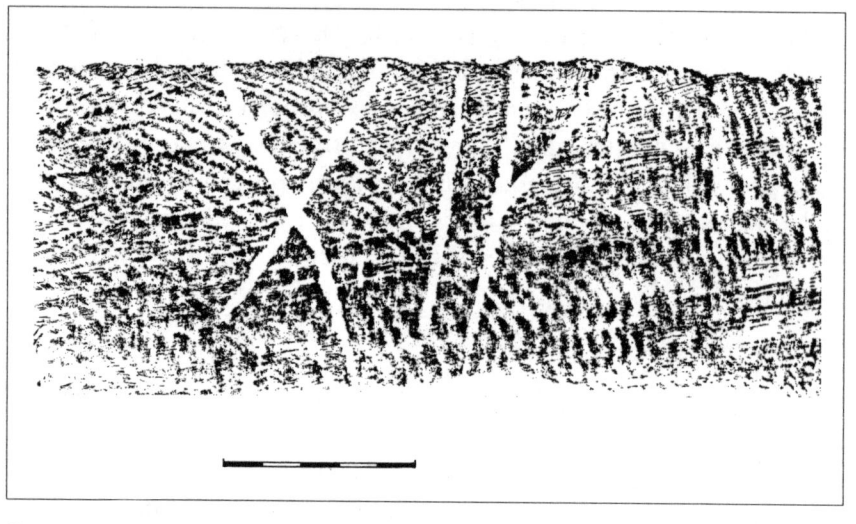

Figure 4.16 Carpenter's numeral XII (with a tag on the second I) from the roof of Westminster Hall, as may be seen on part of a wall-post now in the Museum of London. The scale bar is 50mm.

between masons and carpenters. The mason nominally in charge at Westminster Hall was Henry Yevele (or Yeveley) but he was quite elderly and it is thought that a mason named Walton working under Yevele was responsible for much of the detailed work. The master carpenter was Hugh Herland (d. 1405), who had long experience in the king's works and had also worked for William of Wykeham, possibly in building the chapel roofs at New College, Oxford and Winchester College.

The roof of Westminster Hall has been described as a combination of a hammerbeam roof with an arch.[55] It has a clear span of about 68ft (20.7m), which is much larger than could be roofed with the available oak timber if deployed in the usual way. Herland therefore developed a method of building up composite components.[56] For example, the great arch rib that is incorporated into each truss is formed of three timbers placed side by side and pinned together. Each of these three components is itself formed of several individual lengths. The core timber in the arch rib is interrupted by the hammerbeam, into which it is mortised, but the other timbers pass either side of it giving the arch a degree of continuity.[57]

These composite arch ribs rise from a series of timber wall posts which stand on corbels within the stone walls of the building. Near the centre of each wall post is a complex joint with tenons that receive the

Figure 4.17 Detail of the roof of Westminster Hall, with cutaway section (inset, left) showing the complex joint where the arch rib and brace meet the wall post. The perspective (right) shows the shape to which the wall post is cut to make this joint, indicating also the carpenter's numbers. The right-hand drawing, based on a timber in the Museum of London, is not to scale; the scale bar for the left-hand drawing shows 1m.

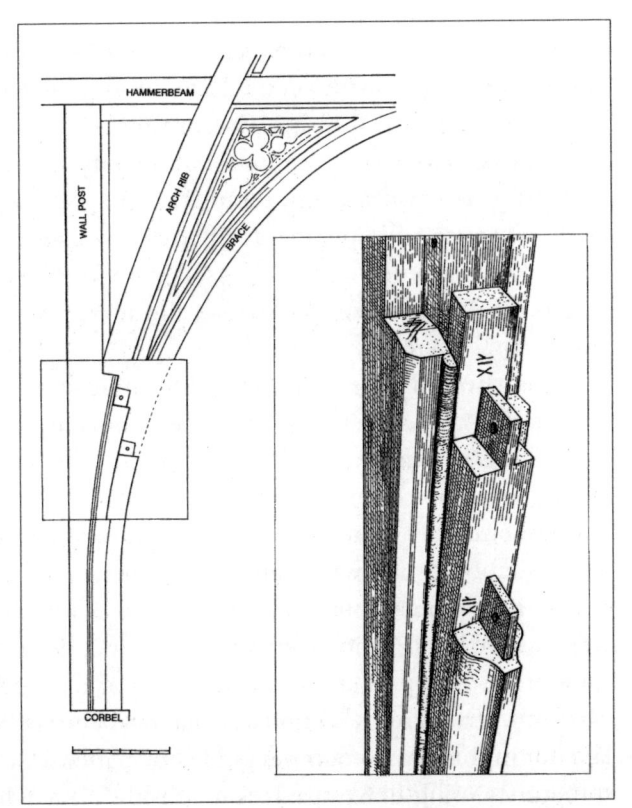

core timber of the arch and a brace to the hammerbeam, and there are housings for the two other arch timbers.[58] Assembly marks in Roman numerals (*Figure 4.16*) were cut on inside faces of the joints (*Figure 4.17*) so that once assembly was complete, they would not be seen.[59]

The length of the hall was such that 13 trusses were needed, hence 26 wall posts had to be cut to shape with this complex joint. Templates or patterns of some kind would be used to ensure that each wall post was the same shape, and that the joint was correctly formed. Each of the three timbers forming every arch rib sprang from slightly different levels on the wall posts, and adjustments would no doubt be made here to allow for irregularities in the timbers.

In the making of smaller roofs at Caister, Norfolk and Wistanstow, Shropshire, more than 150 years before the reconstruction of Westminster Hall, it seems that patterns were used, probably without separate drawings of the roofs. The more complex framing of the Cressing Temple barns was made with such precision that it seems likely that full-size drawings of some kind were made on the barn floors, if not on a separate framing floor. The highly ambitious Westminster roof must have called on all available methods of designing and executing a carpentry structure, including use of drawings, templates, gauges and patterns. However in the absence of explicit information, we can only speculate about precisely what procedures were used. As with most of the other timber structures discussed, our questions about carpenter's drawings remain largely unanswered.

Even though this chapter is inconclusive in that respect, the relationships noted between carpenters' working methods and those of masons raise a number of important points. The numbering of timbers, and of stones in some masonry structures, seems to be fundamental. If components in a structure have been numbered, this shows that they were assembled somewhere else, or at least in a different position, before being incorporated into the building. Usually that means that they were assembled in a horizontal position on a floor, or on open ground, sometimes on top of an outline drawing of the intended structure. For carpentry structures, it seems clear that timbers were cut and fitted while laid out in this way, sometimes guided by patterns of one sort or another, sometimes using drawings. It is much less clear what happened when the stonework for an arch, doorway or window was assembled on the ground, with the stones then numbered before being moved for re-assembly on site. However, it seems likely that, in these instances, stones were cut and fitted using an outline drawn on the ground as a guide, but without templates. This suggestion of a 'carpenters' method' for working with masonry challenges the view encountered in Chapter 2 that the standard procedure was always to make templates from the full-size drawing and then use them to guide cutting of the stone.

CHAPTER 5

LATER MEDIEVAL ARCHITECTURAL DRAWINGS

(masons' drawings for mouldings, sculpture and tracery, to 1550)

PLATTES AND MOULDINGS

Most of the drawings by masons (and carpenters) considered so far have been from the century and a half before *c.*1360. The one later example has been a drawing from the Wells tracing floor which appears to date from *c.*1420. For the period after 1360, there are more documentary references to drawings and, later still, to 'plattes' meaning plans or other architectural drawings 'plotted' on parchment. More particularly, after 1450 there are contracts for new buildings which specified that the mason must build according to the 'platte' agreed with the owner.[1] But although contracts worded this way became fairly common, the plattes to which they referred do not usually survive until a later period than is dealt with in this chapter. For example a contract for extending a house in Sussex, signed in 1586 by a freemason from Arundel, was accompanied by four drawings.[2] One of two that survive is illustrated below in Chapter 7 (*Figure 7.9*).

The careers of leading masons are now sometimes better documented than earlier and show that they often advised on structures they did not build. The implication is sometimes that they made drawings for others to follow. This happened, for example, during the multi-faceted career of Henry Yevele (or Yeveley, *c.*1330-1400) who was the royal mason – that is head of the king's Office of Works – for 30 years. Another example is one of Yevele's successors, Thomas Mapilton, when he was giving advice in 1430 about a bell tower at Bury St Edmunds.[3] There is a definite implication that drawings were sometimes made in these situations, but again none survive.

One other kind of record that needs to be mentioned is associated uniquely with William Worcestre (1415-85), a man from Bristol who spent most of his working life in Norfolk as secretary to Sir John Fastoff of Caister. After Sir John died, Worcestre was able to devote himself to his personal enthusiasm for travel and he wrote a journal or itinerary of a trip he made from Norfolk to St Michael's Mount in Cornwall. He also visited his old home town and compiled a survey of Bristol which overlaps the itinerary in places.

One peculiarity of William Worcestre's approach is that he was fascinated by measurements and statistics and noted any that he came across, including a calculation of the number of seconds in a year by a monk at Norwich. Bringing this approach to bear on the many buildings he visited, Worcestre always wanted to know their leading dimensions, and if there was nobody to ask, he would pace out the length and breadth of a building, noting the result as a number of 'steppys' (steps). At Exeter Cathedral he noted the lengths of the choir and nave as:

Longitudo navis. 100. steppys
Longitudo chori. 90. steppys

This entry using Arabic numerals stands out because Worcestre more often noted dimensions in Roman. His 'steppys' are fairly consistent, apparently amounting to about half a metre (slightly shorter than we might expect for 'paces') making these estimates for Exeter reasonably accurate. And whilst at times he seemed only interested in the dimensions of a building, at Exeter he mentioned how the 'whole church is vaulted over in the most beautiful way'.[4]

In some places Worcestre quoted dimensions in feet or yards, which probably meant that he had borrowed a measuring rod or line. Harvey noted that, on a visit to Tintern Abbey, Worcestre seems to have had the use of a six-foot measuring rod. Often, though, he spoke to the masons working on a structure and quoted the dimensions they gave. At Wells, he wrote down some dimensions in yards, noting that the cloister was 53 yards square. He rarely quoted fractions of a foot or gave a measurement to the nearest inch, so when describing the cloister windows mentioned in Chapter 3, he quoted their width as 3 yards and 1 foot (equivalent to about 3.05m) whereas the dimension given above was 10ft 8ins (3.25m).[5]

Although Worcestre never drew the plan of a building he described, one could say that he had a good sense of how plans worked, and his descriptions and measurements have allowed outline plans to be reconstructed for buildings that no longer exist. What is more significant, though, is the fact that he quoted linear dimensions of buildings so frequently. Not only that, but he often met masons who would quote the height of a tower or length of a building in feet. This is significant for the way people thought about plans and generally about design. In earlier centuries, the laying out of the plan of a building on the ground had been so much a geometrical procedure that people would probably think about the extent of a building geometrically, that is in terms of squares and diagonals, rather than thinking numerically in terms of feet. As Eric Fernie has put it, when the plan of a building was being set out on the ground, many dimensions were not laid out in feet (or other units) because the length arose 'from a particular geometric sequence'.[6]

By contrast, Worcestre was clearly thinking numerically and in terms of units of measurement (feet or steps) as were some of the masons he met, and this is probably characteristic of late medieval practice. Even so, in referring to dimensions in feet but rarely fractions of a foot, Worcestre still reflected the masons' traditional ways. Carpenters may have differed from masons in this respect, and may have been accustomed to using the inch (understood as a twelfth part of a foot) from an earlier date. Details of their practice are not well recorded, but it is striking that when rulers began to be graduated in inches, they were at first known as 'carpenters' rulers' (as will be seen in Chapter 7).

An early example of the prominent use of inches is an agreement made by the carpenter Robert Giles who contracted to build a row of seven houses in York for the parishioners of St Martin's, Coney Street, in 1335. The agreement is remarkable for the way it not only specified the dimensions of the row (in feet) but also gave the required sizes of individual timbers. Thus the massive corner posts of the house were intended to be 16ins wide and 13ins deep, and dimensions were given for numerous other members down to a small timber on the upper floor which was 8ins x 6ins.[7]

In Bristol a century and a half later, William Worcestre's surveys led him to make contact with several masons, notably John Norton, master mason at St Mary Redcliffe, who told him that the spire had been 300ft (91m) high, but the top 100ft (30m) had been thrown down by lightning.

At St Stephen's Church he spoke to Benedict (Benet) Crosse, a freemason who was working on the south porch, and who was probably the source from whom Worcestre was able to quote the height of the tower as 125ft (38m). Crosse's doorway to the south porch had an elaborate moulding and he drew the profile of it for Worcestre. It is to be seen on a page of Worcestre's notebook where Worcestre wrote (*Plate 11*): 'Thys ys the Jambmuold of the porch & door'. The drawing is in what Harvey described as 'red chalk' although the lines are really a dark brown colour. Worcestre carefully noted the names that Crosse gave to the different shapes within the moulding[8] and the end of this list of names can be seen on the extreme right of Plate 11, where the last word reads 'Battelle' or boutelle.

Figure 5.1 shows part of the moulding redrawn to illustrate the nomenclature. For example, a bowtel (or boutelle) is a plain round moulding, whereas a 'fillet' is (for Crosse) almost any flat surface that comes to a sharp corner or edge. A 'casement' is a hollow moulding, and Worcestre noted that in this doorway, the larger casements shown were to be filled with a band of carving showing a 'trail of leaves'. The curves in the drawing indicate the depth of undercutting in the carving.

This building survives as a fine late Perpendicular church, a unified design of the 1470s, and such a building, combined with documentation for its master mason and an architectural drawing in the mason's hand, is 'a rare combination of survivals'.[9] A detail of the arched doorway for which Benedict Crosse drew this feature is illustrated in Plate 12, together with a glimpse of the vault within the porch. At the top of the picture is Benedict's moulding with the two hollowed 'casements' very prominent, but instead of a continuous trail of leaves carved within the casements, small panels of foliage or flowers are inserted at intervals. Apart from this, the mouldings around the doorway were executed largely as Benedict drew them except that the bowtels are omitted. Perhaps they were included in the drawing merely to explain to William Worcestre what a bowtel was, but perhaps the bowtels and the trails of leaves had to be omitted to save expense in what was still an elaborate design. The series of fretwork cusps which decorate the arch is not indicated at all in the drawing, but this is above the level of the jambs, which is all that the drawing attempts to show. Figure 5.1 not only explains Benedict Crosse's nomenclature as noted by Worcestre, but is also intended to aid comparison between the original drawing (*Plate 11*) and the moulding as executed (*Plate 12*).

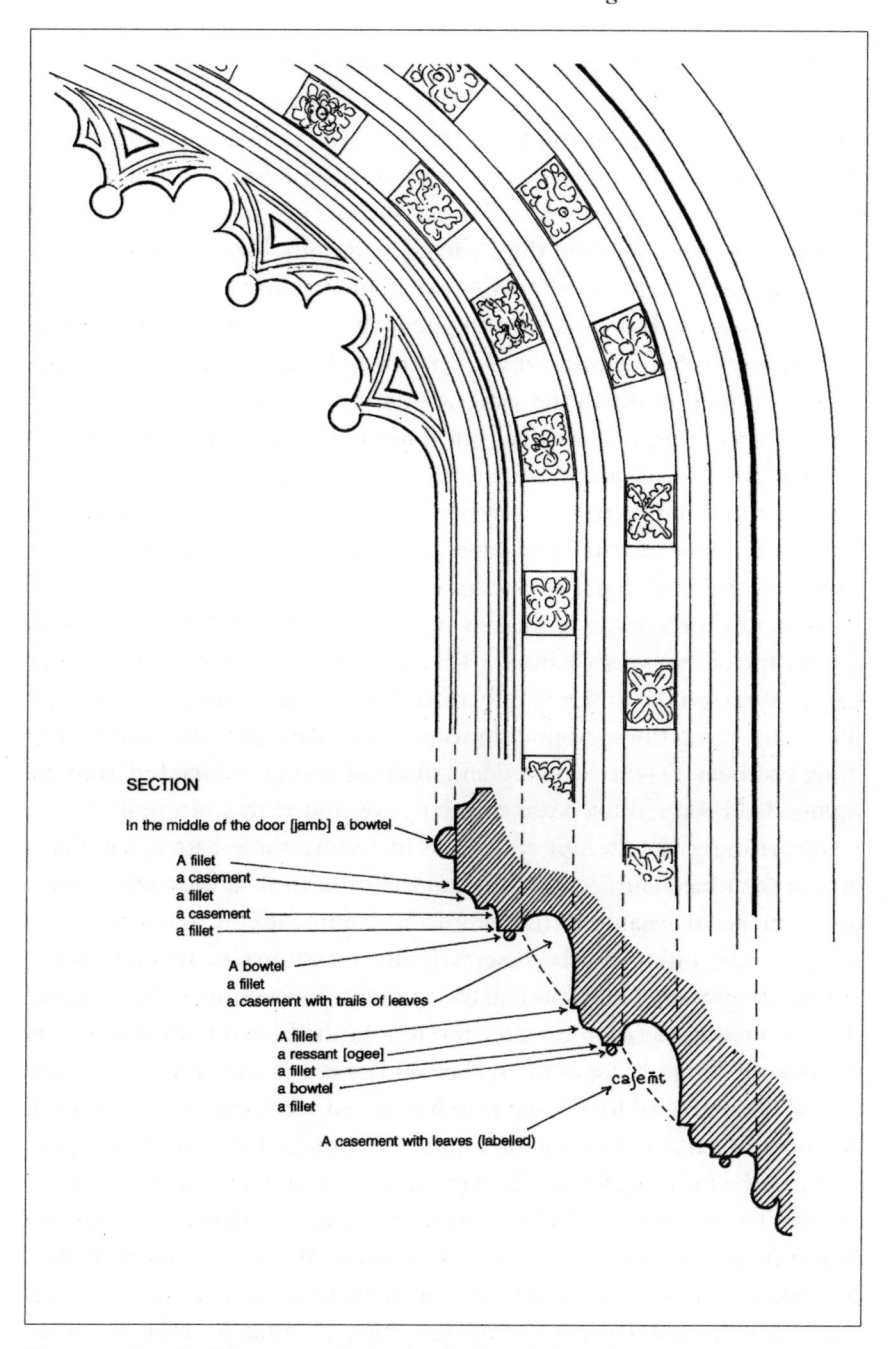

Figure 5.1 Detail of doorway at St Stephen's Church, Bristol, with names for different parts of the moulding. The names are those quoted by Benedict Crosse, mason, and recorded by William Worcestre in his notes on the drawing reproduced as Plate 11. Spellings are modernised.

A SCULPTOR'S DRAWING

At Gloucester, there are two examples of medieval masons' drawings in the buildings of the former abbey church of St Peter, now Gloucester Cathedral. In many ways the most important is in the monastic buildings, in what is called the Parliament Room. Here there is a stone chimneypiece with a large, plain overmantel that was once used as a 'mason's setting-out table'.[10] On it can be seen full-size outlines of moulding profiles, compass-drawn circles and a grid of lines suggesting that it was used in much the same way as the tracing floors at Wells and York. It is an important survival, but is not in its original position.

What also merits attention, not least because it exemplifies a kind of drawing not so far discussed, is to be seen in the lady chapel, built around 1480. Behind the altar in this chapel was an elaborate reredos which also dates from around 1480. The reredos was designed as a display of sculpture with niches for a series of statues of saints. Inevitably, since this was a lady chapel, there was a statue of Our Lady at the centre. However, the statues attracted the wrath of reformation iconoclasts who smashed all of them, damaging the surrounding stonework in the process.[11] The whole thing had been brightly painted and such paintwork as survived after the statues had been removed was unevenly covered with whitewash.

Surprisingly, no attempt was made to restore these battered remains during the nineteenth century and on the stonework at the back of most of the niches the name of the saint to be represented is roughly scribed or scratched, often in a bold scrawl, but sometimes in smaller, neater handwriting. Some letters overlap the mortar between stones, showing that the names were written up after the reredos had been built, and not in the masons' lodge. Most of the niches are labelled in this way (but not the central one intended for the statue of Mary) and a historian of the cathedral has supplied a transcript of all the names.[12] What is of particular interest here is one of the lower niches to the right of centre where the name Benefrida appears. This is a variant Welsh spelling of the name Winifred, patron saint in North Wales and associated with healing miracles. What some commentators have missed is that, as well as a name, this niche (and one or two others) also contains a drawing. There is a centre line down the middle of the niche and around it an outline showing a silhouette of the statue to be placed there. An irregular curve forming the right-hand half of the outline can be clearly seen below the large patch of whitewash in Plate 27.

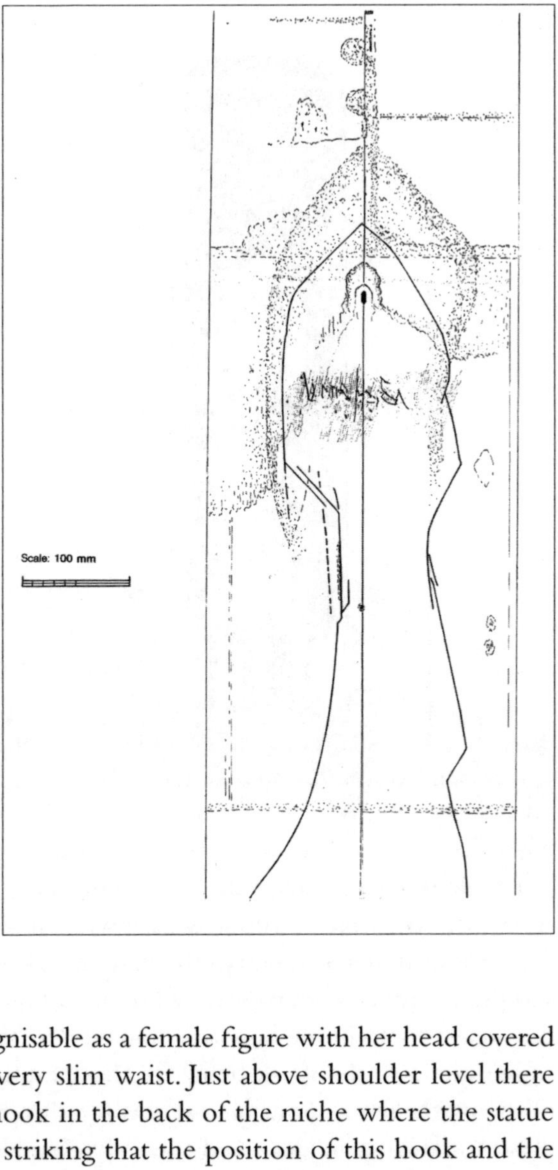

Figure 5.2 Gloucester Cathedral: Drawing on the back of a niche in the Lady Chapel reredos, *c*.1480. The lettering 'benefrida' is shown with its background of mason's tooling. Above it, a dark object in the centre is the remains of an iron hook, intended to hold the sculpture in place. The vertical ruled lines represent, firstly, the scribed centre line, and then the sides of the niche to left and right. Stippled areas represent painted or whitewashed surfaces, and also a mortared joint (crossing the top of the drawing).

The silhouette is recognisable as a female figure with her head covered (*Figure 5.2*) and with a very slim waist. Just above shoulder level there are remains of an iron hook in the back of the niche where the statue was once attached. It is striking that the position of this hook and the size of the silhouette together indicate quite a small statue (560mm tall) compared with the height available in the niche (about 800mm). Figure 5.3 is an impression of how the statue may have looked relative to the size of the niche. However the iconoclasts may have obscured evidence of what was intended, for under their whitewash is the suggestion of a taller, painted figure. Was this a revised design, or did the small statue stand in front of a painted background which filled the niche more completely?

Figure 5.3
Reconstruction of the missing sculpture of St Benefrida at Gloucester showing the tall proportions of the niche relative to the sculpture. The shaft on the left was painted with the spiral pattern indicated.

The drawing also raises questions about how the work was organised, as between the clergy (who may have written up the names of the saints) the artist or designer (perhaps the master mason) who drew the outline, and the sculptor(s) and painters who carried out the work. It would also be interesting to know how the drawing was transferred from the back of the niche to the work bench of the sculptor(s). Nothing is known of the craftsmen responsible for this reredos. Even the identity of the master mason who designed the lady chapel is unknown, although one suggestion is that he could have been John Hobs (or Hobbes) a prominent Gloucester mason who did similar work elsewhere. John Harvey sees him as having a practice that extended to Worcester and Ludlow (where the church tower was built under the supervision of an unnamed mason from Gloucester).[13]

However, there is also a possibility that there were two masons known by this name, father and son, because 40 years earlier there is a well documented episode when wages were paid to 'John Hobbys, mason' for riding to the quarries at Upton and Freme to pick out good stone for work on the castle at Gloucester. Hobbys was 'marking and scappling and proving the stones so picked out, so that the King should not be deceived therein, at 6d a day. And to William his servant, working there at the marking, scappling and proving of the said stones at 4d a day'. The reference to scappling implies that they were cutting sample pieces of stone to a flat surface. They also marked some stone in the quarry, which is a reminder of the distinction between marks made by masons to indicate ownership or quality of stone and the 'masons' marks' that identified individual masons for the purposes of paying wages.[14] Masons' assembly marks are different again as explained in Chapter 3.

DRAWINGS OF WINDOWS: DECORATED TO PERPENDICULAR

The drawing of the moulding at St Stephen's in Bristol was made on paper. It was, in fact, a page of William Worcestre's notebook. It is likely, though, that many of the missing drawings that accompanied contracts during this period were on parchment, and a few high-quality drawings surviving from around 1500 were on vellum.[15] Parchment was used for some drawings throughout the period covered by earlier chapters, although no mason's or carpenter's work on parchment survives from before 1300.

However, a rare example of parchment drawings used by craftsmen from the late fourteenth century takes the form of a series of patterns and drawings, presumed to have been used as models for copying by artists as well as by craftsmen. The drawings were sewn together to form what looks like a sketchbook with rather miscellaneous contents. Much later it belonged to Samuel Pepys and it is now held by Magdalene College, Cambridge.[16] Pepys himself thought of the document as a 'monk's drawing book'. It contains 24 folios with drawings made by several different people over a long period. Three of the drawings represent architectural detail, and were apparently drawn by masons. For the rest, which includes sheets covered with animals, birds and human figures, the drawing book has been interpreted as a 'model book', intended to provide patterns or models which makers of stained glass windows might copy, or perhaps manuscript illuminators and embroiderers.[17] Grössinger notes that the high quality of many drawings of animals would have made it a good source for carvers of minor sculpture in churches, and especially carvers of misericords.[18]

There is no clue as to where the model book originated beyond a general likelihood that it was in London or south-east England. At least one of the masons' drawings has been trimmed down to the same size as other leaves in the collection (248 x 205mm), and this may indicate that the model book was compiled from loose sheets of parchment some of which had previously been used by masons for their drawings. Hence the masons' drawings may be earlier than the rest of its contents. One view is that they date from c.1350, whereas the drawings by other artists are probably of the 1380s or a little later.[19] Pepys may have been right in thinking that it came from a monastery. It is certainly possible to imagine old masons' drawings being salvaged in such an institution for re-use by other artists, but it is likely that the artists responsible were specialist laymen employed by the monastery rather than monks.

Two of the masons' drawings in the book show profiles of mouldings, but do not refer to any known building. They are earlier and simpler mouldings than the one drawn by Benedict Crosse (*Plate 11*), but the drawings are presented in much the same way. What is more important, though, is a traceried window with its curves drawn on the parchment using the point of a pair of compasses as a dry-point scorer.[20] The lines were never inked in, and in order for the drawing to be clearly reproduced, it has had to be redrawn, as in Figure 5.4. This outline is on one of the parchment sheets that had to be cut down when the model book was put together in the late fourteenth century, and the vertical lines to right and left show the existing edges of the drawing.

Almost a third of the window was lost from the drawing when it was cut down. Black dots in Figure 5.4 show holes in the parchment where the compass point was placed to draw some of the curves. If the sheet had not been trimmed so drastically, we would probably have seen that the method used in setting out the drawing was the same as may be observed on tracing floors and mural drawings. A base line was drawn across the lowest part of the tracery. In this case, the line would have extended some way further to left and right than is now apparent (*Figure 5.5*). The mason placed his compass point at various locations along this line to trace out the curves that form the main outline of the design. In this instance, curves were first drawn for a taller, more sharply pointed

Figure 5.4 Drawing from the fourteenth-century model book in the Pepysian Library, Magdalene College, Cambridge (redrawn with kind permission of the Pepysian Library).

window, and then were abandoned in favour of a more rounded shape. It should be noted that the compasses were kept to the same radius in drawing the main lines of the curves that subdivide the window. Then much smaller-radius curves were used to draw in the cusping.

In discussing drawings inscribed on stone or plaster surfaces, previous chapters have illustrated several masons' drawings for windows, including a two-light window with a cusped circle filling the window head (*Figure 2.1*). Another series of drawings, often reproduced and so not illustrated here, includes three different versions of a common type of window in the 'Geometrical' style with three circles in the window head. One of this series is a little sketch in the church at Leighton Linslade (Leighton Buzzard), Bedfordshire[21] and another small drawing, carefully set out with compasses, is scribed on a block of stone (clunch) and was found at St John's College, Cambridge.[22] A third, much larger drawing was set out very precisely on a wall at Christchurch Priory, Hampshire.[23] All three probably date from the end of the thirteenth century.

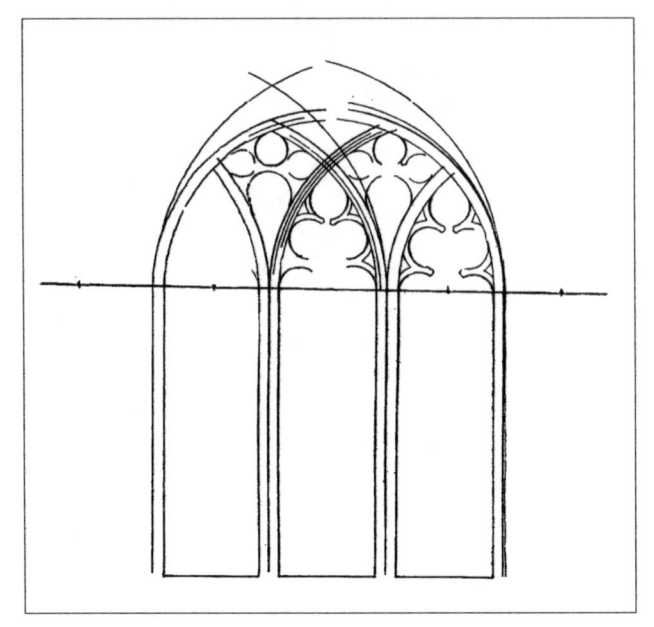

Figure 5.5 Reconstruction of the window in the fourteenth-century drawing illustrated in Figure 5.4 with missing curves added. The base line for drawing the tracery is also shown.

In later windows, particularly of the fourteenth century, a common design was one in which a central mullion in a window would divide to form a Y shape, with curves going to right and left, and several surviving drawings demonstrate this feature. The drawing in Figures 5.4 and 5.5 is similar but shows two mullions dividing, not just one, and the resulting curves intersect one another in a manner that became a common motif.

At York, the tracing floor has one more elaborate mid-fourteenth-century design (*Figure 2.9A* above), but other fourteenth-century window designs are poorly represented in surviving drawings. Indeed, to find designs representative of the great variety of tracery to which the Decorated style gave rise we need to pay more attention to some much rougher sketches, and also to carvings on fonts and screens that sometimes seem to show a mason reviewing options for a project, or looking through a sketchbook.

In Lincolnshire, for example, there is a six-sided font at Ewerby, a church associated with the 'Heckington masons',[24] five sides of which are decorated with different window designs (*Plate 28*). The sixth side is blank, probably because the font was designed to stand against a pier or a wall. There is a similar, somewhat earlier, tracery 'sketchbook' on a font at Stamford, also in Lincolnshire.[25]

On a thirteenth-century pier in the church at Gamlingay, Cambridgeshire, is a very rough sketch of window tracery partly obscured among the vertical tooling left on the stone when it was dressed in the quarry. The sketch has been reproduced by several authors who regularly comment that there is no window in Gamlingay church anything like it.[26] Hence it seems to be just another item in the very varied graffiti for which this church is famous. However, it seems to be a genuine mason's sketch, showing a recognisable pattern of Decorated tracery resembling windows in several fourteenth-century churches (*Figure 2.4*). It is quite possible that there was once a window like this at Gamlingay, or it could be a preliminary design by a mason planning the unusual east window in the church at Bassingbourn, not far away to the south-east, and thought to date from 1330 or 1340.

In the fifteenth century, there was a preference for flatter window heads. In making drawings for such windows compass points could be brought quite close to the centre line of the window to give it a much more rounded shape, as in the drawing at Wells discussed at length in Chapter 3. A very late drawing that illustrates this point is on a wall inside the church at Old Basing, Hampshire and may date from about 1550. It is a design for the main west window of this church and is of interest for its neat proportions. The radius of the main arch of the window head is very close to 1.83m (6ft), whereas the overall width of the window is 2.76m, which John Crook interprets as precisely 9ft (measured in feet of 307mm).[27] The simple ratio of width to radius is striking although, in late Perpendicular windows, proportions close to this may be quite common.

LATER DRAWINGS ON THE YORK TRACING FLOOR

One characteristic of late Perpendicular architecture is the four-centred arch or window head, much less sharply pointed in shape than earlier forms that were drawn with the compass points placed at two locations on a base line. In a four-centred arch, the shape changes from a sharp curve near the springing to a much flatter curve near the centre of the span. To draw the sharp curves on each side, the compass points would usually be placed on two centres on the base line, but for the flatter part of the curve, two centres well below the base line would be used.

On the tracing floor at York Minster, there is a series of drawings such as this for four-centred arches. The geometry need not concern us, but what is of much greater interest is that all these drawings can be identified with doorways, windows and arches in the church of St Michael-le-Belfrey which stands just across the road from south-west tower of York Minster. This relatively small church was originally inside the Minster's cathedral close, and its maintenance was the responsibility of the Minster. When it was decided, around 1525, to rebuild the church almost entirely (with the exception of parts of the north wall) its design was placed in the hands of the master mason at the Minster, John Forman, and he is presumed to have made the drawings for St Michael's which survive on the tracing floor.[28]

Identifying the subject of each drawing depends not only on recognising the geometrical shapes underlying each detail, but also on remembering that these are full-size drawings and their dimensions must match measurements of the architectural features they are supposed to represent.

Figure 5.6 illustrates a part of the western edge of the tracing floor on which several drawings overlap. At the top of the illustration is evidence of a rough patch of floor on which it was difficult to draw and where a short, broad footprint can be seen – the print of somebody employed in 'puddling' the gypsum plaster to consolidate the surface when it was laid in the fourteenth century.[29] However, the feature of most immediate interest is the set of curves that run from bottom left to top right in this drawing. They are the lines of half of a four-centred arch, and above them, at top left, is a complex pattern of circles.

These details appear to be related to doorways in the north and south walls at the west end of St Michael-le-Belfrey Church. Details of both were modified when stonework was replaced during a Victorian restoration, but their overall four-centred shape was retained.[30] Both doorways also still have quatrefoil tracery patterns in the spandrels (*Plate 13*) corresponding in dimensions to the circles at top left in the drawing (*Figure 5.6*).

Among other drawings represented in Figure 5.6 are an ogee shape below the curves representing the doorway, also some arcs from a large circle to the right and long curves dipping gently downward from left to right. When the latter are followed across the tracing floor past the right-hand edge of this illustration, they turn out to be part of the drawing of an arch.

130

Figure 5.6 Drawing on the tracing floor at York Minster showing part of a four-centred doorway with a circle pattern in the spandrel. Doorways following this design were used in the rebuilding of St Michael-le-Belfrey Church, *c.*1525-35. The curves below the four-centred arch belong to unrelated drawings. *Copyright © Dean & Chapter of York*

Disentangling this arch from other detail on the tracing floor and eliminating the majority of lines connected with other drawings, we arrive at Figure 5.7, which appears to show half of a very flat four-centred arch. In order to check whether this drawing is related to arches in St Michael-le-Belfrey Church, a measured drawing of a typical arch was matched against the tracing-floor drawing. Dimensions of the spandrel

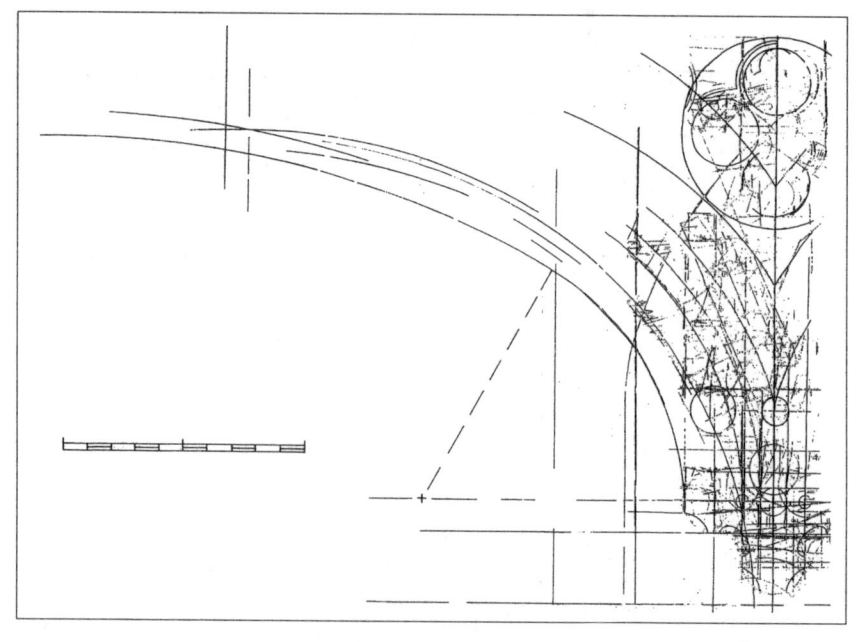

Figure 5.7 Curves on the tracing floor at York Minster showing part of an arch with a circle pattern in the spandrel on the right. The dashed lines represents a radius of 1.070m and the scale bar is of 1m. *Copyright © Dean & Chapter of York*

and its moulding were especially carefully measured (they are within easy reach from the west gallery of the church). Once that was done, it seemed that detail of the actual building matched the drawing on the tracing floor very well. There could be no real doubt that this is a drawing for the arches in St Michael's.

The lowest of the curves drawn on the tracing floor (*Figure 5.7*) seems to correspond with the four-centred curve of the soffit of the arch as built. At the right-hand end of the drawing, near the springing of the arch, the lowest curve has a radius of 1.02m (3ft 4in) and is drawn from the centre marked, whereas the upper, flatter part of the arch has a radius of 3.96m (about 13ft) and the centre is below the lower edge of the illustration. The only line in Figure 5.7 that does not appear on the tracing floor is the dashed line representing a radius, drawn at the point where the more sharply curving, lower end of the arch meets the long-radius upper curve.

Apart from the straightforward four-centred arch, there are curves on the tracing floor which seem to represent an alternative design. These curves are not always easy to follow, but they seem to comprise three or four parallel arcs, representing a three-centred rather than a four-centred arch.

Having settled on the lines of his daringly flat, four-centred arches, Forman considered how their springing would relate to the capitals of the supporting piers. In the spandrel, there was to be a decorative circle in blank tracery with a carved face or shield at its centre (*Plate 14*). An incomplete outline of this circle appears on the tracing floor (on the right in *Figure 5.7*). Dimensions match, with the circle measuring 762mm (30ins) in diameter both on the drawing and in the building itself.

At the lowest point on the drawing in Figure 5.7, the elevation of the arch and spandrel merges into a plan view showing the mouldings on the arch as they converge on the abacus above the capital. This is another example of the medieval drawing method mentioned in Chapter 3 whereby plan views and elevations of detail are sometimes combined in one drawing.

The windows in the north and south aisles of St Michael-le-Belfrey Church are of uniform design, each with four lights under a four-centred arched head (glimpsed through the arches in *Plate 14*). An outline of the geometry for the right-hand half of this design was drawn out on the tracing floor and can still be seen, although it is a more fragmentary drawing than the others relating to St Michael's.[31]

It appears, then, that the set of drawings for St Michael-le-Belfrey Church on the tracing floor at York is more comprehensive than the surviving drawings for most buildings of the period, and it might be worth asking what other details in the building were sufficiently complex for templates to be needed? What further drawings might we expect to find?

Here it is worth noting evidence from the rebuilding of St Mary's Church, Beverley (in the East Riding of Yorkshire) whose nave had been destroyed in 1520 by the collapse of the central crossing tower.[32] The piers in the rebuilt nave have almost exactly the same section as the piers in St Michael-le-Belfrey. There is a suggestion that, before going to York as master mason, John Forman worked briefly on the repair of St Mary's. If he did work there, perhaps between 1520 and 1523, and then worked on St Michael-le-Belfrey in York from 1525, it is possible that he was able to transfer some templates from one site to the other and hence did not need to make new drawings for these details.

There is a degree of surmise in this, but it fits well with what is known about John Forman's career. He is first heard of in 1515, when he was working on Wolsey's new buildings at Hampton Court Palace and had become warden of the masons there.[33] When the tower of St Mary's, Beverley, collapsed, one who responded with donations to pay for repairs was a local man, Sir Richard Rokeby, who had become comptroller of Wolsey's household.[34] In that role he would know the masons working on Wolsey's buildings and may have picked out John Forman as somebody who could help with the rebuilding at Beverley.

In 1523, with reconstruction at St Mary's complete (except for some carpenter's and roofer's work) Forman was appointed to the post of master mason at York Minster. Biographical details are missing for the time he may have been at Beverley, but from 1523 his work at York is well documented as is his work on more distant properties of the Archbishop of York, notably his palace at Southwell. However, the one building that is most characteristic of Forman is St Michael-le-Belfrey. It appears to show the influence of his formative experience at Beverley very clearly in the pier sections and in the tracery circles of the spandrels of arches and doorways. These tracery designs also suggest the influence of John Wastell, the East Anglian mason-designer, famous for his work at Great St Mary's and King's College Chapel, both in Cambridge.[35]

DRAWINGS IN SECULAR CONTEXTS

Although reference has been made to documentary evidence for tracing houses in secular buildings, such as the royal castles at Knaresborough and Scarborough (both in Yorkshire)[36] almost all the examples of craftsmen's drawings discussed or illustrated here have come from churches. This is largely because it is hard to find extant examples in secular buildings. The two castles mentioned are in ruins and, in any case, their tracing houses were probably constructed as temporary buildings. Most other secular or domestic buildings surviving from before 1550 have been so much altered that few mural drawings by craftsmen are likely to have escaped being destroyed or obscured.

However, even in the absence of any obvious location for drawing, there is sometimes a strong case for systematically and minutely examining the fabric of a building to catalogue such evidence as masons' marks, carpenters' numbers, plumb-and-level marks, setting-out lines and design drawings or sketches. Systematic studies of this kind have been pioneered by Jenny Alexander at Lincoln Cathedral and Southwell Minster,[37] but the most complete survey of the fabric of a building to result in a published record of such evidence is from a secular context, and refers to a Tudor courtier's house, Acton Court, at Iron Acton, Gloucestershire. Although much of this house disappeared long ago, the part that survives was later used as a farmhouse without significant alteration or refurbishment. As a result, extensive traces of wall paintings and graffiti remain which would have been lost if the house had ever been modernised in the eighteenth or nineteenth centuries, and these have been recorded with great thoroughness by Kirsty Rodwell.[38]

Acton Court was once a moated medieval house, but the part that survives consists mainly of an east range built in 1535 so that the owner, Sir Nicholas Poyntz, could entertain Henry VIII. Attached to it is a north range added a little later and roofed using trusses removed from Kingswood Abbey (6 miles or 10km north of Acton Court) after its dissolution.[39]

The range built in the 1530s has a series of rooms on the first floor designed to be used by the king during his visit. The walls were panelled, but above the panelling was a painted frieze which was notable for its use of an up-to-date Renaissance design including roundels and columns. Whilst the paint survives well in places, in other parts the roundels are discernible only by 'scribed setting-out lines' on the plastered wall. There are also the setting-out lines for a semicircular arc which may have framed a recess with a coat of arms.[40] In other words, although the subject matter of this painting is secular and classical, the techniques used are reminiscent of the fourteenth-century wall paintings discussed in Chapter 3, several of them in churches, but some also in a domestic context at Longthorpe Tower, Peterborough. One technique that is common to all these examples and also Acton Court is that compass-drawn circles were set out using metal points which left incised curves in the plaster. Some ruled lines were also scribed or incised. These curves and lines can still be traced even where the paint has flaked away.

Graffiti on the walls at Acton Court recorded by Kirsty Rodwell include several drawings of architectural detail, again scribed with metal points on plastered walls. These architectural or 'constructional' drawings seem to refer mainly to alterations being made to the house during the 1550s, and are located on the walls of two ground-floor passages or corridors. In one instance, a whole wall, 2.25m high, is covered with

Medieval Architectural Drawing

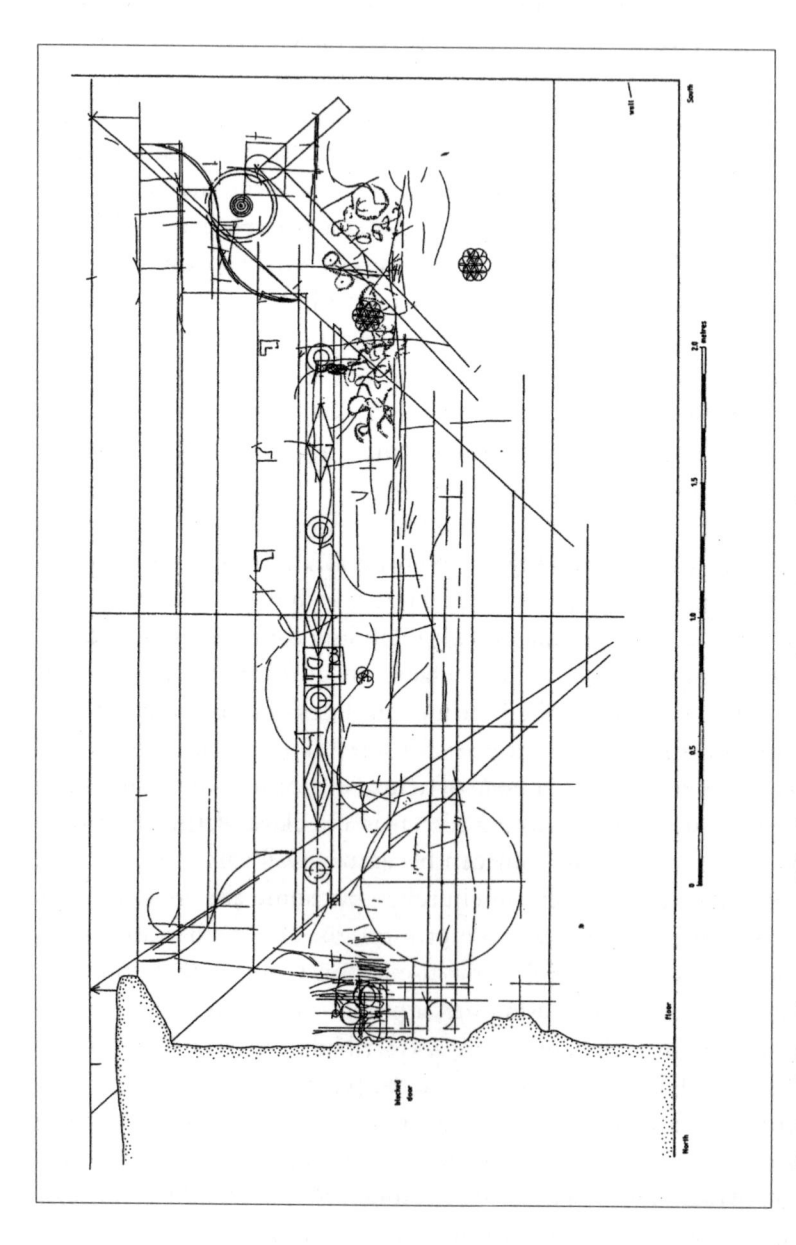

Figure 5.8 Drawings on a wall in the east range at Acton Court, Gloucestershire, including structural detail for the lower part of an oriel window. (Recorded by Kirsty Rodwell, and reproduced from the book *Acton Court: the Evolution of an Early Tudor Courtier's House*, 2004). Copyright © English Heritage

drawings. The largest of these consists of some inclined lines that splay outwards and upwards and are related to reverse curves (on the right in *Figure 5.8*) and a series of horizontal lines. The drawing has been identified as showing the projection that would be required to support a first-floor oriel window from below.[41]

The north range of the building once had such a window. It was later reconstructed as a conventional transomed window, but the dimensions of what remains show that the original oriel was 3.36m wide. The splayed lines in the drawing imply two options for the window, one 2.58m wide and the other 3.48m. That tends to confirm that the second option shown on the wall was a full-size representation of what was constructed.

Other drawings on this wall include a row of lozenges and roundels (with visible compass marks) which may have been part of the oriel window design and which are also related to a screen which no longer exists. There are also drawings which seem to represent the apex and slopes of a roof and the outline of a finial, along with patterns of intersecting circles to which many commentators would attach apotropaic significance (*Figure 5.8*).

On the wall of another passage, which crosses the wing from east to west, is another drawing of a baluster or finial, alongside the quoined jamb of a door. This does not refer to any extant feature of the house, and when the present author copied it he had the impression that it may have been drawn as an exercise to show how complete a design could be produced just from arcs of circles. Other graffiti in this passage include several small drawings of ships, and here and elsewhere in the house are several scrawled names and dates, the earliest being 1556. Most of these graffiti were scribed with metal points, but some are in red chalk.[42]

The ship drawings prompt the comment that in other parts of the country, also, where medieval and sixteenth-century drawings are found on walls, ships are quite widely portrayed, notably at Dartington Hall, Devon, in medieval churches on the coasts of Kent and Norfolk,[43] and in a fifteenth-century house at Whitby (Yorkshire).[44] Many of these examples are on the coast where ships were among the largest ships occur at inland sites, and where they are accurate with respect to constructional detail, they may sometimes prompt suspicion that carpenters working on a house, barn or church had prior experience as ships' carpenters.

DESIGN CHANGES

The drawings discussed in this chapter represent work from about two centuries, between 1350 and 1550, and include drawings on paper and parchment as well as lines on stone or scribed on plastered walls. There is no record of who the craftsmen were at Acton Court, although the sophistication of the wall painting suggests that painters employed by the king's works may have been involved. That leaves the best instances of identifiable craftsmen discussed here as Benedict Crosse at Bristol and John Forman at York, and the drawings attributed to them are, in many ways, more revealing than others quoted here. By studying the drawings together with the extant buildings to which they refer, one can observe where changes in design may have occurred, and John Forman's drawings on the tracing floor at York show evidence of several changes of mind, particularly about the curvature of arches in the church he was designing.

What is also striking, though, is that plans and elevations are still lacking, as in earlier periods, among surviving drawings. Also, despite the enormous variety that can be observed in the design of window tracery, and despite the prominence of windows among the drawings, tracery of the late Decorated and Perpendicular phases in medieval building is poorly represented. One reason must be that many of the most spectacular windows were too big to be drawn on walls, or on either of the two surviving tracing floors. Much larger areas of floor must have been used, perhaps in the transepts and naves of churches, or in other places where long-term survival of drawings cannot be expected. Another answer, though, is that the smaller sketches for such windows have not been found because very few buildings have been subjected to the kind of close examination that Jenny Alexander has given to Lincoln cathedral and Southwell Minster, or that Kirsty Rodwell has exercised at Acton Court.[46] Thus even if few large tracing-floor designs can be expected to survive, many smaller drawings may remain to be discovered.

CHAPTER 6

HOUSE CARPENTERS AND CHURCH CARVERS

(drawings and woodwork, *c*.1450-1550)

A CARPENTER'S ELEVATION

Craftsmen's drawings discussed in previous chapters have been mainly limited to architectural detail. There have been very few elevations and sections of buildings. In Plate 29, however, we may at last examine a late medieval drawing showing the front of a three-storey building. The drawing is on parchment and belongs to the Diocese of Worcester.[1] The building illustrated is timber-framed and the elevation was apparently drawn by a carpenter.

An indication of how architectural drawings were rarely thought to be worth keeping is that this example survived only because, after being discarded, it was reused in the binding of a book. Groups of small holes show where the parchment was sewn to attach the binding to the volume which it covered. When the book was rebound in modern times, the value of the drawing was recognised and it was incorporated within the volume in a way that allows it to be more adequately examined.

What can now be seen, then, is a folded sheet of parchment with drawings on both sides. Most prominent is the elevation of a timber-framed structure with shops on the ground floor (*Plate 29*). The elevation extends from the ground to eaves level, although only part of the upper floor elevation is drawn and the roof above the eaves is not included. This was probably the kind of drawing that would be shown to the client for whom the carpenter was working. It may have been used to discuss details and to form the basis of a contract for construction of the building.

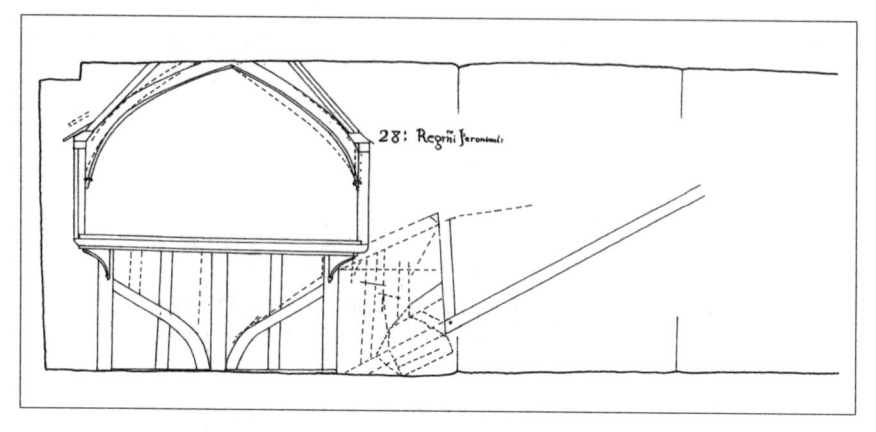

Figure 6.1 Interpretation of the verso side of the carpenter's drawing from Worcester showing how the cross-section of a building with an arch-braced roof merges with another drawing that has been partially erased (dashed lines) by scraping the surface of the parchment.

The drawing measures 1100mm x 600mm. On the verso side of the sheet is marked the title of the volume for which it was once the cover: '28: Registrum Jeronimis' (*Plate 30*). In other words, this was a register in which were the collected records associated with a cleric named Jerome de Ghinucci. He was an Italian who served as Bishop of Worcester between 1522 and 1535. Below this title can be discerned the remains of a drawing which has been partially erased, but is redrawn in Figure 6.1. The main feature is two long inclined beams, roughly parallel with each other, with various near-vertical timbers jointed to them. This looks like a detailed drawing for a repair to a building, or the beginnings of a design abandoned at an early stage.

To the left of the title, '28: Registrum', is a faint drawing of an arch-braced roof truss. Even fainter are drawn the timber posts supporting the roof which are part of the jettied upper floor of a building. Below this is a representation of the braces and studs of a timber-framed wall merging in places with the partly erased drawing to the right. What is depicted, then, is a cross section representing two storeys of a building and it incorporates the elevation of a cross wall. This is much rougher work than the elevation on the other side of the parchment sheet and looks like a drawing the carpenter did while working out details, and before he had arrived at a final design.

Comparing this drawing with the more finished work, suitable for showing a client, on the other side of the sheet, we can recognise two stages in the process of drawing as used by this particular carpenter. He began by drawing in very thin, watery ink, using a set-square with straight edges to ensure that lines were precisely drawn and where necessary were at right angles. Then, in finishing the drawing, he went over lines that he was satisfied were fully correct with undiluted ink. With the pen used freehand, and without a straight edge, he followed the ruled lines very closely.

On comparing the finished drawing on one side of the sheet with the fainter, much rougher drawing on the other side, F.W.B. Charles and Kevin Down wondered whether the section (with roof truss) refers to the same building as the elevation on the other side of the sheet, and concluded that it probably does.[2] The elevation shows a three-storey building, but stops short at eaves level (possibly because the parchment was trimmed when turned into a book cover) but the section shows a roof with only two storeys below. However, Charles drew a reconstruction that showed with greater clarity the carpentry of the upper floors implied by the section, and which also demonstrated how the Worcester drawing might represent a three-storey structure with the ground floor omitted (*Figure 6.2*).

Looking at the main elevation, the arrangement of doorways and ground-floor window openings is reminiscent of late medieval shops such as survive in Tewkesbury and Shrewsbury and which may well have existed in Worcester also. Paired shop-window openings in timber-framed buildings can be paralleled in south-east England also.[3] The accommodation indicated in the drawing above the shops seems more unusual, however. Charles and Down thought that, if the drawing had been finished, the very large window would extend along the full length of the building and would perhaps light a long workroom, possibly for weaving or finishing cloth. Such a window would not be glazed, but rather would be fitted with wooden shutters. The rooms on the top floor, open to the arch-braced roof, provided more elegant accommodation and, if this was wholly a business premises, there may have been a showroom here. Alternatively it may have been a lodging where people lived.

In attempting to establish the date of this carpenter's drawing, Charles and Down noted that the book for which it formed the binding was the register of a bishop who left office in 1535 and the volume would only have been bound after that date. A few notes written on the parchment

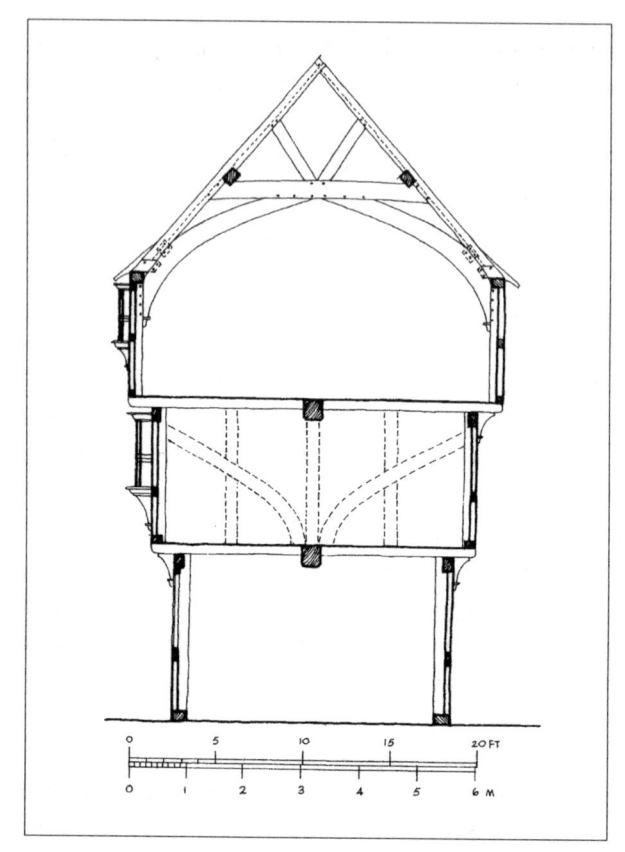

Figure 6.2 Section of a timber-framed building of three storeys, reconstructed by F.W.B. Charles from the two storeys represented on the Worcester drawing. *Reproduced from* Transactions of the Worcestershire Archaeological Society, *3rd series, 3, 1970-72: 78, by kind permission of the Society and by courtesy of the Worcestershire Record Office, where the papers of the late F.W.B. Charles are deposited*

seem to belong to the time when it was being used as a book cover and do not refer to the carpenter's work. For example, where the elevation of a first-floor corner post is depicted, some words which appear to label it (on the right in *Plate 29*) actually say, 'In the name of God, A[men]', as if a clerk was about to start writing out a will beginning with these words and was trying out his pen. In the margin at the other end of the drawing are some names identified as referring to a court case that occurred in the 1540s and it may be about this time that the parchment was used to bind the bishop's register.

One conclusion that may be drawn is that the sheet of parchment was lying around in the bishop's registry in the 1530s or 1540s and was regarded as scrap. It may have been lying there for some time, but even so, one might expect that the drawing was most probably made in the 1520s or 1530s. The fact that such a drawing was in the bishop's registry at all probably indicates that the building depicted was a project at one time being planned for some church property in or near Worcester. It was not at all unusual for an ecclesiastical body to build a structure such as this as an investment, to produce an income from rents. At Battle (Sussex) there are building accounts dating from 1498-9 for a house built by Battle Abbey, and elsewhere in the town is a row of eight houses also built by the abbey in the fifteenth century.[4] Similarly there are houses with shops in Tewkesbury built by the abbey there. The whereabouts of houses in Worcester that may have been built by the church is uncertain, although Nash House, New Street, is a four-storey timber-framed house that has some similarities with the drawing.

Ranging further afield in the West Midlands, Charles and Down found a much closer match to the drawing in the Abbot's House, Butcher Row, Shrewsbury.[5] They did not think this was the same building as the one in the drawing, but it had 'remarkable' similarities. It is a three-storey building of much the same size and has a similar range of doorways and shop windows on the ground floor (*Plate 15*). As in the drawn elevation at Worcester, the main posts in the elevation at Shrewsbury are each carved with a slender pilaster moulding which supports a bracket under the jettied floor above.

At the time when Charles and Down did their research, the Abbot's House was thought to date from the early sixteenth century (but before the dissolution) and so seemed to fit the estimated date of the drawing. Despite its name, Pevsner commented that it was 'wrongly said to have been the town house of the abbots of Lilleshall'.[6] Since then, however, tree-ring analysis (dendrochronology) has shown that the Abbot's House is rather earlier than expected.[7] Trees were felled for its construction in the summer of 1457 and the late spring of 1458. These dates almost coincide with a documentary reference showing that, after all, the house did belong to the abbots of Lilleshall, for in April 1459 the frame was ready for assembly and there was some sort of foundation-laying ceremony. The Borough Bailiff's accounts record that the abbot and his carpenter were present and 20*d* was paid 'to the carpenter of the abbot of Lilleshall as his reward'.[8]

The carpenter is not named, but the wording suggests that he regularly worked for the abbot. Thus he was probably not a local Shrewsbury carpenter. Meanwhile, since the building in the Worcester drawing is so similar to the Abbot's House, it may be that the house and the drawing are by carpenters from the same 'workshop'. If so, this must have been a workshop that built the better quality timber-framed structures required for the more prominent ecclesiastical estates in the area.

However, this conclusion is not compatible with the evidence cited above that the drawing may date from after 1520, that is, much later than the Abbot's House. There are also detailed differences which make the Worcester drawing seem later than the house. If the roof drawn on the verso side of the parchment refers to the same building as the main drawing, then the arch-braced truss delineated there is certainly very different from the tie-beam trusses with queen posts supporting collars in the Abbot's House.[9]

Another difference is that on the elevation in the drawing, slender pilaster mouldings are carved on the main posts and studs in a manner that in most respects corresponds to practice in the West Midlands after 1480 or 1500. However, the Abbot's House at Shrewsbury, now dated to 1458-59 also has carved pilaster mouldings, but of more substantial form such as might be found on a rood screen, or in other examples of fifteenth-century church carpentry.

In order to investigate further the similarities and differences between the Abbot's House and the parchment drawing, corresponding details were copied from both and also from a third building, a merchant's house in Friar Street, Worcester, misleadingly called The Greyfriars (*Figure 6.3*). In all three cases, the posts with pilaster mouldings support a bracket under the projecting jetty of the floor above. The convention used in the parchment drawing is to show the posts and pilasters in elevation, but to combine this with a side view of the brackets and, in Figure 6.3, the same convention is followed for the other two buildings. The Greyfriars in Worcester is said to date from 1480 and one of the brackets is carved with the initials of Thomas Grene who died in 1499 (although of course this may have been done retrospectively).[10]

Comparisons underline the fact that the parchment drawing at Worcester is not to scale but tends to exaggerate the width and reduce the height of each post and its mouldings. Figure 6.3 does not distort the proportions of the other buildings represented to the same extent. Even so, the simpler and more slender design of the pilaster mouldings at The Greyfriars stands out. The odd, elongated base of the pilaster from the Worcester drawing is also evident. And a distinctive feature of the Abbot's House is that pilasters on the first-floor elevation have the addition of a ring or subsidiary capital at mid-height.

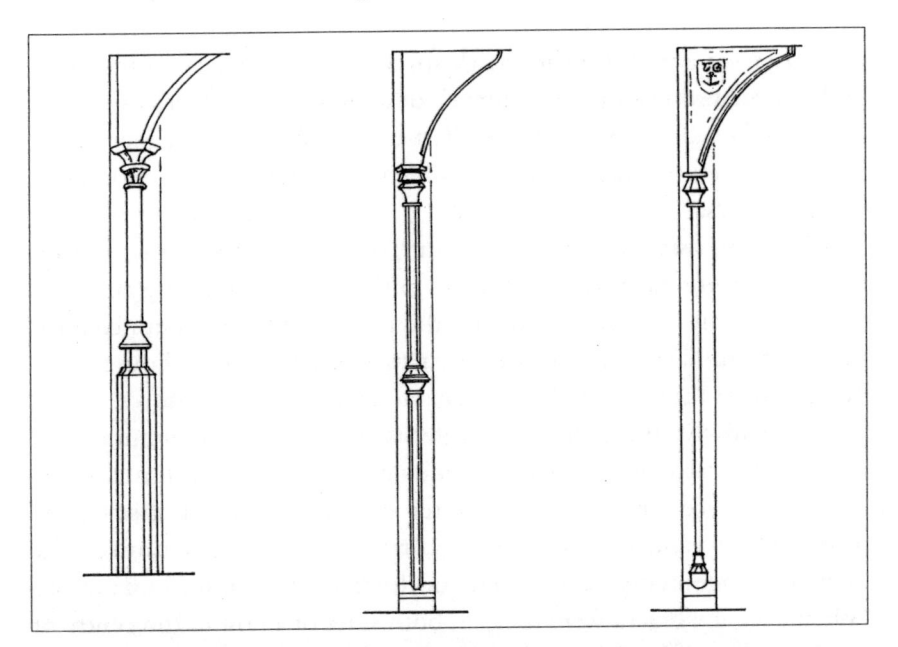

Figure 6.3 Timber posts carved with pilaster mouldings. From left to right they are a detail from the parchment drawing at Worcester, a first-floor post at the Abbot's House Shrewsbury and a ground-floor detail from The Greyfriars, Worcester. The convention of combining a side view of the bracket with a front elevation of the post is adopted from the Worcester drawing. In two cases brackets are plain, but at The Greyfriars one is carved with initials TG and an anchor. Not to scale.

These and other considerations tend to show that, although the detail in the parchment drawing seems later and less like church woodwork than the detail from the Abbot's House, it does not have such slender forms as many later pilaster mouldings. Hence the drawing is likely to be earlier than previously thought (perhaps even late fifteenth century) and can still be seen as related to the Abbot's House in terms of the kind of house-carpentry that was produced for ecclesiastical clients.

YORK AND SCARBOROUGH CARPENTERS

Shrewsbury is famous as a town of timber-framed houses and, in the sixteenth century, a so-called 'Shrewsbury school' of carpentry developed with some distinctive ways of ornamenting timber frames. For example, the slender pilaster mouldings carved in the surface of the main posts of houses were now finished with spiral or cable patterns. Vine trails, perhaps derived from the woodwork of church screens, were carved on horizontal timbers. One of the earliest exponents of this style was John Sandford (d.1566) who was also a leading figure in the Shrewsbury Guild of Carpenters.[11]

At the opposite side of the country, the city of York was another place of strong carpentry traditions, although the building industry there was somewhat depressed after the middle of the fifteenth century. Perhaps by the 1480s, however, or perhaps a little later, more houses were being built, some of which were characterised by a decorative device just as distinctive (though less delicate) than the later Shrewsbury cable mouldings and vine patterns. This device consisted of a doubling up of curved braces and where Worcester and Shrewsbury timber frames displayed few and relatively small curved braces in elevations, York carpenters often emphasised them, or duplicated them for extra effect. When doubled braces were used on both sides of a post in the centre of an elevation, this could give the house a very emphatic presence, as seen in Plate 31, and could make it stand out from the other timber-framed buildings in the vicinity.[12]

Although the names of most York carpenters active at this time are known and the history of their guild is well documented,[13] it is impossible to say which favoured the doubled-brace design. However, one or two who used it seem also to have worked in Scarborough, then the most important Yorkshire port between the Humber and the Tees. The dates of the buildings they erected in Scarborough are uncertain, although the early 1480s seems possible because, at that time, an effort to develop the port and town was being made on orders from Richard III. This was a project that he had begun privately some years before he became king, and there are records of him ordering that 300 oaks from the Forest of Pickering should be used in the quay at Scarborough.[14] So much timber implies much work for sawyers and carpenters, but there is no documentation to show where such craftsmen were recruited.

It is likely that improvements to the harbour stimulated the construction of buildings nearby and one which shows especially close affinities with the York carpentry tradition survives in fragmentary form alongside a public house known as the Newcastle Packet. The remains are from a substantial timber-framed house of hall and cross-wings plan which stood here until the present pub was built in 1898-9 (and extended

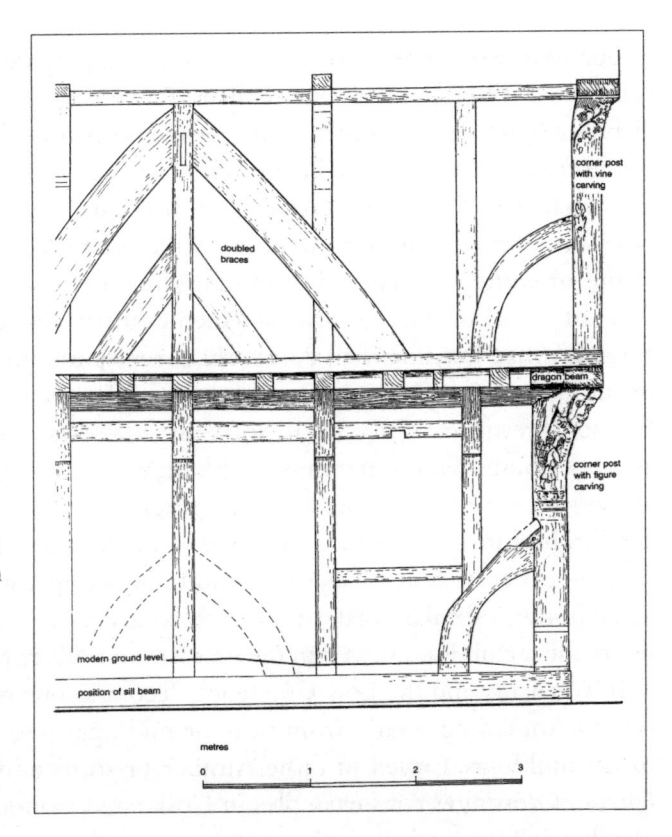

Figure 6.4 West elevation of the Newcastle Packet public house, Scarborough (North Riding). The drawing shows the existing timber framing (in 2003) except for the sill beam, the dragon beam and two other timbers attached to the first-floor corner post, which are reconstructed.

1923) to designs by the local architects F.A. and S. Tugwell. Framing from one side of the old building was preserved *in situ* by attaching it to the brickwork of the west wall of the new structure. This can be seen in a narrow alley beside the pub, now used as the fire exit.[15]

The framing is part of the side elevation of a building with jettied upper floors and, in the centre of the first-floor elevation is an instance of the doubled curved braces that are so characteristic of late fifteenth-century York. Here, though, the outer braces are planks of exaggerated width (*Figure 6.4*). At the corner where this elevation meets the original front wall, which faced the harbour, there are the remains of carved corner posts at ground-floor and first-floor levels. Both posts are angled to support dragon beams (diagonal floor beams, now missing) that were intended to carry the joists of the first and second floors. However, sketches of the house made by the architect Frank Tugwell before he began rebuilding show it as only two storeys high and it is likely that an intended second floor was never built.[16]

The first-floor corner post, preserved in a slightly displaced position, is carved with grapes and vine tendrils. The ground-floor post is more elaborately decorated with a carved head and two smaller figures. One of the latter is a woman carrying on her back a basket of loaves or, since this is close to the harbour, perhaps fish (*Figure 6.5*). Another corner post was recorded before demolition of the old building began.[17] It was at the opposite, eastern end of the building and was carved with the head of a fool or jester. Many late-medieval timber-framed houses in English urban locations had decorated corner posts, but the decoration on surviving examples often consists of tracery panels, as at the Abbot's House, Shrewsbury (*Plate 16*). In York, carved corner posts on fifteenth-century houses tend to be simpler, although one has quatrefoil patterns and others have brattishing. Carved figures are much less common on English houses, but there are examples at Lincoln and there was at one time a corner post in Bury St Edmunds depicting a wild man with a hairy body. A similar corner post with a carving of a hairy man with boots and a club is preserved in the Victoria and Albert Museum.[18]

In Germany and the Low Countries, decoration representing human figures (including scenes from peasant life) appeared more often on urban buildings, carved in either timber or stone and often painted. Christa Grössinger cites examples in Goslar and mentions buildings in Flanders.[19] The carving on the corner post at the Newcastle Packet in Scarborough seems to be related to this continental tradition which, at first sight, seems explicable by Scarborough's importance as a port with direct links to the Low Countries.

In more detail, the carvings on the corner post at the Newcastle Packet can be related to the work of German artists who took advantage of developments in engraving and printing to publish prints which circulated in England far beyond the immediate vicinity of coastal towns. The subject matter of such prints is also noteworthy, in that there was a vogue for humorous and often bawdy scenes deriving amusement from the lives of working people. On the Scarborough corner post the woman carrying the basket on her back is typical of this. She closely resembles in posture a differently dressed woman with a similar load depicted by a German artist whose prints appeared from the late 1470s. His name is not known, but he always signed himself 'bxg' and around 1480 was evidently working in Frankfurt. Some of his designs were redrawn about 1520 by Hans Schäufelein, a pupil of Dürer, for use on a

Figure 6.5 The Newcastle Packet, Scarborough (North Riding). Studies of the two smaller carved figures on a corner post of the former house. The woman with a basket on her back is on the north-west face of the post and the man with the jar or flask is on the south-west face. Dashed lines and hatching show surfaces that are badly decayed and hard to interpret. The post is decorated with brattishing below the feet of both figures.

set of playing cards.[20] Figure 6.6 is Schäufelein's playing-card version of Master bxg's depiction of the woman carrying a basket and is an accurate mirror-image version of the original. Prints by Master bxg circulated in England during the 1480s and, although there is no carpenter's drawing for the Scarborough house, these prints by bxg seem to have been used by the carver of the corner post.

Detailed study of the carving in Scarborough is difficult (and photography nearly impossible) because of its confined position relative to the Victorian brickwork of the pub and because of decay in the timber, but the subject matter of the carving has three components. The woman carrying the back-pack basket is on the north-west face of the post and a male figure of similar size is on the south-west

Figure 6.6 Playing card illustration by Hans Schäufelein based on an earlier engraving by Master bxg. A woman carrying a basket on her back is accompanied by a man with his right leg bent back and supported on a crutch. *From Hans Joachim Raupp,* Bauernsatiren, *Nierderzier, 1986; reproduced by kind permission of the publisher, Franz J. Lucassen*

face (*Figure 6.5*). These two figures seem to be related to the the bxg print shown in Schäufelein's reworked version in Figure 6.6, notable similarities being the woman's posture, the basket she is carrying, the flask carried by the man and, possibly (as will be indicated below) the man's legs. The third element in the carving is a large head looking outward from the building (*Figure 6.4*). Associated with this are arms and hands on both north-west and south-west faces of the corner post. On the south-west face is also the male figure with the flask (of beer?) which seems too large in comparison with the size of the man and almost in scale with the hand that is probably about to take it.

The large head on the corner post is now badly weathered, but has some similarities in posture to a woman's head in another print by bxg (on which his initials are clearly seen: *Figure 6.7*). The hands holding a jar in this scene are also faintly reminiscent of the hand that is about to take the beer in the carving. In this way the carving may seem to be combining two pictures so that the woman in Figure 6.7 is taking her jar of beer from the man in Figure 6.6. However, the carving is so

Figure 6.7 Engraving signed bxg showing a peasant woman with a goblet and a blank shield. The diameter of the original is 90mm. *From Christa Grössinger,* Humour and Folly in Secular and Profane Prints of Northern Europe, 1430-1540, *London, 2002, p. 45; reproduced by kind permission of Harvey Miller Publishers*

badly decayed that this interpretation can only be tentative. The head and torso of the man have almost entirely rotted away, but his arm and legs are well preserved. In the relevant prints by Master bxg and Schäufelein (*Figure 6.6*), the man is shown as a cripple, with one leg bent back and supported by a crutch. In the Scarborough carving, one leg seems shorter than the other and, below the shorter leg, there does seem to be a peg-like extension. This may correspond to the crutch in the print although this detail in the carving is too weathered to be clear.

Referring to the woman who accompanies the man in Figure 6.6, it appears in the carving as if the large hand on the north-west face of the corner post is taking loaves (or fish?) from the woman's basket in much the same way as the large hand on the other face is taking the man's beer. The carving includes some lettering which has been read as the word JUSTICE or JUSTITIA which may indicate that the building functioned as a customs house or court room, although this hardly fits the humour in the German prints.[21] The lettering may be a late addition, intended to modify the meaning of the carving at a late stage in its production.

There is no independent evidence for the date of the timber-framed house to which this corner post belongs, but if the identification of the carving with prints by Master bxg is accepted, the structure must clearly be later than the prints, that is later than $c.1475$. This is consistent with the similarity between the doubled braces in the elevation of the Scarborough house and the doubled braces in houses in York, which are thought to date from the later fifteenth century or $c.1500$. It is significant, too, that prints by the German who signed himself bxg were used, not only in Scarborough, but also on the other side of Yorkshire by carvers working in Ripon Minster in 1489 and up to 1494.

These points support a late fifteenth-century date for the Scarborough carving. They also suggest a relationship with the work of craftsmen elsewhere in northern England, indicating that the unusual features of the Newcastle Packet are not solely the result of the alien influences to be expected in a seaport.

USE OF PRINTS BY CHURCH CARVERS

The prints by Master bxg used by carvers at Scarborough belong to a context in which many similar prints were being imported and copied elsewhere in England. In earlier centuries, manuscript illumination had sometimes been a source of ideas for carvers and there were probably more 'model books' and manuscript 'model drawings' in circulation than we know of. One such book of drawings that has survived is the fourteenth-century example in the Pepysian Library in Cambridge (Chapter 5). However, few such exemplars used by craftsmen have survived, making it hard to trace a carver's sources.

Once prints became available, though, the fact that they were produced in multiple copies (even if sometimes only a dozen of one illustration) means that the chances that a design would survive were greatly increased. An example is a series illustrating the story of Reynard the Fox produced by William Caxton.[22] However, English printmakers were few and many more prints were produced on the continent. A considerable import trade developed and there are customs house records for 1479-80 of books and prints being shipped into London from such places as Paris and Antwerp.[23]

Three kinds of illustration that could be used as patterns for carving need to be distinguished. Firstly, there were Flemish woodblock illustrations of Bible stories such as Jonah and the Whale, or Samson, mostly from what was known as the *Paupers' Bible* and similar works;[24] secondly there were the German prints of peasant life and bawdy humour, as exemplified by those used at Scarborough; thirdly, after 1500 there were prints which, in their decorative detail and mode of representing the nude human figure, reflect Renaissance influence.[25] These often came from Paris in books rather than as separate prints or cards.

All three kinds of illustration were used at one time or another by carvers of misericords, the decorated tip-up seats in church choir stalls. One particularly well-known example of a print by Master bxg, used by carvers in Ripon Minster, is a humorous picture of a peasant giving his wife a ride in a three-wheeled barrow. As Grössinger notes, this print circulated widely and was copied by carvers of wood and stone on the continent as well as at Ripon.[26]

German prints, especially those by Master bxg, could have been introduced into northern England by a group of Flemish craftsmen based in York that included John Dam, a goldsmith whose family may have originated from Damme, near Bruges.[27] Many printmakers on the continent (and perhaps also Master bxg) were goldsmiths, because that trade gave them the necessary skills in engraving.[28] Through practising this trade, John Dam would have had contacts with printmakers and he also had potential users of the prints in his own family. His father (James Dam) and an uncle (David) were woodcarvers who had been working on York Minster, probably from about 1470.[29] Carved wooden bosses by one of them, David Dam, alias David Carver, are to be seen decorating a vault above the crossing in the Minster.[30] However, there is no evidence for the use of German prints there.

As for Ripon Minster, Charles Tracy's study suggests that the carving of misericords in the choir stalls there was done by three 'hands',[31] and the subject matter of the carving indicates that the three men

Figure 6.8 Ways of writing the date at Ripon and Fountains Abbey: in timber, on the choir stalls in Ripon Minster, [Ann]o dni 1494 (left) and 1489 (top), and in stone in the abbey church, [An]no Domini 1483. Not to scale, with the stonework detail much reduced relative to the others.

concerned may have had prior experience not only in York, but perhaps also at nearby Fountains Abbey. The church at Fountains inspired a style for placing dates on carved work, beginning with a window repair in which an awkward joint is partly masked by a carved stone angel carrying a scroll with the date 1483 in Arabic numerals. A wooden angel on a misericord at Ripon displays the date 1489 in similar style. Then, five years later, a scroll held by another angel, carved as the stalls were being completed, was marked 1494 (*Figure 6.8*). Was a drawing of the stone angel used by the later woodcarvers, one wonders? In each case the digit four was carved as a loop in the medieval manner (Chapter 4, Figure 4.11).

The choir stalls at Ripon have an unusually interesting set of misericords of which several are based on woodcuts from the *Paupers' Bible* (including representations of Jonah and Samson) and one is based on the print by Master bxg mentioned above with the three-wheeled barrow. Other aspects of the choir stalls at Ripon include the desks on which clergy and choristers placed their service books. These were

Figure 6.9 Comparison of desk-ends made for major churches in Yorkshire demonstrating their similar dimensions. The Jervaulx Abbey desk-end (now at Aysgrath, left) carries the initial W, with hazel leaves and a tun, to commemorate William Heslington or Hazelton, abbot from 1472. The Ripon Minster example (right) is surmounted by an elephant-and-castle instead of a poppy head, and bears the date 1494 on a scroll carried by the angel below the bishop's mitre and the shield.

supported at each end by heavy carved vertical boards which sometimes also functioned as bench ends for the next row of seats. Many were topped with 'poppy heads' and had heraldic animals (such as a lion or wyvern) in front, but one is engagingly topped with an elephant (with castle, *Figure 6.9*). Drawings of elephants had circulated in England since the thirteenth century and appeared in bestiaries. One without a castle is to be found in the Pepysian model book, but it is hard to identify the model for the Ripon version. However, on a screen made for Jervaulx Abbey,[32] not far from Ripon, about 1506, the elephant-and-castle theme appears again, though on a smaller scale (*Plate 32*).

It has long been thought that the same craftsmen worked at Ripon Minster and Jervaulx, and it has also been claimed that this so-called 'Ripon school of carvers'[33] produced desk-ends for a variety of different churches to standard dimensions. This has been largely disproved by measuring many examples, but a fairly clear instance of furniture in one building measuring the same as in another is that the desk-ends made for Jervaulx Abbey, now at Aysgarth (North Riding), are very close in some dimensions to the principal desk-ends at Ripon. The width and thickness of the basic planks of timber from which each one was made (excluding the detached shaft and tabernacle at the front) are 342mm and 115mm respectively.[34] There is a roll moulding near the base of each desk-end and the total height measured from here is the same for each one (*Figure 6.9*).

These similarities in dimensions combined with differences in design suggest two different carvers accustomed to working together and perhaps using the same outline drawing, or at least the same measuring rod marked with set dimensions. Alternatively, perhaps the timber came from the same woodyard where a standard template was used when preparing material for the desk ends. As with the similarities in ways of showing dates at Ripon and Fountains Abbey, this parallel between work at Ripon and another Cistercian abbey shows evidence of designs being transmitted without evidence for whether drawings were involved, and of what sort.

Evidence for the identities of the woodcarvers is not entirely conclusive either. A carver named William Bromflet was working in York during 1482-3 and could well be a link between the Dam family at York Minster and the Ripon carvers.[35] But there is no documentation to show whether he was at Ripon when work was in progress on the choir stalls in 1489. Twenty years later, though, in 1518 and 1520, a William Bromflet was mentioned as the leading carver at Ripon.[36] However, we cannot be sure whether this was the same Bromflet as before, or perhaps his son or nephew. The wood carving in the choir at Ripon seems to be the work of at least three craftsmen and the later woodwork from Jervaulx was apparently made by yet another carver,[37] though using Ripon measurements. It is tempting to think that William Bromflet was involved, but there is no record.

What is most relevant here is that one misericord carved at Ripon during the undocumented period after 1489 has the design mentioned above based on a print by Master bxg. Since pictures by this printmaker also informed carving on the Newcastle Packet in Scarborough, where unidentified York craftsmen seem to have worked, it is worth wondering whether York was the centre from which these prints circulated. Alternatively, it is possible that the prints were first imported by the carvers working in Scarborough before others took them to York and Ripon.

RENAISSANCE DESIGNS

Many of the prints used by woodcarvers were very small. Some, indeed, were produced as playing cards, not always for use at the card table, but for circulation as models for copying. They were an alternative to books as a means of disseminating designs and artists were stimulated by this medium to produce suits and sets on related themes.

Such small illustrations had to be enlarged before carvers could use them. In many instances, as probably at Scarborough, the carver was not aiming at an exact copy of the print and could make his own sketches interpreting the print at the size he required. Sometimes, no doubt, he would sketch directly on the wood that was to be carved. In other instances, though, it is clear that the carver was aiming at a fairly exact copy and there are examples where he enlarged a design painstakingly on paper. The design would then be transferred to the timber surface by 'pricking through' the paper in such a way as to mark the timber. It may be significant that some of the best evidence for the use of this technique is where carvers were working to Renaissance designs whose style was novel and unfamiliar and which they would perhaps not feel comfortable sketching freehand.

One such example is in Bristol Cathedral, which, at the time when the carving was done, around 1520, was the abbey church of St Augustine. The context is another set of choir stalls with misericords and, in her book on the subject,[38] M.D. Anderson identifies the source of some of these designs as engraved decoration used by Thielman Kerver and others to ornament the books they were printing in Paris around 1500.

One engraving shows three nude boys running away from a dragon with two heads. The boys look backwards at the dragon as they run and, in enlarging the engraving onto paper (and probably not parchment),

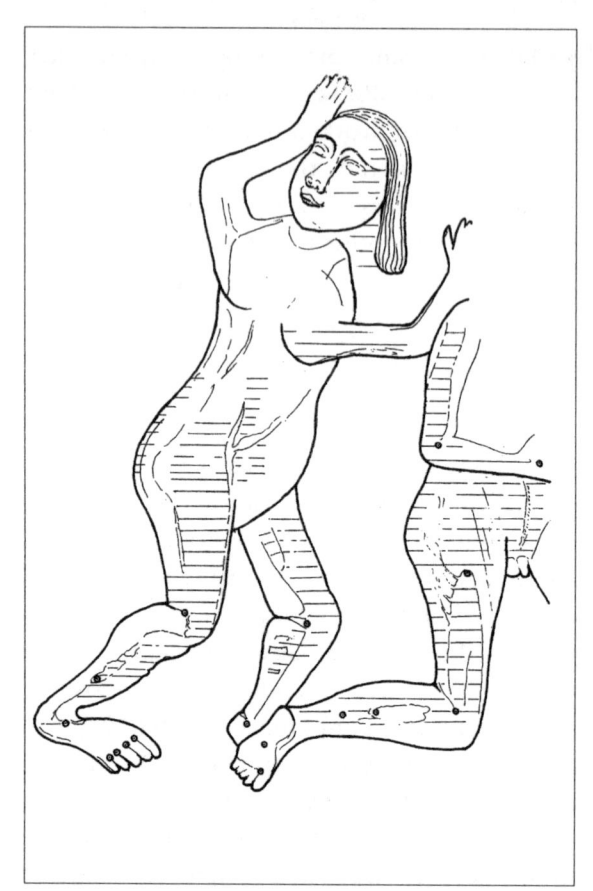

Figure 6.10 Outline of a carved figure on a misericord in Bristol Cathedral. On the lower limbs, many of the holes caused by 'pricking through' from the drawing can be seen and are emphasised in this outline. The predominant surface pattern is the horizontal grain of the wood. Not to scale, but the figures are around 200mm tall.

the woodcarver has not copied the original exactly and has made one of the heads turn at an anatomically impossible angle.

Discussing the same misericords, Christa Grössinger notes evidence that some designs were pricked through onto the wood from a drawing, which is how we know that there was indeed a separate drawing in this instance.[39] The term 'pricked through' rather understates the process, though, for the carver must have applied his metal point quite forcefully to penetrate the wood as deeply as he did. Figure 6.10 is the outline of one of three nude figures being chased by the dragon showing where some of the prick marks occur. They are clearest between the toes of one foot, and at ankle and knee joints.

Another example of Renaissance detail in wood carving is at St Helen's Church, Sefton, Lancashire, a village church just beyond the northern outskirts of Liverpool. The church was substantially rebuilt, except for its tower and north aisle, soon after 1500 and was provided with the richest of furnishings: pews, choir stalls and screens. Extensive, high quality restoration of roofs and screens was carried out by W.D. Caroë from 1919, but the detail of most lower parts of the rood screen is original and presents a striking parade of putti (cherubs) supporting horns of plenty in a frieze. This Renaissance detail contrasts sharply in style with the late Gothic structure in which it is set. The frieze includes a series of shields bearing the initials I and M, for James Molyneux, rector of the church, who commissioned the work but who died in 1509. This may date the woodwork but, if it is really as early as 1509, such notable Renaissance work is truly 'remarkable'.[40]

To ensure that the putti were identical they had to be pricked through from a paper drawing, with the mirror image figure in each pair pricked through from the back of the paper. The technique used was the same as for the much earlier mirror-image foliage designs at Southwell (*Figures 1.1, 1.2*). As at Bristol, points pricked through were at knee and ankle joints, and also at the navel and nipples. Small circles and arcs of circles appear in many places in these carvers' work and were marked around some pricked points, particularly at the leg and arm joints (which make these look like the limbs of mechanical figures). Small circles were marked at the navel and breasts, with two large arcs also inscribed from these points, one outlining the stomach and the other the torso. Strangely, the head was not dealt with in this way and does not have the rounded shape one expects of the more cherubic kind of putti (*Figure 6.11*).

In this instance, the recurrence of identical putti and their mirror images across the length of the screen demonstrates the use of a drawing. In other instances, the repetition of similar designs in different buildings suggests strongly that drawings were regularly circulated among craftsmen. M.D. Anderson has noted that among glaziers, it sometimes happens that their wills mention rolled drawings (scrolls) with designs for stained glass windows which were left to apprentices, colleagues or relatives following the same trade.[41] Similar references in wills are rare among carvers or carpenters. The drawings they used seem more elusive except in the instances quoted where the subject matter of a print (and the postures of the figures depicted) demonstrates that a carver must have known it, or where the marks left by pricking out parts of a design from a drawing provide the evidence.

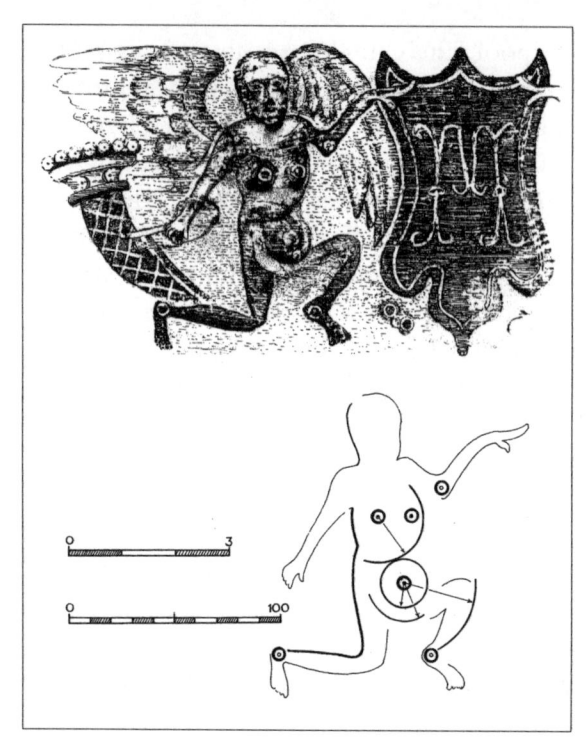

Figure 6.11 St Helen's Church, Sefton, Lancashire: One of the putti in a frieze along the top of the dado in the rood screen. The outline below shows where holes were pricked through from a drawing, and where arcs of circles were drawn before carving began. The scales represent 3in and 100mm.

What has also usefully emerged from this chapter is that such prints and drawings did not just circulate among carvers of church furniture. They could occasionally influence carvings made for the decoration of houses and may sometimes indicate that craftsmen had moved from ecclesiastical to domestic work. At the Scarborough house, however, where the carving on one of its corner posts has parallels in misericords, the church carving may be a little later. The author of the Worcester drawing in Plate 29, like the Abbot of Lilleshall's carpenter, probably worked for ecclesiastical patrons and may have had to work on both domestic and church buildings at various times. This may account for the elaborate blank tracery design with which the corner post of the Abbot's House in Shrewsbury is decorated (*Plate 16*). After the dissolution, the work of the Shrewsbury school of carpenters, with its vine trails and quatrefoils, gives a strong impression that decoration previously used on church screens and roofs was being adapted for domestic contexts. In all these episodes, there are the occasional clues to the drawings that craftsmen used, and there is the one unique drawing at Worcester.

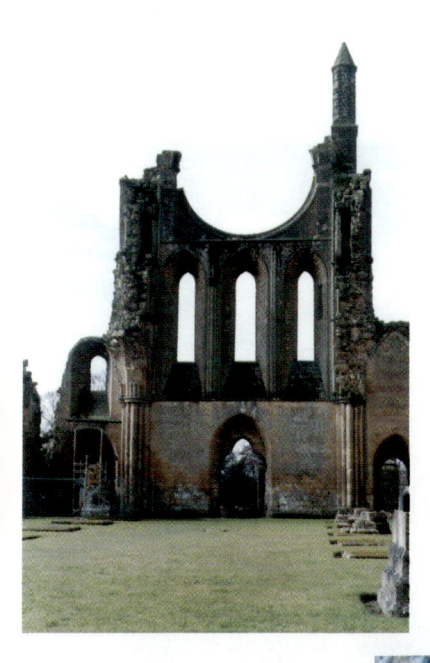

Plate 19 The ruined nave at Byland Abbey (North Riding) with plain walling to the right of the doorway on which is the detail shown in *Plate 20*. Photo: A. Pacey

Plate 20 Byland Abbey: detail of stonework inside the west wall with an incised curve remaining from a former drawing. Photo: A. Pacey

Above: Plate 26 Carpentry joints, roof of the north porch, Wells Cathedral, Somerset. *Photo: A. Pacey*

Right: Plate 27 Gloucester Cathedral: niche with whitewashed upper parts and incised line from drawing in the damaged reredos in the Lady Chapel. *Photo: A. Pacey*

Plate 28 Window design on the font at St Andrew's Church, Ewerby, Lincolnshire. *Photo: A. Pacey*

Plate 29 A carpenter's drawing, now bound in Bishop Ghinucci's register, Worcestershire Record Office. Copyright © *Diocese of Worcester, reproduced by kind permission of the Diocese*

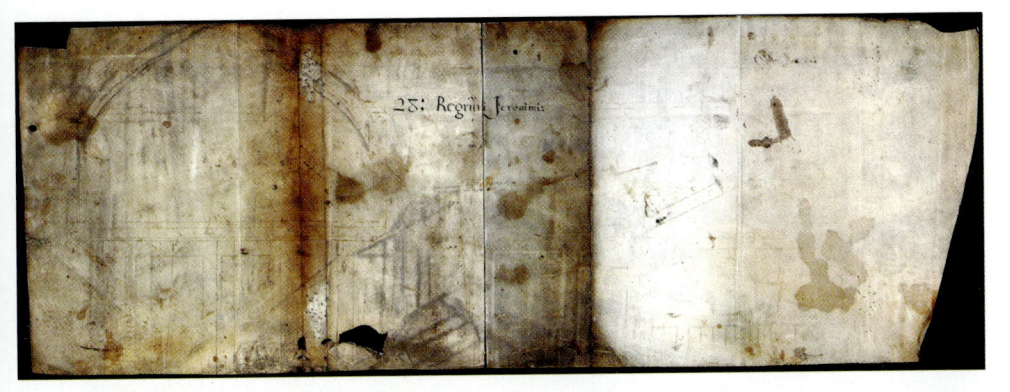

Plate 30 Faint lines on the back of the drawing in the previous plate. On the left is shown an arch-braced roof. Extending across the centre is another drawing with the timbers sloping upward. Some vertical and horizontal lines show through from the other side. *Copyright © Diocese of Worcester, reproduced by kind permission of the Diocese*

Plate 31 Timber-framed house in Goodramgate, York, with doubled curved braces. *Photo: J.D. Pacey*

Plate 32 Detail of a screen made for Jervaulx Abbey, now in the church at Aysgarth (North Riding). Note the small elephant towards the left in the gold-painted frieze. *Photo: Pamela Maryfield*

Plate 33 Rood screen by William Jake, carpenter, at Hubberholme in the Yorkshire Dales. *Photo: Pamela Maryfield*

Plate 34 Churche's Mansion, Nantwich, Cheshire, built in 1577, the work of Thomas Cleese, carpenter. *Photo: A. Pacey*

Above: Plate 35 A jettied and gabled dormer at 14 Old Street, Ludlow, Shropshire, made in 1622 by Francis Bebb, carpenter. *Photo: A. Pacey*

Left: Plate 36 Detail of the former town hall at Leominster (Herefordshire), now known as Grange Court. *Photo: A. Pacey*

Plate 37 Detail of the roof of a house at Eastburn, West Riding. Setting-out lines drawn on the face of the timber include a centre line (in black) and lines showing the slope of the principals (in red). *Photo: Jean Ainsworth*

Plate 38 Red-ochre lines on a barn roof truss at Prospect House, High Bradley, near Skipton, West Riding. *Photo: Sara Baggaley*

Right: Plate 39 Drawing in water colour recording carpenters' setting-out lines on a king-post roof truss at Cuckoo Nest Farm in the Yorkshire Dales near Ilkley.

Below: Plate 40 Middle Temple Hall, London: detail of the roof above the main collar (the top of which is seen at the bottom of the picture) and below the high-level ceiling. *Photo by permission of the Honourable Society of the Middle Temple*

Plate 41 Drawing on plaster dating from the 1660s concealed by slightly later panelling at Pembroke College, Cambridge. *Photo: A. Pacey*

CHAPTER 7

CIRCLES AND SCALE DRAWINGS

(masons, carpenters and surveyors, 1520-1620)

DISSOLUTION CIRCLES AND ELIZABETHAN DEVICES

The middle decades of the sixteenth century might be expected to mark the end of the story told in previous chapters, partly for the conventional reason that the dissolution of the monasteries in the 1530s and the gathering pace of reformation in the church during the next decade can be seen as marking a decisive end of the Middle Ages. The dissolution, in particular, radically changed the lives of many craftsmen who had previously worked for monastic houses.

However, other policies of Henry VIII would, in the long run, have a more positive impact on the work of masons and carpenters, including the Statute of Bridges (1531), which gave responsibility for the construction and repair of bridges to the 'shires and ridings' of England,[1] and policies on naval matters, which led to the first accurate surveys of parts of the coastline. This added to already expanding opportunities for land surveyors, some of whom, before the end of the century, also undertook surveys of buildings.

Consistent with these divergent trends, there are contrasting tendencies in drawings done by sixteenth-century craftsmen. On the one hand, ritual marks, such as were occasionally made during the Middle Ages, proliferated in some places to a surprising degree. On the other hand, by 1600 some stone masons were making accurate drawings to scale and a few seem to have been able to conceptualise buildings so well through the medium of drawing that they were comfortable designing buildings on paper rather than on site, or on a tracing floor.

For landowners who gained by the dissolution and for surveyors, masons and carpenters in their employ, these were interesting times. Conversely, for craftsmen who had previously worked regularly for abbeys or other monastic houses, the effect was sometimes devastating. There were some craftsmen who had quite recently been constructing ambitious new works for abbeys, but who were now employed to destroy them. Lay patrons also saw works they had paid for destroyed and, because they had invested in the monasteries, felt that they had a proprietorial interest that ought to be respected. When such people applied for the purchase of monastic lands, they often stressed their family endowments and, whatever regrets they may have had, looked forward to extending their control of the monastic estate.[2]

In the north of England in 1536 there was a movement of resistance to the dissolution of the smaller monasteries which had just then taken place. Known as the Pilgrimage of Grace, this briefly reinstated the monks at three abbeys before it was crushed. One of the leaders of the Pilgrimage in Yorkshire was a man named Jake or Jakes, from a family of farmers and craftsmen living in Wharfedale.[3] Twenty years later, when the local church at Hubberholme was being partially rebuilt, a relative who was a carpenter named William Jake constructed a rood screen for the restored building.[4] He mainly used fragments of two earlier screens and began the job during the reign of Mary I, when Catholic furnishings were being put back into some churches. However Mary died and policies changed again before the screen was complete and Jake's work has survived in an unfinished state. One story has it that he used parts salvaged from a screen at Coverham Abbey,[5] one of the monasteries that the Pilgrimage of Grace had tried to reopen. However, the old workmanship in the screen at Hubberholme is not of the standard that might be expected of monastic carpentry and is more likely to include remains of parclose screens from this same church. Plate 33 shows the traceried parapet which is carved with small replica windows that have three-sided rather than pointed heads. They are clearly not of the same workmanship and date as the openings in the screen seen in shadow below, and the joists intended to support the rood-loft floor are very rough indeed.

There are other places where craftsmen can be seen to have contributed actively, sometimes apparently on their own initiative, to saving artefacts threatened with destruction by the dissolution.[6] However, a contrary instance, where craftsmen were employed in the particularly thorough demolition of an abbey was at Chertsey in Surrey. The large monastery there was dissolved at a relatively early stage because doorways and windows from its buildings, and stone from its walls, were wanted for reuse in construction of the nearby royal palace at Oatlands. The king was insistent that his scheme at Oatlands should be pushed forward as fast as possible and in 1538 the drinking times of masons demolishing the abbey were reduced to ensure the 'hasty' expedition of materials to the new site. James Nedeham was the master craftsman from the King's Office of Works in charge of removing material from Chertsey. He later went on to demolish Barking Abbey (Essex), a former nunnery, where he employed miners to destroy the solidly built towers by tunnelling under their foundations.[7]

In contrast to the drastic destruction of some monastic churches, the more usual policy was for the Crown to take certain valuables, especially lead from roofs, then for enough of the church to be destroyed to make its reuse by monks impossible. Other buildings would be left standing if they had potential for conversion to domestic use. Hence there are several well-known instances of the buildings surrounding a monastic cloister being turned into a private house, as happened at Newstead Abbey (Nottinghamshire) and Lacock Abbey (Wiltshire). At Lacock, the mason in charge of the conversion was John Chapman,[8] who later worked at Longleat. There were even places where parts of the monastic church were turned into living accommodation, as at Titchfield Abbey (Hampshire) and Buckland Abbey (Devon).[9]

Care was usually taken to ensure that farming operations managed by monastic houses on their lands were not disrupted by the dissolution, so buildings that could be used for farm purposes often survived. An example in north Somerset is the tithe barn at Englishcombe which once belonged to Bath Abbey. The impressive roof structure has four trusses, of which two are raised crucks and two are base-crucks (also raised). These have been dated by dendrochronology to the mid-fourteenth century.[10] They stand within substantial walls of Bath stone on which masons' marks from the time when the barn was being built survive. There is also an array of graffiti drawings and in one instance, where a small drawing of a plough is repeated several times, it is hard to know whether this was a graffito or a mason's mark. Some small drawings of animals may also be medieval. However, the circle pattern superimposed on one of the plough drawings (*Figure 7.1*) is likely to date from after the dissolution.

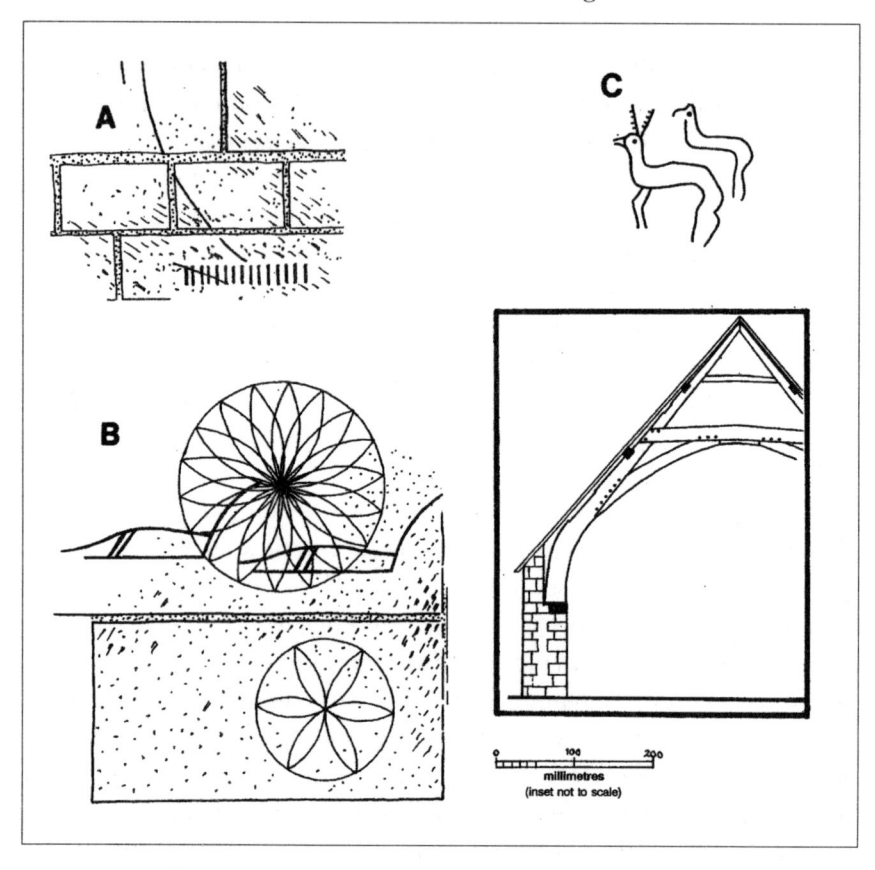

Figure 7.1 Graffiti inside the tithe barn at Englishcombe, Somerset, formerly belonging to Bath Abbey. A: tally marks, east wall of the entrance porch. B: part of a row of ploughs with later circles, west end of the south wall. C: animals, south wall, east of entrance. The scale-bar gives the size of the drawings. Inset is a section showing one of two raised-cruck trusses. Not to scale.

There are large numbers of other circle drawings distributed around the interior of the barn which are almost all drawn with compasses. They must either be the work of craftsmen, or of people sufficiently close to working craftsmen to borrow their tools, and they are all likely to be post-dissolution.

Similar graffiti are found so frequently in all parts of England dating from the late sixteenth century and even more profusely, the seventeenth century, that they must be taken into account in any discussion of craftsmen's drawings of the period. The view that they are ritual protective marks or charms rather than geometrical exercises or random doodles has recently gained wide acceptance and is perceptively discussed by Bob Meeson.[11] He asks whether such marks are mere curiosities, or meaningful symbols. What makes them seem more meaningful in some places (though not in this Somerset building) is where they are associated with letters or signs having unambiguous religious significance. These may include M or VV (monograms for Mary, Virgin of Virgins) or IHS (for Jesus, as in the medieval example discussed above in Chapter 3). Meeson illustrates monograms for the Virgin Mary on seventeenth-century work in a house in Chester and comments that a curious feature of examples with religious meaning is that many come from a period when it was dangerous to use Catholic symbols. However sometimes it seems as if the austerity of the reformation church left so little outlet for practices through which people sought divine protection that these impulses were displaced to the context of domestic folk practices.

However, an interest in pattern-making for its own sake is also, surely, expressed in the profusion of circle drawings in some buildings. When the educated classes of the time showed a similar enthusiasm for pattern-making, and used circles or other emblematic shapes in design, such patterns were often referred to as 'devices', and were deployed with a good deal of ingenuity and wit.[12] When the word 'device' was used in architecture or in the other arts, it often denoted an interesting visual shape imposed on something to which it did not really belong, as when shapes such as triangles were applied to the plans, windows, or other features of buildings.[13] Elizabethan examples include houses laid out to represent letters of the alphabet (such as E as a religious symbol standing for Emmanuel). There were also a handful of circular buildings and the Triangular Lodge at Rushton in Northamptonshire, which was designed to represent the Holy Trinity and was intended by its owner, Sir Thomas Tresham, as a symbol of his Catholic faith.[14]

A striking example of a circular building is Beamsley Hospital in the West Riding of Yorkshire near Skipton. It provided almshouse accommodation for 12 elderly women plus a warden (or 'mother') and was founded by Lady Margaret Russell, Countess of Cumberland. The building was planned in 1593, but construction did not begin until after 1600 and was still incomplete when Lady Margaret died in 1616. The project was finished by her daughter, Lady Anne Clifford. Of the two structures seen today, the circular one was Lady Margaret's brainchild.[15]

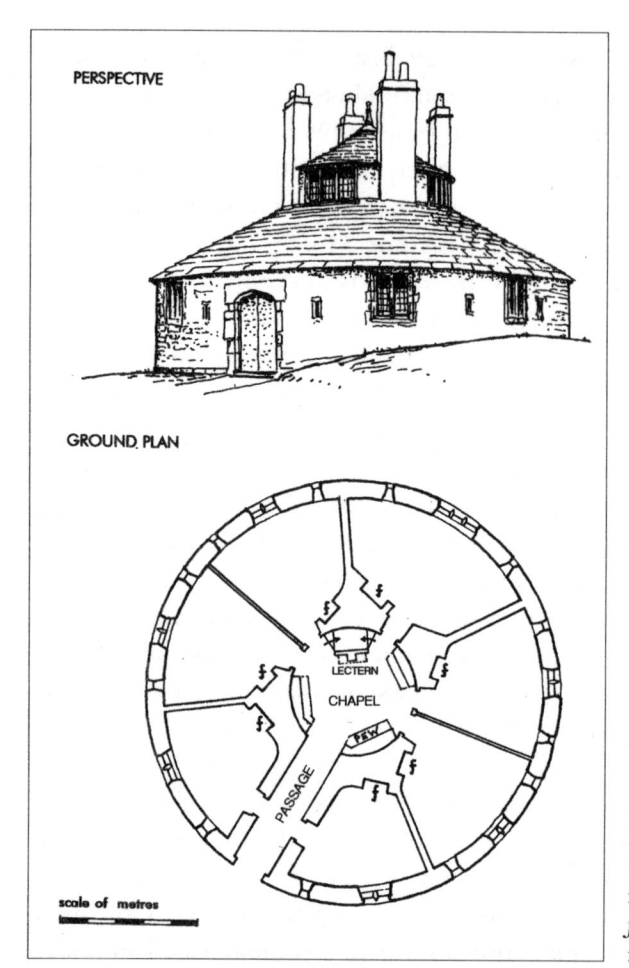

Figure 7.2 Beamsley Hospital, near Skipton (West Riding). There is a fireplace, marked *f*, in each of the seven residents' rooms.

It contains seven rooms for residents arranged around a tiny circular chapel equipped with a lectern and pews (*Figure 7.2*).

One obvious interpretation, given that Lady Margaret had spent part of her youth in Northamptonshire and was sometimes resident in London, is that the design was based on medieval churches with circular plans such as the Temple Church in London and Holy Sepulchre in Northampton. However, a recent writer interprets the building more convincingly as an Elizabethan 'device'.[16] Lady Margaret may have taken ideas from the churches mentioned, but as somebody actively involved in Elizabethan intellectual life, she would undoubtedly have looked at the design in relation to ideas of her own time as well. Hence note should be taken of her business associate Richard Cavendish[17] and his interest in poetic devices and in Euclid's geometry.

So perhaps Lady Margaret's intention in the design of the hospital was to celebrate the Euclidian interests of her associates by making the geometry of a building more explicit than usual. Or perhaps the circle plan had other layers of symbolism for her, given her remarkably varied scientific, scholarly and (Puritanical) religious interests.

Another example of a round building of this period was a lodge erected by Henry Oxinden on his estate in Kent, and this definitely did have religious significance. When asked about it at the end of his life, Oxinden replied: 'I imitated the great Architector … Both Earth & Heaven, hee hath framed soe'.[18] It might be argued that if circles had religious meaning for those who could afford such buildings, they might also do so for the more ordinary people who inscribed circles on walls.

But apart from that, there was certainly a general interest in pattern-making, and in many instances different meanings overlap. Except where religious symbolism is explicit, it is usually impossible to decide whether a particular instance of pattern-making also has geometrical, religious or apotropaic intentions, or whether it was just done for fun.

DRAWINGS NOT TO SCALE

On turning from Elizabethan devices and craftsmen's ritual marks to the architectural drawings of the period, we can seem to be moving into a different world where only practical considerations prevailed. It is clear from building contracts and accounts that many more drawings were now being made, most of them on paper. Relatively few have been preserved, though, and those that have were often presentation copies made for house owners rather than preliminary designs or working drawings. From what can be deduced about drawings of the latter kind it is clear that, although they were of real practical value, they were neither accurate enough nor sufficiently detailed for builders to rely on them entirely. It was still usual to make full-size drawings where it was important to get detail right and architectural drawings were still being made on walls and tracing floors. Examples in churches from York ($c.$1525) and Hampshire ($c.$1550) were quoted in Chapter 5, and drawings in the house at Acton Court, Gloucestershire, from the 1550s were also mentioned.[19]

One of the reasons why such drawings were still important is that, at the beginning of the sixteenth century, the smaller drawings that were made on paper or parchment were not to scale and did not represent dimensions accurately. Some drawings look precise and could certainly have been useful during construction, but close examination always shows that the conventions adopted later for scale drawing were not yet being employed. For example, the master mason William Vertue made a drawing for the Henry VII Chapel at Westminster (on which he was working). This shows a detail of the parapet and has been retrospectively identified as being to the scale of 3ft to 1in.[20] But although this may be approximately true, it seems unlikely that William Vertue had a clear concept of how to draw buildings to scale.

There are two other architectural drawings of the period which have sometimes been attributed to Vertue. Both are of high quality and are set out with great precision, but both include perspective effects incompatible with a true representation to scale.[21] Figure 7.3 is a detail from one of them, a large pen-and-ink drawing measuring 959mm x 290mm. It represents part of Bishop Richard Fox's chantry in Winchester Cathedral (Hampshire) which was constructed in 1518 while alterations were being made to the aisles of the cathedral.[22] The representation of tracery, drawn with a ruler and compasses, can certainly be read as a scale drawing, but the niches on either side and below the tracery are drawn pictorially, so that one sees the floors of the lower niches but also looks up into their canopies. The drawing differs from the chantry as built by the mason Thomas Berty and has been attributed to William Vertue because Vertue worked under the patronage of Bishop Fox, notably on a college building in Oxford. It has also been suggested that the drawing was made about 1525, after the actual chantry was completed, and was intended as some kind of record.[23]

Another illustration of an elevation that intermittently uses perspective is the drawing of a row of shops in a timber-framed building discussed earlier. This was probably drawn at Worcester some time before or about 1500 (*Plate 29*). Looking at the left-hand side of this drawing, Freddie Charles noted some consistency in dimensions and remarked that it seemed to be drawn to a scale of 'about three-quarters of an inch to a foot',[24] which corresponds to 1:16. Then he noted that horizontal dimensions tend to be compressed towards the right of the drawing, probably in order to fit the elevation onto the limited area of the

Circles and scale drawings

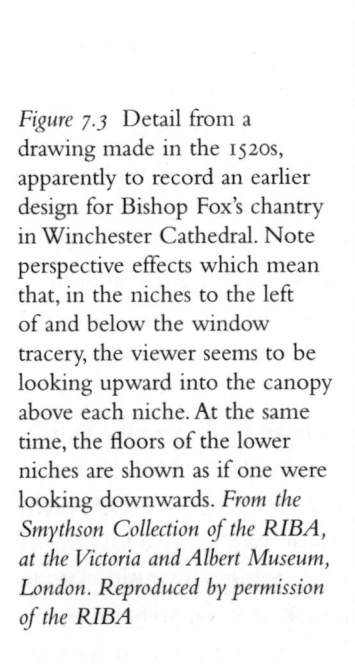

Figure 7.3 Detail from a drawing made in the 1520s, apparently to record an earlier design for Bishop Fox's chantry in Winchester Cathedral. Note perspective effects which mean that, in the niches to the left of and below the window tracery, the viewer seems to be looking upward into the canopy above each niche. At the same time, the floors of the lower niches are shown as if one were looking downwards. *From the Smythson Collection of the RIBA, at the Victoria and Albert Museum, London. Reproduced by permission of the RIBA*

parchment sheet. So the apparent scale of horizontal dimensions altered while the vertical scale remained the same.

The other aspect of this elevation which is not consistent with the conventions of scale drawing is the representation of the window projections and the brackets supporting the jetty. As noted in Chapter 6, most of these brackets are shown sideways-on to the rest of the drawing or else in an approximation of a perspective view. The point here is that, to make a scale drawing, a draughtsman not only needs a clear idea that everything in the drawing is reduced in the same proportion, but also requires an awareness that any protruding parts of an elevation, and any surfaces seen obliquely, cannot be shown as they ordinarily appear. Instead, a drawing convention known as orthogonal projection has to be used in which everything is drawn as if seen from exactly at right angles to the plane of the picture. This has the effect of compressing the third dimension of the object being drawn, which preserves dimensional accuracy where perspective distorts it.

A drawing in which this sort of clarity is achieved, avoiding the temptation to present some parts of an elevation in perspective, is an elevation by John Thorpe dating from soon after 1600 (*Plate 17*). The drawing does not correspond with any existing building, but may be related to Theobalds or 'Tibbals',[25] a great house in Hertfordshire demolished during the Civil War period.[26] Comparing this with the carpenter's drawing in Plate 29, one striking difference is that the oriel window in the centre of the elevation is drawn correctly in orthogonal projection, as is the section through a wing on the right. John Thorpe has been tempted to introduce pictorial effects in showing plumes of smoke from the chimneys, but his drawing of architectural detail avoids the pictorial in order to follow a strict convention of scale drawing. This includes the provision of a scale bar under the elevation (although rather faintly in pencil, *Plate 17*).

In between the Worcester carpenter's drawing of probably just before 1500 and Thorpe's drawing made just over a century later, there are many more surviving drawings by building craftsmen and it would be possible to go through them systematically to analyse the extent to which each was intended as a scale drawing and what other drawing conventions were used, especially with regard to protruding oriels and similar structures.

Commenting on the many drawings which incorporated pictorial representations of such features, John Summerson remarked that their inaccuracy implied that builders cannot have worked out designs fully on paper; they must have done this, as in previous centuries, on 'traceries' at the building site.[27] In other words, the tradition of using tracing floors or full-size drawings on walls continued to be the usual method for working out detail. Malcolm Airs amplifies this by noting that while drawings on paper clearly played an important part in building, their inaccuracy meant that detail had to be provided in other ways. Mouldings were made from 'full-size templates', as in medieval practice, outlines for the templates having been drawn out by a master craftsman.[28]

Four such outlines are to be found among drawings by the surveyor John Thorpe. He was active up to the 1620s, but the templates recall the fact that his father was a stone mason and they may perhaps belong to an early part of his career.[29] The templates were for window mullions and related detail, and for the hand rail of a stone staircase (*Plate 18*).

Discussing these drawings by Thorpe, Airs mentions the mural drawings at Acton Court, Gloucestershire, suggesting that they were used to work out the precise jointing of individual stones in the base of an oriel window. When it came to turning drawings into templates, he adds, a joiner would often be employed and would usually make the templates of deal, but he also cites instances where templates were made from pasteboard or paper, or occasionally by plumbers, presumably of lead.[30]

Our perceptions of what drawings were used in these and other contexts are influenced by the need to rely on documentary references in circumstances where there is still a poor rate of survival of plans from any date prior to 1580 or 1590. After that time, architectural drawings on paper came to be more highly valued, most conspicuously by the Cecil family of Hatfield House (Hertfordshire) whose collection of drawings, formed during this period, is still preserved there.[31] However, these drawings include several plans and elevations made for the Cecils as houseowners rather than working drawings used by craftsmen. They were nearly always drawn to scale, sometimes by men who are best regarded as surveyors rather than by the actual masons or carpenters who built the houses.

ORIGINS OF THE SCALE-DRAWING CONVENTIONS USED IN ENGLAND

This brings us back to the question of how scale drawing techniques came to be adopted in England. Three kinds of development can be noted: the empirical evolution of drawing conventions; the influence of mapmakers and surveyors; and the influence of continental (especially Italian) theories of scale drawing and perspective.

With regard to the last point, James S. Ackerman has argued that interest in producing illusions of depth in their pictures encouraged Italian artists and draughtsmen to introduce perspective effects into drawings of buildings, and hence worked against the production of accurate elevations. However, those who read the Roman architect Vitruvius found that he distinguished elevations from more scenic forms of drawing. Then Alberti, in the treatise on architecture he completed in 1450, opposed the use of either perspective or shading in elevations. He made a sharp distinction between 'the drawing of a painter and that of an architect' noting that the painter aimed to give the appearance of depth 'through shadows and foreshortened lines and angles', whereas the architect should aim at dimensional accuracy and avoid foreshortening. He encouraged the use of a separate sheet for drawing each elevation of a building to discourage the practice of trying to show side elevations in perspective alongside the main elevation.[32]

At first Italian artists and designers ignored this advice and continued to draw curves to indicate the shapes of round columns, and to portray protruding brackets in quasi-perspective. However, by the time Sebastian Serlio was beginning to write on architecture in the 1530s, his contemporaries were much more consistent in drawing the elevations of buildings in orthogonal projection. In the third book of his treatise, published in 1540, Serlio included a statement that he did not use foreshortening in elevations because he wanted to show 'only the heights properly measured'. He wanted to avoid the loss of measured forms and their dimensions that would result if some features were foreshortened.[33]

Serlio's treatise was published in parts with the first book appearing in 1537. It strongly influenced the earliest English printed book on architecture. Entitled *The First and Chief Groundes of Architecture,*[34] this was published in 1563 by John Shute, a self-styled 'Paynter and Archytecte' who had travelled in Italy. Serlio's book itself also circulated in England, mainly in a new edition published in Frankfurt in 1575, and then in an English translation of 1611. Another continental writer whose books had influence in England, not only on design but also on styles of drawing and ideas about perspective, was Vredeman de Vries, whose works were published in Antwerp from the 1560s onwards.[35]

Undoubtedly the style of illustrations in such books influenced drawing conventions adopted by English draughtsmen by the end of the sixteenth century, but before that there were craftsmen whose drawings show that new habits of measurement had encouraged something approaching scale drawing to develop in a more empirical manner. As mentioned in Chapter 6, the experience of craftsmen who enlarged small prints and pictures to the size of the item they were carving may have been formative. In many cases, they merely sketched out the enlarged drawing, but quite often it seems that measurements were taken and the enlargement was then fairly precise. Occasionally, a grid of lines would be drawn over the picture being enlarged and the contents of each square would be sketched into the corresponding square of an enlarged grid. Where measurements were taken or a grid was used, the craftsman would be aware that all dimensions were being enlarged by, say, three times and hence that the drawing or print the craftsman started from was consistently one-third of the size of the finished object.

However, for craftsmen to acquire this kind of experience they had to be taking measurements with rulers or measuring rods. Such instruments were not consistently marked out in feet and inches during the earlier Middle Ages when buildings were designed by the geometrical methods, but the concept of a fixed ratio between lengths on a drawing and the dimensions of an object could only become clear when measurements were easy to check. Hence a clear concept of scale drawing was unlikely to arise until the geometrical methods of the thirteenth and fourteenth centuries became less dominant and building dimensions were more often quoted as numbers of feet. This increasing emphasis on measurement, at the point it had reached in the 1480s, can be observed in the writings of William Worcestre (Chapter 5). Although he seems to have borrowed measuring rods or staffs on occasion, he nowhere described these instruments.[36] Medieval illustrations that show masons with their staffs seem to show that the rod or staff had few or no graduations.[37] Its function seems often to have been to provide a standard of length, not to take detailed measurements. By the 1480s, the likelihood is that William Worcestre was using measuring rods marked off in feet, but it is not until later that there are good illustrations or surviving instruments that may be examined.

Graduated rulers of a kind completely different from the rods seen in medieval illustrations were found among tools possessed by the ship's carpenter on the *Mary Rose*, the ship from Henry VIII's navy which sank in 1545 and which has been salvaged by archaeologists. Along with such things as a gauge for measuring the depths of mortices and a chalk line for snapping straight lines onto timber was a twelve-inch rule on which the central four inches were subdivided into quarters of an inch using dividers or compasses to ensure that the divisions were equal.[38] In the centre was a circle of quarter-inch radius and an arc of half-inch radius which constituted a miniature drawing, marked on the wood as a kind of hallmark to show that the ruler had been accurately divided. These wooden rulers are a link with the geometrical past, showing perhaps that the carpenter wished to be reminded that geometry was the true source of the proportions of what he made (*Figure 7.4*). Any painted numbers

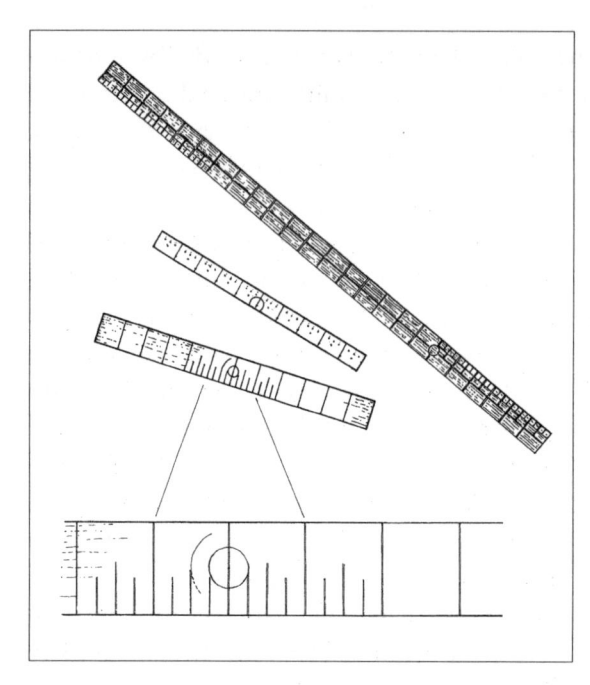

Figure 7.4 Three wooden rulers belonging to the carpenter on the ship *Mary Rose*. The rulers are graduated in inches of 25.4 mm, and are in 24-, 10-, and 12-inch lengths. Below is an enlarged view of the centre of the 12-inch ruler drawn from a display at the Mary Rose Museum, Portsmouth.

or marks have been removed by long immersion in sea water and a ten-inch rule which may have lost its markings is divided by a series of small holes, perhaps where the points of dividers were placed. The hallmark circle at the centre of this ruler seems to be unrelated to the quarter-inch divisions and is perhaps entirely decorative. By contrast, a 24-inch ruler is more roughly set out with longitudinal lines dividing the scale into three bands at the ends, two bands in the centre.

Rulers such as this must have been commonplace among carpenters, masons and other building craftsmen in the sixteenth century although hardly any examples survive from before the time when the *Mary Rose* sank. The next good evidence of sixteenth-century craftsmen's rulers and measuring rods comes from a short book or pamphlet printed for its author, Leonard Digges, in 1556 and entitled *A Boke named Tectonicon*. The title page explained that the printer was John Daye and the book was on sale at a shop in Blackfriars, London, kept by Thomas Gemini, who was 'ready exactly to make all the instruments appertaining to this book'.[39]

Leonard Digges enjoyed inventing new words, including 'theodolitus' or theodolite when referring to a newly-invented surveying instrument

Circles and scale drawings

which he modified or simplified.[40] What 'tectonicon' meant was explained as 'how to measure truly and very speedily' all manner of land, timber and stone, emphasising the equipment needed. The book was addressed to carpenters and masons, and also to 'landemeaters' (another invented word, referring to land surveyors). The particular equipment discussed in *A Boke named Tectonicon* included the carpenter's square, the carpenter's 'ruler', the quadrant (for measuring angles relative to the vertical) and a measuring rod or staff designed so that two 3ft lengths could be fitted together to provide a 6ft staff (with an alternative version having two 5ft lengths).

The carpenter's ruler illustrated (*Figure 7.5*) is very like the 12in example from the *Mary Rose*, though with the figures on its surface now visible. It is almost quarter of an inch (6mm) thick and, unlike modern rulers, does not have a bevelled edge. Digges commented that a 24in ruler is often more useful, but he was limited in what he could illustrate by the quarto page size of his book.

Part of the book is concerned with surveying land, but with regard to the work of carpenters (and masons) Digges discussed one problem in detail, that of estimating quantities. This was of great importance to craftsmen when they were bidding for contracts, because although some craftsmen did work that was paid by the day or 'by measure', many undertook contracts which were said to be 'by great'. In other words they took responsibility for the whole of a job, employing what labour they needed and buying the timber and other materials. There was a considerable financial risk involved, because if quantities of materials were under-estimated and more had to be bought to finish the job, those purchases would be at the contractor's expense. On the other hand, if he over-estimated quantities and submitted an excessively large estimate, he would be liable to lose the contract to a lower bidder.

Digges did not discuss contracts or give other general advice, but recognised the problem of estimating quantities as crucial. So he focused closely on how to estimate the number of (cubic) feet of timber (or stone) that would be required for a particular job. He explicitly assumed that the carpenters for whom he was writing would not know the art of 'numbering', that is, multiplication and division, but that they would be able to read numbers off quite intricate tables. Thus he provided tables to assist with such calculations as how many cubic feet of timber are represented by beams or joists of various dimensions, which he referred

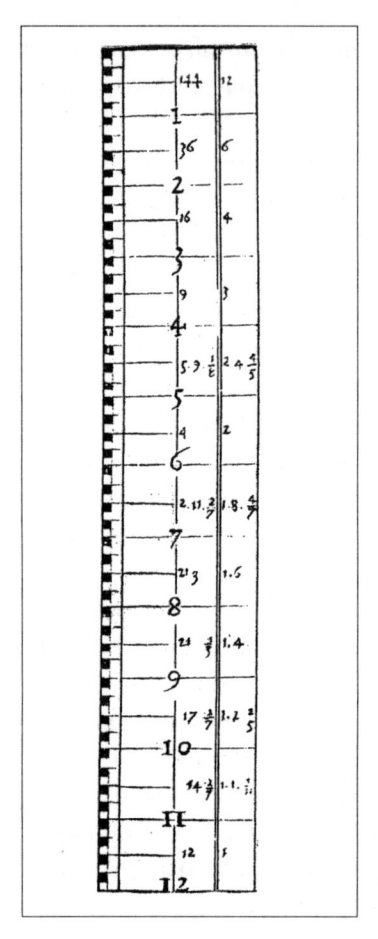

Figure 7.5 Illustration of the carpenter's ruler in *A Boke named Tectonicon*, by Leonard Digges, 1556.

to as 'tymber measure'. Other tables showed what length boards of specified width would be needed to make a floor covering a particular area in square feet. He called this 'borde measure'.[41]

The carpenter's rule he illustrated (*Figure 7.5*) has numbers on it to help with these calculations. For example, if the carpenter were purchasing timber rafters measuring 4 x 4ins, then he would look along his ruler to the 4in mark, and would notice just above it the number 9. This would tell him that a 9ft length of his rafter contains one cubic foot of timber. Small numerals towards the lower end of the rule as it appears in the illustration are in inches rather than feet, so if the carpenter was faced with a great baulk measuring 12 x 12ins, the ruler would give him the obvious information that a 12in length would contain one cubic foot.

176

Figures on the right-hand side of the ruler provided a similar ready-reckoner for 'borde measure'. So if he had a board 3ins wide, he would look against the 3in mark on the ruler and see, to the right, the number 4. This would tell him that a 4ft length of 3in board had an area of one square foot.

Digges did not discuss scale drawing at all, but the possession of rulers such as this would assist thinking about the subject. For example, if inches on a ruler were divided into eighths, it became easy to draw to a scale of 1:8, with each of the smaller divisions on the ruler representing an inch. Thus it was significant that when surveyors began to depict the scale of a map by drawing a bar graduated in furlongs or miles, the scale bar was often drawn like a picture of a ruler. In some respects the carpenter's ruler displaced the position long held by compasses as the iconic drawing instrument, but on some maps and plans, scale bars combined illustrations of both instruments (*Figure 7.6A*).

In her study of early British architectural books, Eileen Harris lists only two books printed in England before 1590, one being Shute's *Chief Groundes of Architecture* and the other being Digges's *Tectonicon*. The latter contains no direct comment on buildings, but it proved so useful to craftsmen that it was frequently reprinted. After the first edition in 1556, it was reprinted in 1561, 1562 and 1566, after which there were 13 further editions or reprints down to 1656. Country carpenters all over England are said to have used it and Harris comments that, when the book was not available, the numbers were copied by craftsmen from one ruler onto another, with cumulative inaccuracies.[42]

LAND SURVEYORS AT WORK

Although *A Boke named Tectonicon* was the only work by Digges selected by Eileen Harris as significant for architecture, several other books by Leonard Digges and Thomas his son were important for surveyors and other 'mathematical practitioners'.[43] As well as writing books, Thomas Digges became closely involved in overseeing one of the biggest engineering projects of the time, the improvement of the harbour at Dover (Kent).[44] This project is of significance here because of the large number of accurately scaled plans it spawned. One of the earliest good plans of any part of the English coastline was a survey of Dover harbour

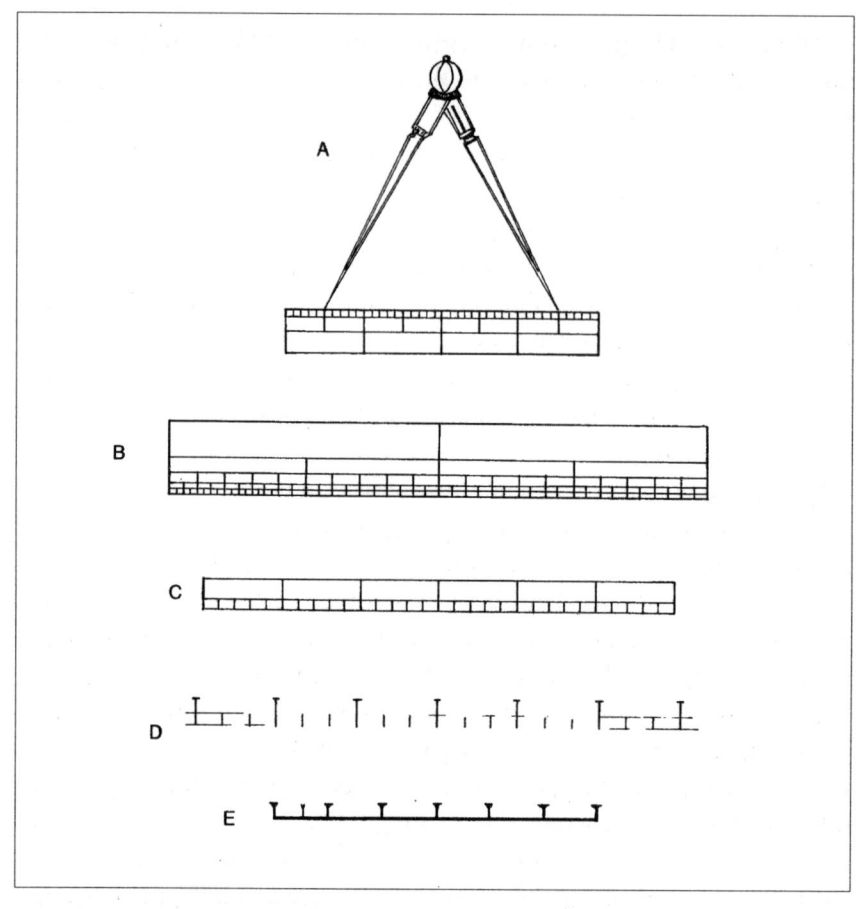

Figure 7.6 Scale-bars on sixteenth-century and early seventeenth-century maps and house plans:

A, B are scale-bars of the type used by land surveyors, and sometimes on house plans by Robert Smythson (who usually added extra decoration). These are realistic depictions of the drawing instruments used at the time.

C, D are scale-bars of a type used by John Thorpe, sometimes with the horizontal lines scribed with a stylus but not inked in, as suggested in D.

E is a linear scale-bar of the kind used by John Symons on house plans and land surveys (see *Figure 7.7*).

by the military engineer Richard Caundish with three others in 1541. John Symons made a plan in 1585 which is illustrated below and Thomas Digges, in 1595, made the most accurate map of all.[45]

At the same time, many more maps of landed estates were being made, and the earliest to be drawn to scale also date from around 1540.

Surveyors quickly learned how to make such maps and, by 1550, some 40 scale maps of private estates are known to have been produced.[46] This undoubtedly owed something to the dissolution of the monasteries in that the new owners of former monastic estates needed to take stock of what they had acquired.

Some land surveyors and mapmakers made scale drawings of buildings, although there is a risk of confusion here, and some real overlap, between a land surveyor and the kind of surveyor who supervised building projects. In the Middle Ages, the latter would often have been referred to as a master of works. Confusion about this second meaning of the word surveyor extended to Leonard Digges himself who certainly did some land surveying but who was also referred to by a later generation as 'the best architect of that age' even though he did not design buildings or supervise building works. A houseowner would more usually employ a carpenter or mason as surveyor for the rebuilding of his home. In that capacity, the surveyor would have responsibility for design, in consultation with the owner, and would supervise construction. By contrast, when a bridge was being built under the provisions of the 1531 Statute of Bridges, the county sessions court would sometimes appoint 'surveyors' who had no real knowledge of bridge design but who could supervise with regard to legal requirements and payment of the masons who did the actual building.[47]

Information about these developments is limited, but there is an impression of a rush of events in the 1540s and 1550s. England was somewhat behind the Continent, but now was catching up, with the appearance of new books, maps and instruments. It can seem that innovation in instruments for surveying and drawing (including the carpenter's rule) coincided with the first scale maps of estates and harbour works in the 1540s, and that the first printed books on surveying came out in the 1550s. A little later, in 1571, Thomas Digges produced a further book entitled *Pantometria*. It was based on a draft by his father to which Thomas made additions and described a wider range of instruments than *Tectonicon*.[48] These included the plane table and theodolite for surveying and the rule, square and compasses for drawing. Quality instruments with brass fittings were described, including a carpenter's rule whose 2ft length would fold down to half. Wooden instruments were also described such as artisans could more readily afford (or make for themselves).

A number of drawings surviving from just before and just after 1600 demonstrate how building craftsmen made use of such instruments. Some particularly clear examples were by John Symons (or Symonds) who was one of several of his generation who made maps of Dover harbour. He did this work about 1585 and signed it: 'P[er] I/Symans' (*Figure 7.7*). Symons began his career as a stone mason, and was later employed by the royal Office of Works in various capacities, both as a craftsman and a clerk.[49] He was also employed by Lord Burghley as surveyor in charge of his London

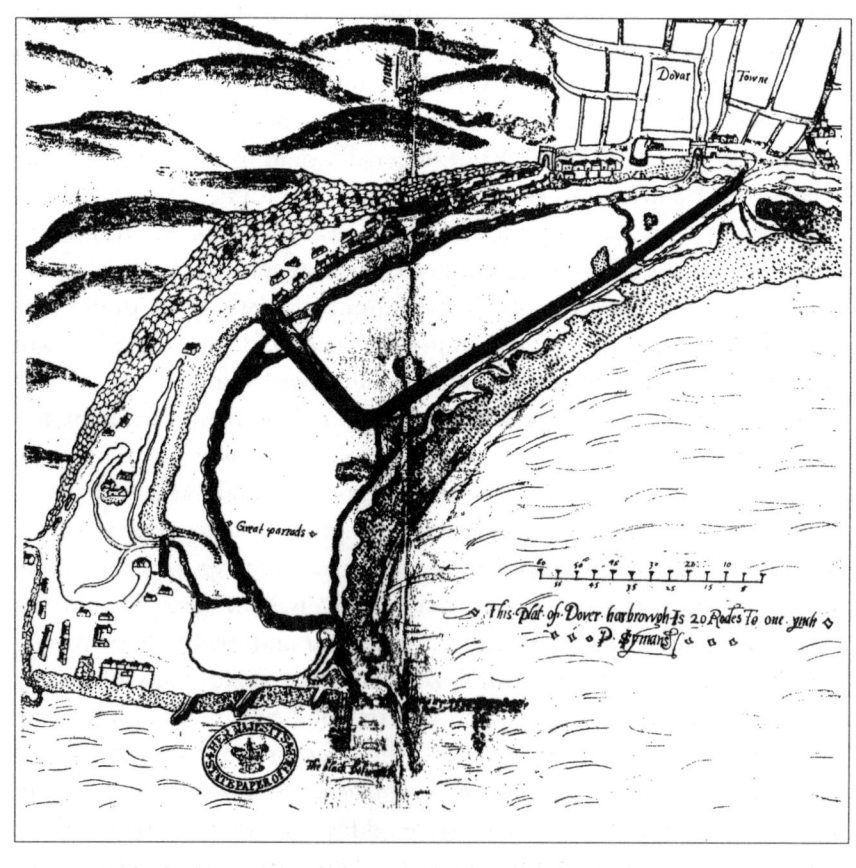

Figure 7.7 The harbour at Dover in a map surveyed by John Symons in the 1580s which illustrates two methods of showing the scale, in words and by a graduated bar. The harbour entrance is close to 'The black Bolwark' (label near the bottom of the map). Above it, a channel shown in black veers left into the main harbour, marked 'Great parrads' (or 'Great paradise' in other documents). The shingle banks have stippled hatching and curve to the right. *National Archives, Kew, map image MPF 1/122, reproduced with permission*

houses, and it was probably Burghley who asked him to make the Dover map because of concern about how shingle banks were continually being reshaped by tides and currents, periodically blocking the harbour entrance.

The map of Dover surveyed by Symons is pictorial in many respects, particularly in the way houses in the town are sketched in, but it can be assumed that the harbour works are to scale, and it is striking how Symons expressed the scale in words as '20 Rodes to one ynch', and also by means of a linear scale bar. Several accurately-scaled plans of buildings that were drawn by John Symons are in the collection at Hatfield House and in each case the scale bar is drawn in the simplest possible way and the convention of providing a picture of a ruler is not adopted.[50]

Nearly everybody with any pretension to practical or technical knowledge was consulted about the chronic problem at Dover at one time or another, not only Thomas Digges and John Symons, but also the carpenter and shipwright Matthew Baker, who was consulted about the wooden structures within which the stonework of piers and breakwater was constructed.[51] Matthew Baker wrote part of a book on 'Shipwrightry' which shows him applying the principles of scale drawing to the design of ships' hulls.[52] Like many masons and carpenters, he may have learned the principles of drawing to scale from contact with surveyors.

John Thorpe also worked as a surveyor, although he was more important as an architectural draughtsman. He was perhaps less skilful with his pen than John Symons, but more of his drawings survive and illustrate a varied career. His early experience as a Northamptonshire stone-mason's son is reflected by drawings in his collection that may have been his father's, and by his own drawings of masons' templates (*Plate 18*). He spent eighteen years in the Office of Works and must have known Symons. However, he was disappointed by lack of promotion and left his post to pursue an independent career as a land surveyor. His work illustrates the relationship between people who drew scale plans for houses and the growth of mapmaking and surveying, for Thorpe was often asked to draw the plans of houses on the estates he was mapping. He may also sometimes have supplied a house owner with a design for a new house or for alterations, but most of his drawings illustrate houses already in existence and, a few designs excepted, it is a mistake to think of him as an architect.[53]

Thorpe's early drawings were usually set out with a stylus or blind point that scored lines on the paper without marking it with ink or colour. For example, the geometrical drawing to the right of the template in Plate 18

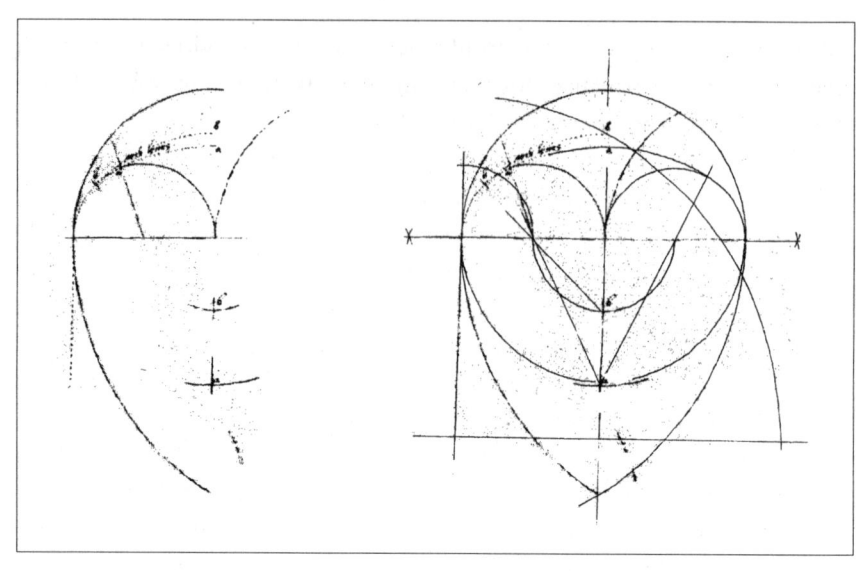

Figure 7.8 Two versions of the geometrical drawing by John Thorpe shown also in Plate 18. On the left are the ink lines and curves seen in ordinary lighting conditions, and on the right are Thorpe's stylus-drawn lines and curves which can be seen in oblique light. The object was partly to construct alternative profiles for a three-centred doorhead which are shown as dotted lines labelled (almost illegibly) 'arch lynes'. The two profiles are marked *a* and *b*, and the central curve of each is drawn with the compass point placed below where the same letters appear again. However, the drawing is more complicated than necessary only to do that. *By kind permission of Sir John Soane's Museum*

has many lines which do not show up in ordinary conditions, but which can easily be seen in oblique light. Figure 7.8 shows the same drawing again and then, to the right, the much more complicated geometry that shows up when the paper is looked at obliquely to see what Thorpe drew with his stylus.[54]

The illustration shows Thorpe working out curves for a three-centred arch that had to span two existing door jambs. He wanted to try two versions, the lower, flatter arch being marked **a** and the other **b**. He drew a circle to establish where the centre point for drawing the main arc of **a** should be, and a semicircle of half the radius to establish the position of centre **b**.

Thorpe was being very particular here about the relationships between different curves, an attitude that seems to reflect a continuing influence from medieval principles of geometrical design. John Forman's drawing for a four-centred arch at York comes to mind (*Figure 5.7*). On the other hand, Thorpe seems to have wanted to elaborate his work with these arcs and circles just as much as the graffiti artists discussed earlier (*Figure 7.1*) and was perhaps enjoying pattern-making in the same way.

If the geometry of this drawing is reminiscent of tracing-floor drawings, so is the draughting technique. Thorpe's use of a stylus when drawing on paper would probably have come naturally to somebody from a family of stone masons, because it was closely similar to the medieval method of drawing on plaster, stone or timber with a metal point, where also lines were drawn without leaving either a black trace or any colour. It seems that Thorpe used a stylus most consistently in his earlier architectural drawings, working on a particular subject with that medium until he was satisfied with the basic shape and layout. Then he would ink in the lines that he thought were correct and perhaps add others. His later work seems more often to have been set out in graphite pencil. A scale of feet was usually marked as a double line with transverse strokes marking intervals of 3, 5 or 10ft.

A prominent scale bar was the hallmark of men from a land-surveying background and Figure 7.6 contrasts different styles of scale bar. Some were like little pictures of carpenters' rulers, while others followed the more abstract form favoured by Symons (*Figure 7.7*).

Robert Smythson, the designer of major houses such as Wollaton Hall near Nottingham and Hardwick Hall in Derbyshire, sometimes decorated his plans with elaborate scale bars of this kind, with strapwork or other ornamentation embellishing the picture,[55] though sometimes he drew only a single line with divisions marked off at right angles, as on the map by John Symons. Yet other drawings by Smythson have no scale bar at all. In these, he followed the convention familiar from many books on architecture in marking dimensions in numbers. In this way, some draughtsmen may reflect the sources they were using by the way they marked the scale.

Another example of a builder who marked dimensions on his plans rather than drawing a scale bar is provided by a set of drawings which accompanied the contract for building a new kitchen wing on a house at Woollavington (East Lavington),[56] Sussex, in 1586. The ground-floor plan is illustrated in Figure 7.9 where rooms are labelled with such names as 'a drye larder' and 'the bak[e] house', both with dimensions given as '17 by 16 [feet]'. A round bread oven is shown in the latter room. The plan is the work of a stone mason, Henry Hunt (alias Hobbes) who also

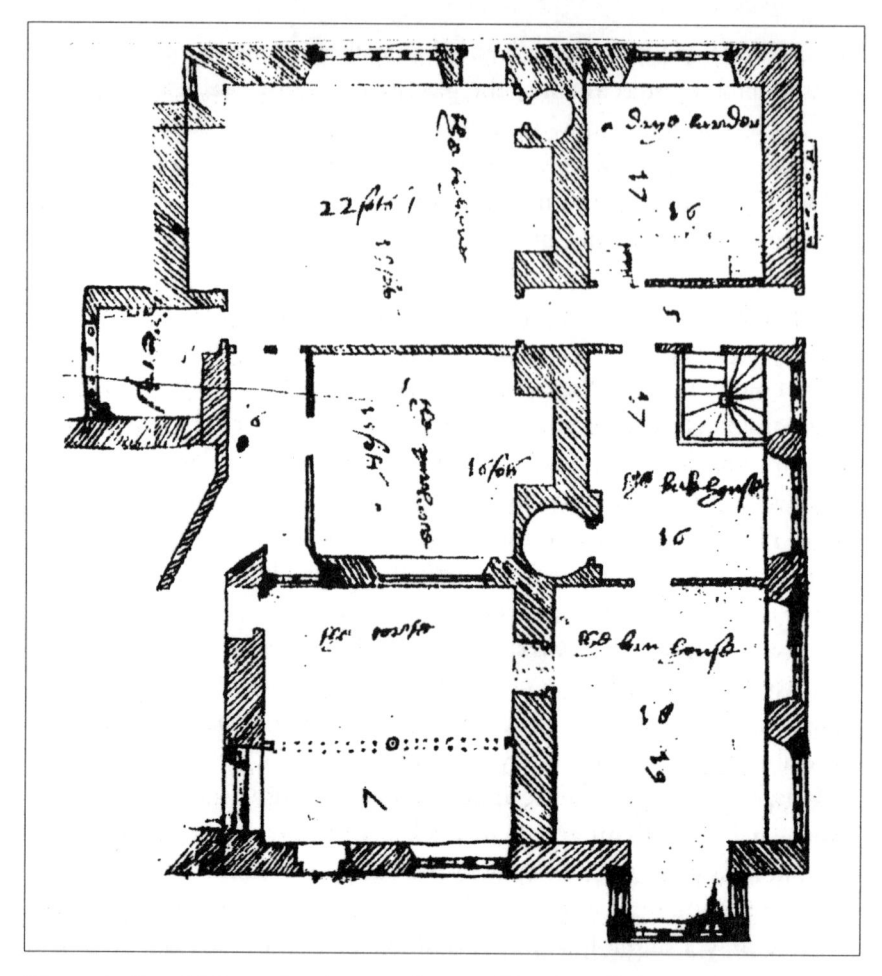

Figure 7.9 Ground-floor plan for extensions to Giles Garton's house at Wollavington (East Lavington), Sussex. The plan accompanied a contract dated 1586 signed by the stone mason Henry Hunt. *By kind permission of the Sussex Archaeological Society*

worked at Petworth House, Sussex. The point has been made that Hunt had a distinctively local practice. He lived in Arundel and the jobs at Woollavington and Petworth were both within 15 miles of home.[57]

DRAWINGS AND DESIGN

John Thorpe's drawings, it was noted earlier, were mostly records of existing buildings rather than designs for new ones. The same can

Circles and scale drawings

be said of many of the drawings collected by the Cecil family, now preserved at Hatfield House, Hertfordshire, particularly plans of their London properties commissioned from John Symons,[58] the surveyor who mapped Dover harbour (*Figure 7.7*). However, it should not be assumed that surveyors were the only people who made scale drawings at this time. While John Thorpe with his stylus may be typical of draughtsmen from a background that included stone masons' work as well as surveying, his contemporary Inigo Jones had begun life as a painter or 'picture-maker'. He had learned about architecture partly through travel on the Continent, and had worked with an Italian artist 'whose style of draughtsmanship had decisively influenced his own'.[59] Not surprisingly, in his architectural work Jones used a very different draughting technique from that of Thorpe. Apart from such contrasts as this among practitioners, there was also the interesting phenomenon of gentlemen such as William Cecil and Sir Nicholas Bacon who attempted to make drawings of their own for building works they planned.[60]

In some instances where no drawings survive, a good deal can be learned about the process of design from account books and other documents. An especially clear example, referred to by several other authors,[61] is the big house at Kyre Park, Worcestershire. Here, a book of accounts kept by the owner, Sir Edward Pytts, identifies the craftsmen he employed to rebuild the house and shows that he commissioned several different men to make drawings for the project.

In 1588, for example, he paid 40s to 'John Symons of London for drawing my first platt for my house', and then a few months later, £3 for drawing another platt, 'according to my newe purpose'.[62] This is the same John Symons who had worked for the Cecils and at Dover harbour. It would appear that he did not visit Kyre Park before drawing the platt. His job was simply to make a drawing that expressed the ideas Pytts put to him. Meanwhile, Sir Edward's account book shows him paying for both stone and bricks, and in 1595 work on the house was completed. A dozen years later, however, Pytts was doing more building at Kyre Park. In February, he bargained with John Chaunce of Bromsgrove 'to be my cheiff mason workman and Survey'r', then in May he arranged a meeting involving Chaunce and a Coventry mason Thomas Sergianson. Also, on his way from London to Kyre, he paused in Oxford and from there, 'I brought John Bentley, ffreemason (where he wrought the newe addition to Sir Thomas Bodleigh his famous library) ... to draw me a newe platte, for I altered my first intent because I wold not encroche on the churchyard ... And for John Bentley's labour I paid him the first of June 1611 for his paines & further labour thereinafter to be taken 30s'.[63] It will be seen that no one person can be regarded as the architect or designer of Kyre Park. Sir Edward's ideas were clearly important, but so were the plans commissioned from Symons in 1588 and Bentley in 1611 and the judgements John Chaunce made in interpreting them.

The freemason from Oxford employed at Kyre Park, John Bentley, was one of a well-known group of masons from the Halifax area in Yorkshire who worked in Oxford, first at Merton College and then on the Bodleian Library. The other masons with whom Bentley worked included the brothers John and Martin Akroyd who are known for building a grammar school near Halifax. This structure incorporated a round window that seems to be related to a design by Robert Smythson.[64]

There are no surviving drawings by this group of masons but, as at Kyre Park, accounts and correspondence relating to the Halifax school and the Oxford buildings give an impression of how designs were formulated by discussion between interested parties and the masons. At Halifax there are passing references to the drawing of a 'form' which was perhaps a ground plan. At Oxford, when John Bentley was accused of 'daubing', that might be a comment on a bad drawing, although it could refer to other inadequate work he did when deputising for John Akroyd on site at the Bodleian Library.[65]

It will be clear from all these references to forms and platts which no longer exist that although many more architectural drawings survive from the late sixteenth century onwards, this still means a tiny minority of all the drawings produced. However, on the basis of the examples that can be identified, it would appear that draughtsmen's practice had been revolutionised by 1600, not least through changed attitudes to measurement and the use of scale drawings. Being able to reduce a whole design to a small drawing probably made it easier to think about the building as a whole, as compared with the earlier position when the only really accurate drawings were those made at full scale. One way of expressing what this meant is to say that changes in drawing methods demonstrate a change in how designers could conceptualise buildings before they were erected.

CHAPTER 8

SETTING OUT CARPENTRY AND DRAWING IN RED

(carpenters' lines and circles, 1500-1700)

CRAFTSMEN'S WRITINGS

By 1600, there were one or two printed books in circulation dealing with subjects related to architecture and building, and there were even a handful of craftsmen who wrote about their trades. It might be thought, therefore, that some of the questions left unanswered in previous chapters might now be capable of resolution by reference to documentary sources. The most important of these unanswered questions concerns the setting-out methods used by *carpenters* and any related drawings on framing floors or on paper. The way *masons* worked up designs and set them out on tracing floors can be illustrated from as early as *c*.1200, but no such clear evidence has so far been found for carpenters (compare Chapter 4).

Two craftsmen in particular whose manuscripts are sometimes cited were John Dee, carpenter at Petworth House, Sussex, and Robert Stickells, a stone mason and joiner who, around 1600, worked for the Office of Works.[1] Taking John Dee as an example, the documents that he helped compile, around 1615, were 'A Booke of Computations for Building' and a detailed estimate for replacing Petworth with a completely new house. The book of computations noted the sizes of rooms (width, length and height in feet) in ten important contemporary houses and also, interestingly, the dimensions of 14 tennis courts in London. A rather different document, Dee's estimates for the proposed new Petworth House, included several pages of costs for stonework, timber construction and panelling. Much of the timber was to come from nearby estate woodland and costs were estimated for felling, hewing and sawing, as well as for construction. Estimates for the proposed hall roof, 80ft long and spanning 40ft, specified £9 for felling and hauling the timber, then: 'for sawinge, framinge and raisinge the roufe ... £240.' This sum implies a fairly elaborate roof, not just a large one.[2]

Apart from notes made by craftsmen such as Dee, another kind of information available in 1600 which did not exist a century earlier was the printed book dealing with particular aspects of building, such as John Shute's book on architecture (1563) quoted in the previous chapter, and the book by Leonard Digges (1556) which gave advice on estimating quantities of timber. The latter was frequently reprinted and would probably have been used by the Petworth carpenter in drawing up his estimates, but it did not deal at all with drawing or design.[3]

A century after Shute and Digges, Joseph Moxon was a publisher and printer in London who brought out a range of books on practical subjects, including basic mathematics. He also produced a work entitled *Vignola, or, The Compleat Architect* (1655), based on a French version of a book on architecture by Giacomo Barozzi. There were also illustrations copied from those provided by the French editor, Pierre de Muet.[4]

A more famous book written and published by Moxon was his *Mechanick Exercises,* which had an important section on carpentry. He had planned to issue this in monthly parts, but it actually came out less regularly, with the fourteen parts of Volume I (on smithing and woodworking) produced in 1677-80 and Volume II (on printing) in 1683-84. To the extent that there was a philosophy behind these volumes, it was that the blacksmith's work was fundamental to the other trades in providing tools, and that geometry was fundamental in a different sense, because all craftsmen, in various ways, were 'working on the Straight, Square or Circle'. The main emphasis of Moxon's discussion of carpentry was his instructions to workmen, 'how to choose their Tools ... that they may use them with more ease and delight.'[5]

Before Moxon published this book there had been no English publication with a detailed description of carpenters' work and even Moxon, with his interest in tools, hardly discussed setting-out methods or drawing. He provided many illustrations of tools, but only one showing the framing of a timber-framed house. Many of the illustrations came from French sources, one in particular from a book published in 1676 by André Félibien.[6]

This is significant, because there were several French authors who discussed carpentry, and they went into greater detail. One of the earliest was Philibert de l'Orme, the son of a stone mason who had acquired a good education and had visited Italy to study the ruins of Roman buildings. He could discuss academic matters, but always remained in touch with the practicalities of both mason's work and carpentry. Philibert wrote two books that were important for their practical detail as well as for architectural design. The first of them, printed in 1561, was *Nouvelles inventions pour bien bastir*, one of the first printed books to discuss the carpentry of buildings as well as masonry. The relevant material reappeared in Philibert's one major work, *Le premier tôme de l'architecture*, printed in 1567, where Book X dealt with the roof structures of buildings, while Book XI dealt with timber ceilings. There was also an innovative design for a vast hall with a curved wooden roof for which Philibert developed ideas for compound or laminated forms of timber construction.[7]

More books that discussed carpentry appeared in France during the next 100 years, including *Le théatre de l'art de charpentier* by Mathurin Jousse, published in 1627. There was also material on carpentry in books by Blanchard, Le Muet, Frézier, Fourneau and Félibien, several of whom wrote about other architectural subjects as well. Quoting these works, Eileen Harris suggests that there was no comparable writing in England about the theory and practice of carpentry until after 1700. This does not mean that carpenters were ignorant of these matters, but that the people who bought expensive books, mainly the gentry, had little interest.[8]

EVIDENCE FROM THE FABRIC OF BUILDINGS

In the absence of any clear discussion of carpenters' setting-out methods by English authors, it would be possible to examine the working methods of carpenters described in French books and ask whether comparable methods were employed in England. However, it seems preferable here to stick to the methods of investigation adopted in earlier chapters and look for evidence provided by the fabric of buildings, especially well-documented examples. It has also seemed useful to work in counties that still had a vigorous tradition of timber-framed building in 1600, such as Shropshire and Cheshire.

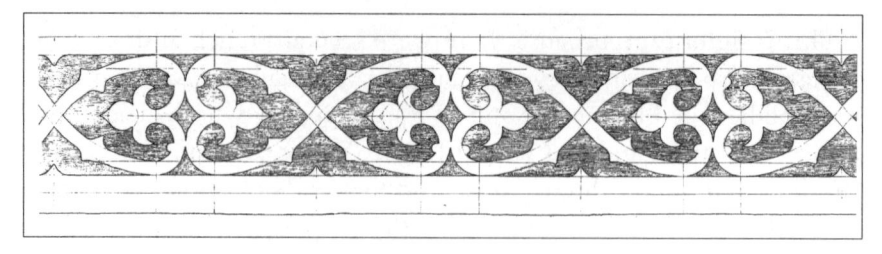

Figure 8.1 Fascia board originally mounted at cornice level below a panelled wood ceiling in St Mary's Church, Nantwich, Cheshire.

Sampling timber structures with a view to identifying setting-out methods actually began in Nantwich (Cheshire), not only because of the wealth of timber buildings there, but also because of the availability of building accounts and other documentation for some houses. For example, the work of several Nantwich carpenters is documented following a catastrophic fire that destroyed a large part of the town in 1583. One instance is the rebuilding of two houses and a stable as recorded by their owner, Thomas Minshull, in accounts which show that the carpenter, John Gambole, made the timber frame at Buerton, six miles south of Nantwich.[9]

In constructing such a building, the frame would be made in sections each of which would be laid out flat on a framing ground (or framing floor). This would often be close to or on the site where the building was to be erected, but sometimes a framing ground could be a few miles away. In certain large towns, carpenters would sometimes attempt to evade guild regulations by framing buildings outside the urban area, but for this Nantwich building the frame was made at Buerton probably because the carpenter, John Gambole, had his workshop there with access to woodland nearby, from where the timber was obtained.[10] When he had completed the frame, the next stage recorded in the accounts was 'bringing home & rearing' or erecting it, by which time the cost (for two houses together) had amounted to £36. After that, finishing them cost another £30, which included roofing and infilling wall panels with wattle and daub. The stable mentioned in these accounts was built separately by Owen a Morre, who was probably one of the Welsh carpenters regularly found working in Shropshire and Cheshire.

Not long before the fire, the roofs of St Mary's parish church at Nantwich had been partly renewed by the carpenter Thomas Cleese

Setting out carpentry and drawing in red

Figure 8.2 Detail of fascia board in Nantwich Church, Cheshire, showing what survives on the surface of the timber (top), with a reconstruction of the original setting-out drawing (below). Some radius lines have been added to clarify where the centres of particular curves are located.

(d. 1610). The church was unaffected by the fire and the low-pitched roofs he constructed have tie-beams spanning the interior supporting a traditional panelled ceiling such as might have been constructed a century earlier.[11] But at cornice level Cleese completed the roof with a series of fascia boards on which he carved not only the names of the churchwardens, but also his own name and then a series of friezes with decorative patterns, some based on intersecting circles, some with strapwork designs (*Figure 8.1*).

The fascia boards are now displayed at a lower level where the carving can be inspected at close enough quarters for the setting-out lines used by Cleese (or by craftsmen he employed) to be clearly seen. It is noticeable that after straight lines had been scribed on the timber to mark borders and the centre line, all the drawing was done with compasses and the design was developed from a series of circles (*Figure 8.2*). This is valuable as evidence for how decorative detail was set out and underlines the continuing importance of work with compasses, but does not tell us anything about setting out structural carpentry.

Among houses in Nantwich designed by Thomas Cleese, one named Churche's Mansion is a particularly impressive building dated 1577 (*Plate 34*). It is notable for a remarkable series of carpenters' numbers, those on the exterior being in Arabic numerals. The interior of the house contains at least one chimney-piece that has survived successive restorations and is marked with the initials of the original owners, Richard and Margery Churche. It is an accomplished example of Renaissance design, with Ionic pilasters carved in wood.

Elsewhere in the region, there were trade guilds in some of the larger towns. Ludlow (unlike Shrewsbury) did not have a separate guild of carpenters because its craft guilds had merged. During most of the sixteenth century, the Ludlow 'Society of Hammermen' contained both masons and carpenters along with smiths and some others.[12] However, carpenters were the most numerous of building craftsmen, reflecting the many timber-framed houses built in the town during that period. With the building boom continuing after 1600, notably with construction of the elaborate elevation of what is now The Feathers hotel,[13] historians speak of the development of a 'Ludlow school of carpentry'[14] or Ludlow style, quite distinct from the Shrewsbury style. This phrase refers mainly to the decorative detail of houses and only in minor ways to structural form,[15] and the kinds of decoration that are characteristic of Ludlow include carved brackets and a distinctive way of infilling the square panels of the structural frame with decorative curved struts or diagonal braces.

A house which exemplifies this tendency (now extensively restored) was built a few years after the alterations at The Feathers and is more typical of the Ludlow style. Above its two main storeys are the gables of an attic which give the building a tall elevation. There is particularly elaborate decoration in the gables and three levels of somewhat more restrained ornamentation lower down the frontage. Each floor is jettied out above the floor below with the ends and centre of each jetty supported by carved brackets. Figure 8.3 illustrates a small part of the elevation with cusped, curved braces high up, plainer decorative braces below and one bracket carved with a leaf pattern.

Looking at the whole building in section (*Figure 8.4*), it will be seen at which levels carved brackets were used and, while several other brackets have variants on the leaf design, two in the centre of the building are

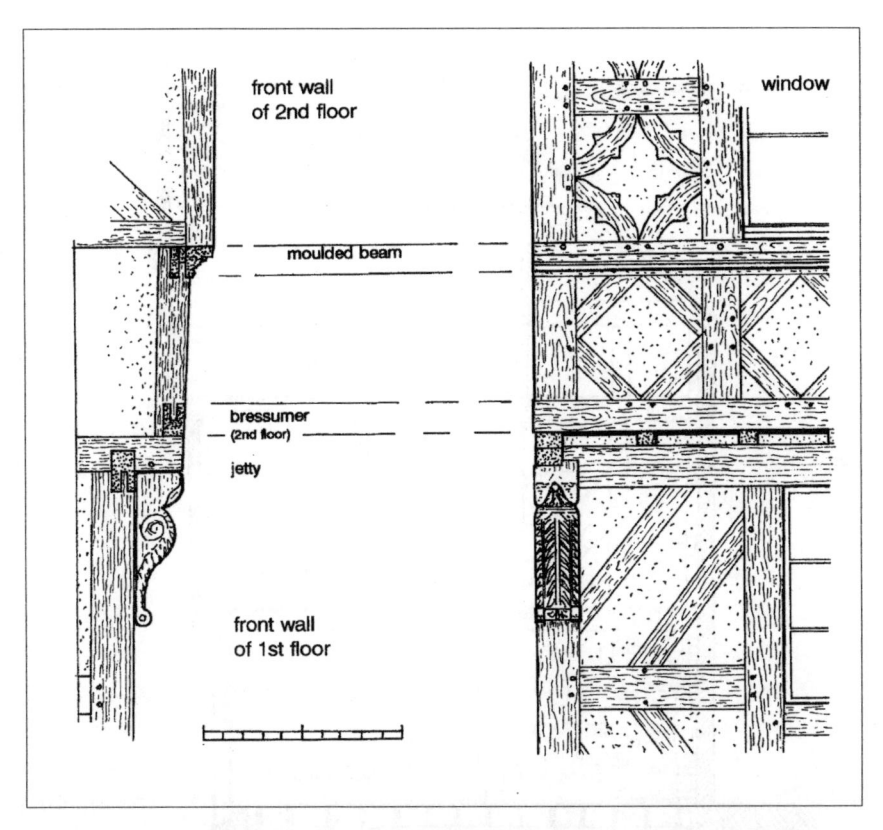

Figure 8.3 Detail of the street elevation of 14-15 Raven Lane, Ludlow, Shropshire. On the left, the jetty below the second floor is seen in section/side elevation, with a carved bracket below the jetty. On the right, the carving of the bracket is seen in front elevation and three ways of infilling wall panels in the timber frame are also evident: small curved and cusped braces at the top, and two ways of using straight braces below. The scale bar represents 1m.

carved as naked human figures. Although part of the structural frame of the house was replaced in brick walling in the nineteenth century, the basic pattern of the framing is still clear. The back of the building was constructed with tall oak posts extending from the sill beam to the eaves, while on the front of the house, each storey was jettied forward to overhang the storey below.

A slightly more unusual example of Ludlow carpentry is to be seen in a pair of jettied dormer windows added to the Preacher's House in Old Street in 1622 (*Plate 35*). Building accounts surviving only for that year identify the carpenters responsible as Francis Bebb assisted by

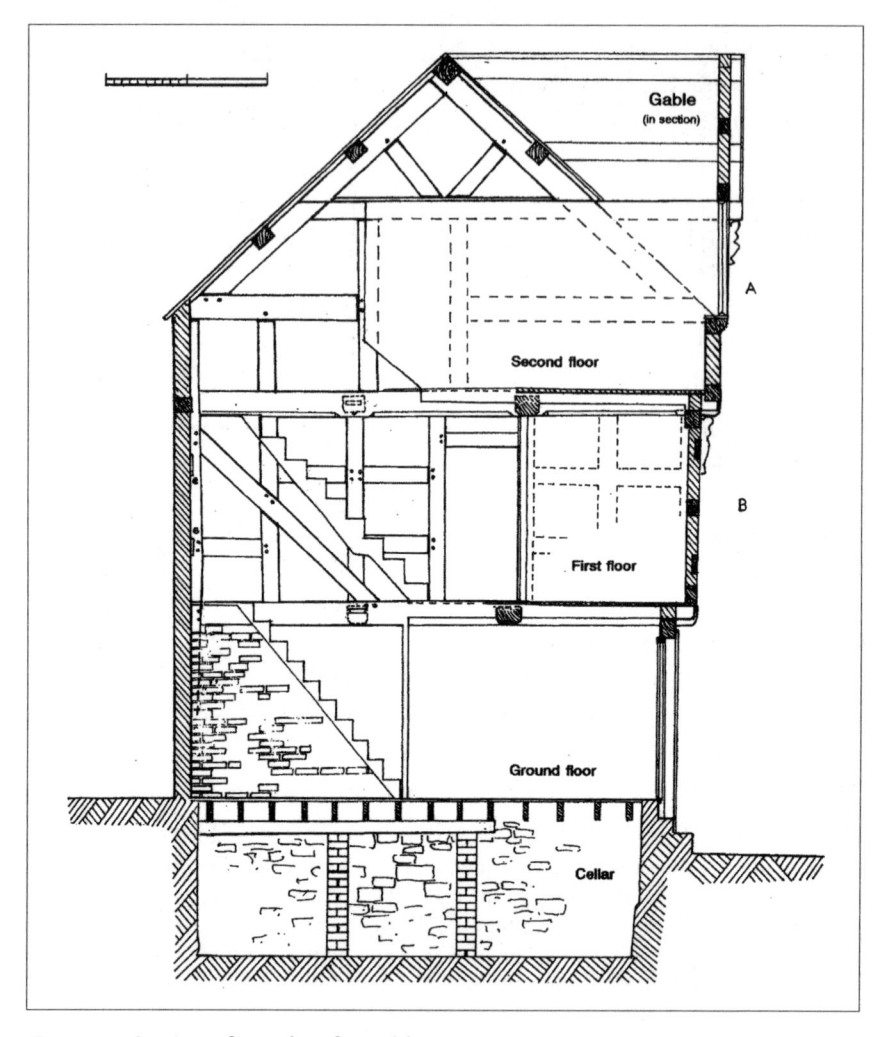

Figure 8.4 Section of a timber-framed house at 14-15 Raven Lane, Ludlow, Shropshire. The back wall and some other ground-floor walls in the house were rebuilt in brick during the nineteenth century, but the house retains its original structural form. The detail illustrated in *Figure 8.3* extends from A to B; the scale bar represents 2m.

John Mytton. The accounts make it clear that the jettied dormers with pendant corners were made during July 1622 and refer to them as the 'clerestory'.[16] Otherwise, most of the work being done on the house consisted of alterations to an older structure. This is nicely illustrated by one of the tie-beams in the roof which has two overlapping sets of carpenters' numbers. A series of long straight strokes scribed with the point of a knife includes numbers VII and VIII, whereas other numbers cut with the end of a gouge are likely to be part of the work done in 1622.

Given the dates of these houses in Cheshire and Shropshire, some of them well after 1600, it is worth asking about their builders' response to Renaissance design. On the exteriors of buildings only minor details show influence from this quarter, as when small blank arches, often paired, occasionally appear, and when carved brackets become consoles decorated with acanthus leaves. One of the few carpenters who were willing to adopt a more complete Renaissance style was Richard Dale the younger, whose design for the grammar school in Nantwich was unusual for a porch with classical columns supporting arches.[17] Dale was the son of a carpenter whose work at Little Moreton Hall,[18] on the east side of Cheshire, included bay windows added in 1559. A later development at Little Moreton was a tall range with a long gallery at attic level. This was probably the model for a similar long gallery at the Crown Inn, Nantwich, a timber-framed building of the 1580s whose roof was reconstructed after 1600 (perhaps by Dale the younger) to incorporate the gallery.[19]

The best-known carpenter by far in the western marches was John Abel in Herefordshire. One drawing by him is known, the ground plan of a small house (or perhaps an extension for a larger house) on which is a bar scale surmounted by compasses.[20] There is also correspondence by him connected with the work he did on the restoration of a former Cistercian abbey church at Abbey Dore, Herefordshire.[21] His design for the choir screen there is of a completely Renaissance character, with Ionic columns, balusters in between and a heavy cornice with brackets supporting three coats of arms.

Another building on which Abel was working in the 1630s was the Town Hall in the centre of Leominster, later reconstructed on a new site in a park where it is known as Grange Court. This originally had an open ground floor, like many other town halls that also functioned as market halls, but the timber posts supporting the first floor were carved in the form of Ionic columns and the braces were made to suggest arches (*Plate 36*). The framing of the jettied first-floor rooms is more typical of the timber-frame tradition. However, below the jetty, among the more classical decoration, is carved the same Latin text as appears on the screen in Abbey Dore church, beginning: 'Vive deo gratus...'[22]

These examples of work by John Abel and Dale the younger are exceptions to the rule which Pevsner enunciates when he says that: 'in timber-framed architecture, structurally at least, the Renaissance made no difference. It is decoration which distinguishes the new from the old, and little of that decoration is Renaissance'.[23]

LANCASHIRE AND YORKSHIRE CARPENTERS

The carpentry traditions of the western margins of England can be traced from Herefordshire, Shropshire and Cheshire northwards into Lancashire, although in Manchester, Bolton and Wigan, a great deal was lost during the later period of industrialisation. However, a search for documented carpenters in this area identifies such people as William and John Charnock and William Weegan, who made the spectacular timber roof of the church at Standish, near Wigan,[24] when it was rebuilt in the 1580s to designs by Lawrence Shipway.[25] There were also families of carpenters in or near Wigan named Southworth and Rigby.[26]

Another Wigan carpenter, John Pryse, signed a contract in 1617 to alter and extend Kenyon Peel Hall at Little Hulton, a village to the south of the town. The alterations comprised changes to the entrance into the hall that would allow for the construction of a new buttery and cellar. The carpenter was also to build an extension at the east end of the house referred to as a 'Crosse Chamber', which was to be 'haulffe Tymbered' probably with a display of decorative bracing such as was then common in Lancashire as much as in Cheshire and Shropshire. The roof was to be made strong enough to bear 'sclate' (meaning sandstone flags, a notoriously heavy roof covering). There is no drawing accompanying the contract, however, and no information about sources of timber. The owner of this building was at that time living in a timber-framed house in Wigan that is mentioned in the contract.[27]

Not far away are several houses built by carpenters who made distinctive use of a rase-knife of the kind adapted for marking small circles on timbers (explained earlier, *Figure 4.9*). They emphasised what this tool could do as if it were their trade-mark. Where dates were inscribed over doorways of houses in this area, the custom had been to carve Arabic numerals in quite angular forms. However a different approach was seen at Crooke Hall, Shevington, a house near Wigan that is now demolished, though with

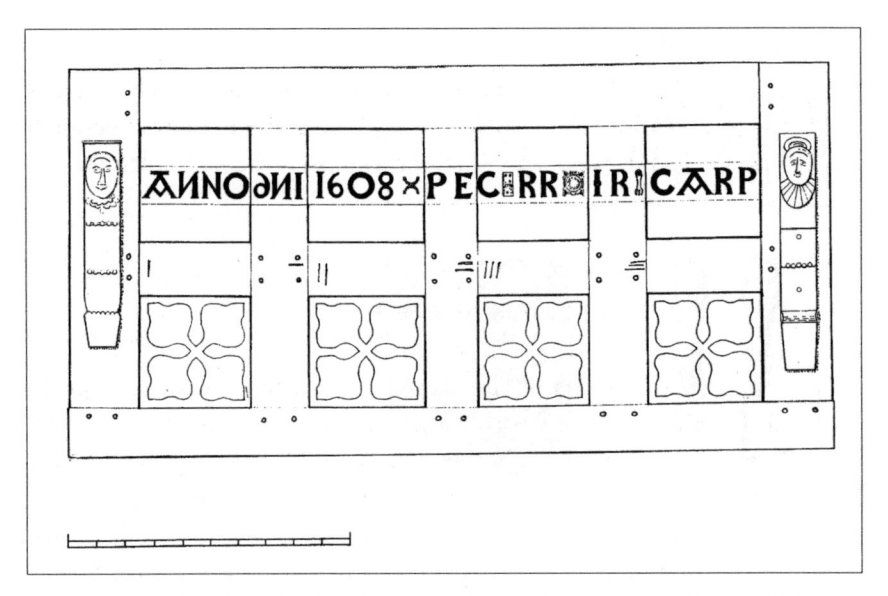

Figure 8.5 Panels and timber-framing above the porch doorway at Crooke Hall, Shevington (Lancashire), now in the History Shop museum, Wigan. The initials represent Peter and Elizabeth Catterall (also represented by busts at either end) and two carpenters (CARP) from the Rigby family. The timbers which frame the central panels are numbered I, II, III. The scale bar represents 1m.

some remains left in a museum.[28] An unusually long inscription on the timbers has the numerals 8 and 0 made up of perfect circles (*Figure 8.5*) These must have been set out using a rase-knife for the smaller circles and compasses for the larger ones. Also in Shevington is Club House Farm, which is probably the work of the same carpenters. Here, the numbering of joints in a timber-framed wall in the housebody consists of a series of large and prominent Arabic numerals in which all the curves in the numerals 3, 5, and 8 are arcs of circles drawn with a rase-knife.

Five miles to the west of Wigan at Holland's House, Dalton, and a little to the north of the town at Giant's Hall, Standish, are more examples of timber framing with similar carpenter's numbers.[29] It has been shown that the same rase-knife used at Club House Farm was used again to mark some of the numbers at Holland's House, which means that the same carpenter must have worked in both houses, and perhaps at Crooke Hall too.[30]

Looking back at the dated inscription on Crooke Hall, these carpenters may even have provided an illustration of their rase-knife, not

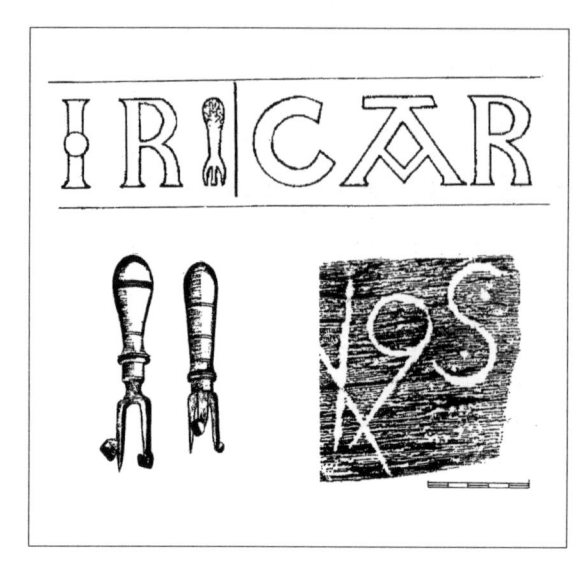

Figure 8.6 Enlarged scan of part of the inscription from Crooke Hall, Shevintgton (see *Figure 8.5*) showing what appears to be a carving of a three-pronged fork, with (below left) illustrations of two rase-knives, one with a third blade. Below right is a rubbing of a carpenter's number at Holland's House, Dalton (near Shevington), which has been scribed with a rase-knife. The latter is reproduced to a larger scale than the other illustration; the scale bar is 50mm.

as a drawing but a relief carving. Inserted as spacers between words and initials in the inscription are a number of devices or symbols, now so weathered that they are hard to recognise. One of them appears to be a three-pronged fork, and it may be intended to represent the type of rase-knife that had three protruberances: the blade for cutting curves, the compass point that went with it, and a further blade for cutting straight lines (*Figure 8.6*).

The initials that form part of this inscription include those of the owners of the house, Peter and Elizabeth Catterall (PEC), and those of two carpenters belonging to the Rigby family (RR and IR).[31] The carpenters' assembly numbers marked on timbers close to this inscription are the Roman numerals I to III, probably because the prominent use of Arabic numerals here would confuse the appearance of the inscription.

At the house referred to as Giant's Hall, the timber frame of about 1610 or 1620 not only has more carpenters' numbers (though cut with a different rase-knife)[32] but it also has some clear setting-out lines at joints in the timber frame. These consist of lines marked on the faces of the timbers which continue the alignment of the edges of connecting members of the frame (*Figure 8.7*).

This may seem an obvious way of marking up a joint and, indeed, it is also used at Holland's House,[33] but some carpenters used different methods, and examples will be encountered later where timbers were

Setting out carpentry and drawing in red

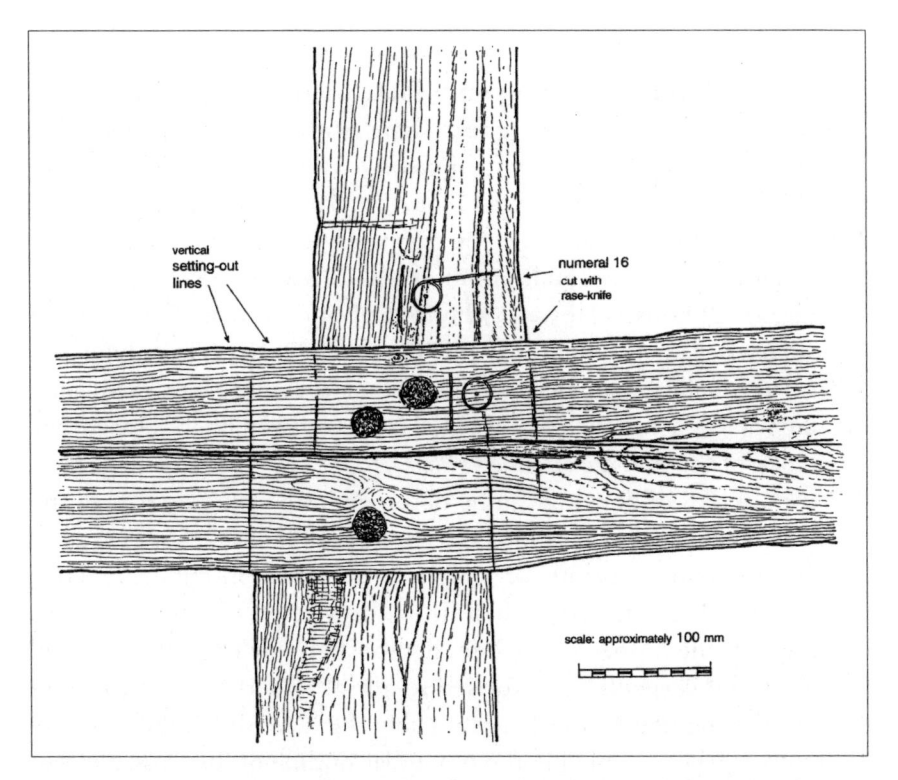

Figure 8.7 Giant's Hall, Standish, near Wigan, Lancashire. Joints in the timber frame at a door opening (below, right) with setting-out lines and a carpenter's version of the Arabic number 16. Pegs are shown darker than the other timber, and one peg appears to be redundant (or to arise from an alteration).

marked along their centre lines rather than their edges. The method used by the Giant's Hall carpenter is sufficiently distinctive to be referred to here as the *edge-line* method of setting out a timber frame (as distinct, especially, from the *centre-line* method).

Many of the timber-framed houses of the Wigan area no longer have a 'half-timbered' appearance because their external walls were later rebuilt in stone (or occasionally brick). At Club House Farm this was done in 1663; at Giant's Hall in 1675; and at Holland's House about 1700. Across the Pennine Hills in the West Riding, displays of half-timbering went out of fashion rather earlier and timber-framed walls were more often rebuilt in stone at a relatively early date. In the northern part of the Riding, the Yorkshire Dales have almost no visibly timber-framed buildings.

One house that illustrates what happened is at Lyon Road in the village of Eastburn, near Skipton.[34] Here there was a timber-framed house to which was added a rear wing with stone walls, probably around 1600. The main part of the house went through various stages of rebuilding in stone until, around 1800, it had a symmetrical front with Palladian windows. Meanwhile, the rear wing was turned into a cottage and other cottages were built onto it so that what we see today is a row of quite small houses. However the roof of one of them remains from the otherwise largely rebuilt structure of *c.* 1600. The truss has a king post whose unusually broad face was used like a drawing board with lines and curves in various media, and chisel-cut Roman numerals where the principals of the roof are attached (*Plate 37*).

Several kinds of drawing can be observed here including part of the circumference of a circle. Some lines are marked in black, but the rest of the drawing consists mainly of straight lines marked in red ochre. They extend onto the principals where they show as parallel lines close to the edges of the timber. These lines demonstrate the edge-line method of setting out carpentry, but applied to a roof rather than, as at Giant's Hall, to the framing of a wall. Presumably there are similar lines on the tie-beam as well, completing the triangular outline of the truss, but that member is obscured by the structure of a ceiling.

Drawings by carpenters on paper or parchment, or on framing floors, very rarely survive, but setting-out lines drawn on the timbers in buildings can quite often be found. This house at Eastburn provides a particularly complete set of lines. The question arises, then, as to whether the lines can be understood in terms of setting-out methods described in sixteenth- or seventeenth-century French books on carpentry, or in terms of southern-English carpentry influenced by such books.[35]

If the Yorkshire carpenters had used roughly similar methods, the procedure they might have adopted in constructing a king-post roof such as the one at Eastburn would have been to start with an outline of the truss drawn out on the framing floor. The tie-beam was then placed on top of the relevant part of the drawing, supported by blocks or battens to raise it slightly above the floor. Next the principals of the roof were placed in position, their ends resting on the tie-beam at the point where tenons would have to be cut to fit into mortices in the tie-beam. At the other end, where the apex of the truss would be, the principals were supported on blocks sufficiently high to ensure that they were precisely

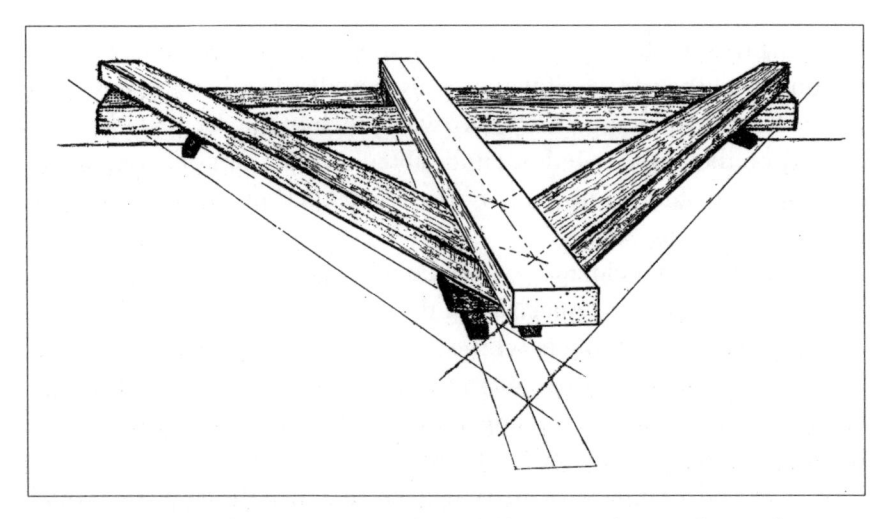

Figure 8.8 Timbers for a king-post roof truss laid out on a framing floor and supported on blocks to ensure that they are accurately level. In this hypothetical reconstruction an outline of the truss has been drawn on the floor, and some lines from the drawing have also been marked on the face of the timber. The king post follows Yorkshire practice in extending upwards some distance above the apex formed by the principals.

level, and finally the timber intended for use as the king post would be placed on top of the whole assembly (*Figure 8.8*).

At every stage levels would be checked and adjusted, with thin pieces of timber inserted above the blocks to ensure that each timber was accurately level. Plumb-and-level marks of the kind described in Chapter 4 might be marked on surfaces which had been thoroughly checked. It was important that every surface was levelled-up as this ensured that surfaces were precisely at right angles to the plumb line that was used to align timbers with the drawing below. For example, the dashed lines in Figure 8.8 show how part of the drawing on the framing floor might be transferred to the face of the king post to show where mortices were to be cut, producing an array of lines like that seen on the Eastburn roof (*Plate 37*). To establish where the lines should be drawn on the timber a plumb line would need to be dropped from the level of the timber surface to the floor at each point where a line came to the edge of the timber.

If a building had several trusses of one type, then use of the same drawing on the framing floor for each one would ensure that they were identical in overall size and shape. However, there is only one surviving truss in the house at Eastburn, and there is so much drawing on the timber of the truss itself that one suspects that less drawing was done on the floor than Figure 8.8 implies, with much of the detail worked out directly on the timber. Methods undoubtedly varied, not only regionally, but also according to how many trusses or sections of framing were being made to one design.

Timber-framed buildings, considered more generally, were made with considerable precision, especially in the cutting of joints, which meant that the levelling of timbers on the framing floor had to be done with great care. Joints would be cut so that, once they were complete and had been fitted together, the upper face of every timber as it lay on the framing floor was at the same level as the upper face of every other timber. This produced a 'fair face' or 'marking face' such that the carpenter could run his hand over the whole frame without encountering any changes of level at the joints, and it was on this face that the carpenter's numbers were scribed before the frame or truss was taken apart for removal to the construction site.[36] The pegs holding the joints were also inserted from this side. Since the fair face generally looked neater, this was designed as the external face of an outside wall or, on internal partitions, the face that overlooked the best rooms.

The implication is that all measurements relating to the thickness of walls were taken from the fair face. However, in making roof trusses for a building it was not always desirable to have all timbers forming a flush face on one side, because this would mean that all members of different thickness would show up on the other side. Looking up at such a truss, the observer might feel it was lop-sided and would certainly notice that it looked different from one side as compared with the other. Hence, in making a truss involving different thicknesses of timber, it was usual to mark centre lines on the sides as well as the face of each timber. Then when timbers were laid on the framing floor, they would be raised on blocks up to the point where centre lines were horizontal, and all measurements would be taken from centre lines instead of from faces or edges.

Compared with centre-line methods, fair-face carpentry and edge-line setting out required much less preliminary marking-up of the timber. Used together, these probably comprised the simpler method if timbers were reasonably straight and regular. So this is thought to have been the standard method in areas where numerous timber-framed houses were being built, as in Shropshire and Lancashire around 1600 (*Figures 8.3, 8.5*). However, the method could not be used in places where much of the timber was rough and irregular, such as that seen in some later barns in the Yorkshire Dales.

DRAWING METHODS AND ROOF TRIANGULATION

Reverting to the small house at Eastburn, near Skipton, although the use of red ochre for the setting-out lines on the timber is striking, other sixteenth-century examples of red ochre lines on timber in the same region are at Milton House, Connonley[37] (where the roof dates from *c.*1500 although the house was largely rebuilt in 1635) and in the Great Barn of Bolton Priory. Both these examples are near Skipton in the West Riding, but another example further south in the same county is Gunthwaite Hall Barn near Penistone.[38]

The Bolton Priory barn is an enormous aisled structure, 11 bays in length, which was built by two teams of carpenters. One team built the six northern post-and-truss frames and the other team built the four southern ones, each marking the timbers with their own distinctive set of assembly marks in Roman numerals.[39] On one truss in the northern part are some faint red ochre marks. They are hard to interpret, but probably include a centre line and some plumb-and-level marks, also in red. The only other drawing of significance is a set of carpenters' circles on one of the braces in the southern part of the building (*Figure 8.9*).

The tree-ring dating work which has established that the barn was built *c.*1518 also demonstrated that the timber came from a local woodland source, possibly one of the woods just to the north of the Priory complex.[40] This is not like the buildings quoted earlier where a timber structure was made some distance from the construction site. In this instance, it has been suggested that the floor of the barn served as a framing floor, not only during construction of the barn itself, but also probably while rebuilding was in progress at the priory church nearby, where a new nave roof may have been constructed prior to work beginning in 1520 on the new west tower.[41]

The four buildings in the Yorkshire Pennines mentioned above show that red ochre was a particularly important material for carpenters' drawings in this area. It can be recalled, then, that red and yellow ochre

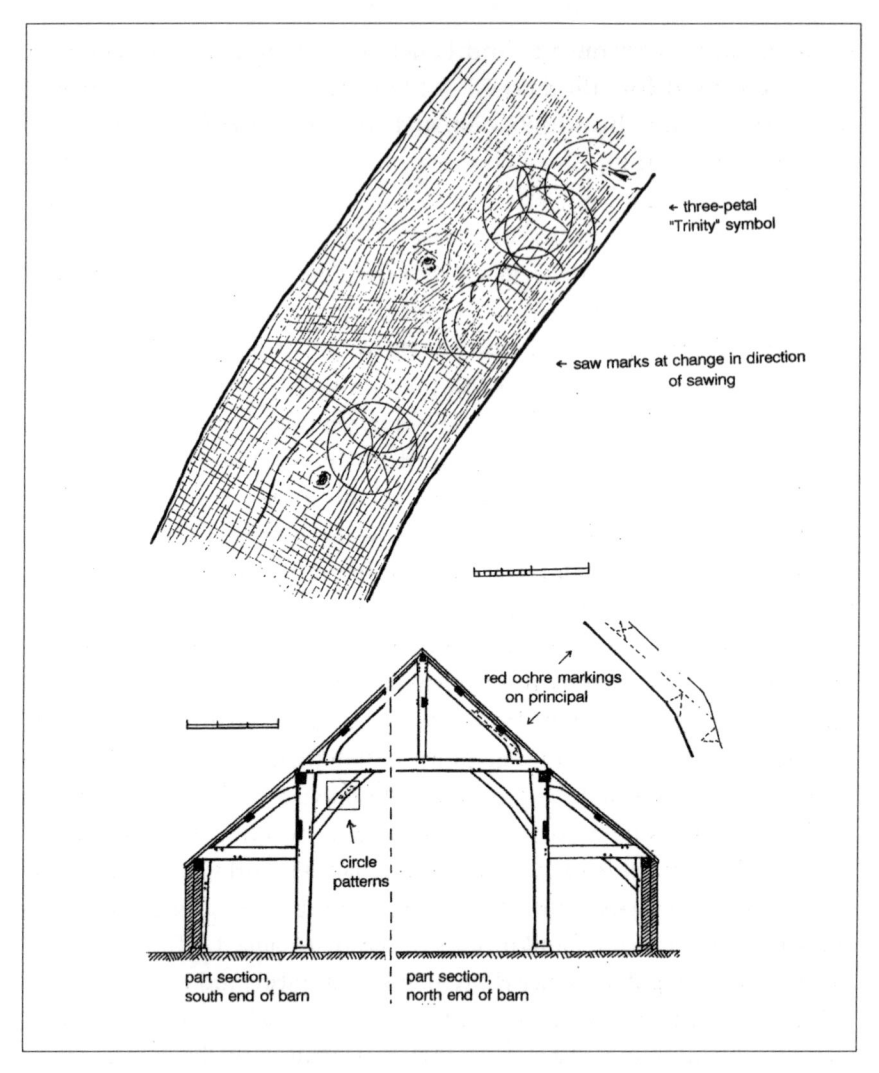

Figure 8.9 Detail of circle patterns in the Great Barn of Bolton Priory with a part section of the barn showing the location of the brace on which the circles appear. The other part section, more towards the north end of the barn, has dashed lines to show the location of a red ochre line and what may be plumb-and-level marks, also in red. The scale bars show 200mm for the detail, and 3m for the section.

are related forms of a naturally occurring mineral and were widely used as pigments, notably in wall paintings. Crayons could also be made by mixing the material with clay, rolling out the mixture and allowing it to dry, but carpenters often applied the colour by mixing it into a slurry, soaking a cord and 'snapping' the taut cord onto the timber. Other media were often used for this purpose, including lampblack, as when the nineteenth-century Buckinghamshire carpenter, Walter Rose, described the process of marking snapped lines when preparing a log for sawing into planks. Using a long string soaked with lampblack and water, the string was stretched out with two men holding the ends and was held taut along the centre of the log. Then there was 'a word or two from the head sawyer as he judged the correctness of the line ... after which he lifted the string and released it to strike the wood as the string of a bow after an arrow has been shot. The strike of the string on the newly chopped wood left an impression, a straight black line to guide the sawing.'[42]

If chalk was used instead of red ochre or lampblack, the technique was similar. The material would be ground up and mixed into a slurry with water and the cord or string would be soaked in this. The string would normally be used damp, but even when it had dried out it would usually have taken up so much material that it could still be used to mark lines.

One difference between these materials, though, is that chalk and lampblack tend to mark only the surface of the timber, whereas red ochre stains it quite deeply. Hence white or black markings less often persist, but red ochre or raddle (ruddle) markings can still be seen on interior timbers, though perhaps more often in barns than in houses.

This way of using red ochre was probably a regional practice. In southern England it is likely that white chalk was more often used for marking snapped lines on timber. There are fifteenth-century references to chalk lines (or cords)[43] and in 1545 a ship's carpenter on the *Mary Rose* had a cord impregnated with white chalk in his tool-chest.[44]

However, in many places it is difficult to know what kind of pigment may have been used by carpenters for setting out, since lines marked on timber were so easily obscured by smoke blackening or paintwork. A further complication is that, in southern counties, particularly Hampshire, the timbers of houses were often painted red with raddle which would mask any red setting-out lines.[45]

It is noticeable, though, that even if chalk or lampblack were preferred for snapped lines in many regions, red ochre might be used by carpenters for other markings, sometimes in the form of raddle crayons. At Paul's Hall, Belchamp St Pauls, Essex, there are red ochre assembly marks, probably dating from the sixteenth century, as also at Borley Lodge Farm, Borley, Essex.[46] In Herefordshire, at Court House Farm, Pembridge, a red ochre line was used in setting out joists in a jettied house (now part of the 'handsome outbuildings').[47]

Other instances have been reported from Worcestershire and Cumberland, but without documentation. At Shapwick House in Somerset, in a roof dated by dendrochronology to 1489, there are plumb-and-level marks in red ochre that are said to have been *painted* onto the adzed surface of the principals.[48]

In parts of Yorkshire, apart from the sixteenth-century examples quoted earlier, there was a continuing tradition after 1700 of marking up roof timbers with snapped red ochre lines. One of the clearest examples is in a barn at Prospect House, High Bradley (again near Skipton, West Riding).[49] The barn has been incorporated into the adjoining house and the two roof trusses each has a collar with an upper king post. The red ochre lines on one truss were in an unusually good state of preservation when photographed in 2001 (*Plate 38*).

Only a few of these Yorkshire examples are associated with named craftsmen. One instance may be Nicholas Bullock, a carpenter who lived at Lower Winskill Farm in Ribblesdale during the 1670s, a site where there are red ochre setting-out lines on a barn roof and compass-drawn circles inscribed on the plastered walls of a first-floor room. In Wharfedale as late as 1758 the carpenter Thomas England probably worked at a farm with the odd name Cuckoo Nest.[50] The barn here has two roof trusses, both with snapped red lines along their tie-beams. On one, there is also a black centre line on the king post that extends downwards onto the tie-beam where a second black line about a foot (300mm) from the king post resulted from a change of plan during construction.

Some of the timber used in this barn is irregular in shape and the tie-beam illustrated in Plate 39 is slightly curved, so there was little scope for drawing lines along the edges of straight timbers. In this building, then, and in many other Yorkshire Dales barns made with rough timber, a notional centre line was snapped onto each timber and used as a datum from which measurements could be taken. In other words, a version of the 'centre-line method' of setting out was being used.

The most significant examples are those in which the red ochre lines to be seen on roof trusses represent the whole triangle of the roof. One instance is a small disused field barn in a remote situation in Wharfedale which has two trusses, both marked with red ochre lines on the tie-beam and principals. In one truss, some lines have been partly lost (on the left

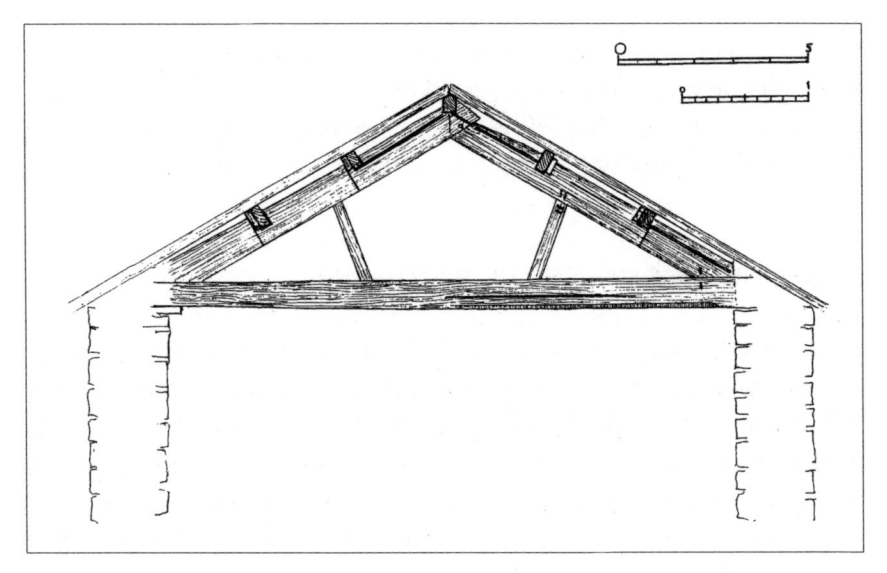

Figure 8.10 Roof truss at North Bounty Barn near Starbotton in Wharfedale (in the West Riding but now North Yorkshire). Bold ruled lines in the illustration represent red ochre setting-out lines marked on the timber. The scale bars represent 5ft and 1m.

in *Figure 8.10*), but all three sides of the triangle are represented and there are additional marks on the principals to show where the purlins were to be placed.[51]

One purpose in drawing out the triangle of a roof was to ensure that every truss was made with the same slope as well as having the correct span. Thus, although the two trusses in this small Dales barn look different, being made of irregular timbers, the same basic low-pitched triangle is represented in both. However, the structure is so simple that very little drawing would be necessary to get it right and it seems likely that a simpler method than envisaged in Figure 8.8 would have been used

In comparing these very basic buildings in the Yorkshire Dales with the much greater range of timber-framing to be seen in the city of York, it is surprising how little evidence for carpenters' setting out has been recorded there. Systematic surveys of houses in the city have identified carpenters' numbers,[52] but not many setting-out lines. At York Minster references to a 'carpenters' tracing house' on the opposite side of the church to the masons' loft raised expectations that some evidence of carpenters' methods might be found there.[53] But investigation led only to a first-floor room above the Zouche Chapel with a low-pitched roof of late date on which various names were chalked, including 'Thomas Morfitt 1760 / M. Potts 1760'. If these were carpenters engaged in maintenance of the building, the only useful evidence they left is that they were using white chalk rather than a raddle crayon for writing their names.

CARPENTRY PRACTICE IN THE SOUTH-EAST

In south-east England carpentry dating from around 1600 illustrates many of the same themes as have been observed in the western marches and in Lancashire and Yorkshire. In Colchester, Essex, there is a timber-framed house in East Stockwell Street to which a small extension or alteration was made around 1600 and the new timber was marked with Arabic numerals cut with a rase-knife in much the same way as the examples cited from Lancashire.[54]

Then in St Albans, Hertfordshire, there are seventeenth-century examples of timber-framed houses whose construction provides a counter-instance to the examples from Shropshire where frames were made in remote woodland areas, for in this town there were complaints, even after 1650, about carpenters who obstructed the highway with saw-pits and timber, and who 'worked up their raw material to a greater or lesser degree in the street'.[55]

However, examples of buildings in country towns such as these, with clear evidence for methods of setting out used by carpenters, have not been well documented in this area of England. Instead, the search for examples led to one of the inns of court in London. At Middle Temple Hall, a double hammerbeam roof was constructed in the 1560s under the direction of the carpenter John Lewis and, in the upper parts of the roof, broad setting-out lines can be seen. They are marked on the face of the timber with the blade of a rase-knife of the type used for cutting straight lines and are relatively shallow, channel-like marks in the timber surface, obscured in places by smoke-blackening. This is partly due to a sixteenth-century open hearth, but further blackening and charring resulted from a World War II incendiary bomb.

The hammerbeams are treated decoratively with classical mouldings and with little wooden columns which have no structural function, although they appear to support a boarded ceiling in the upper part of the roof. Only occasional setting-out lines can be seen below this

Setting out carpentry and drawing in red

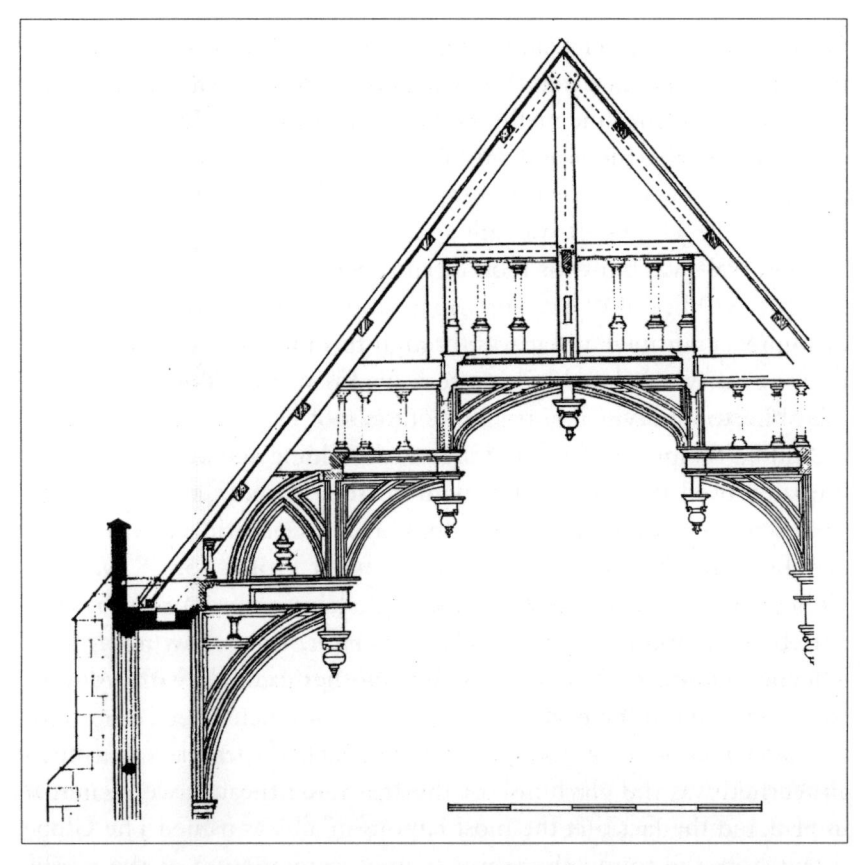

Figure 8.11 Middle Temple Hall, London: part of the roof structure, in a drawing adapted from a nineteenth-century section of the whole building. Dashed lines towards the top of the roof show approximately where scribed setting-out lines have been noted. The top row of small wooden columns (also seen in *Plate 40*) stand on the main structural collar beam, below which are the two hammerbeams on each side. The internal span of the roof is about 12.25m (40ft) and the scale bar represents 5m. *By kind permission of the Honourable Society of the Middle Temple*

ceiling, but in the void above the timbers are rougher and unmoulded and there are 'faint lines marking the intersection of the principal post and the principal rafters'.[56] The approximate alignments of some of these are indicated by the dashed lines in the upper part of Figure 8.11.

In Plate 40, which illustrates the decorative columns and boarded ceiling, one of the central principal posts (or king posts) is to be seen on the right. On this post, just above the carpenter's number IV (probably meaning VI) is a barely discernible centre line. It re-emerges higher up in the roof and careful examination of all the fragmentary lines in that part of the roof shows that the carpenter's setting out was consistently based on the centre-line method rather than using edge lines.

The site of the Inner and Middle Temple, though long tenanted by lawyers, had been a monastic property until the dissolution, when it passed to the Crown. It was still a Crown property when the Middle Temple Hall was built (or rebuilt) and the work was done by Queen Elizabeth's Office of Works. That organisation had the power to conscript or impress craftsmen and it was through this means that the carpenter John Lewis was ordered in 1562 to leave his work at Longleat House, Wiltshire, to supervise construction of the roof.[57]

Middle Temple Hall was an influential building and other carpenters probably used the setting-out methods seen here. In 1604, two men were sent to measure it from Trinity College, Cambridge, with a view to rebuilding the hall at Trinity with similar proportions.[58] Wadham College, Oxford, has a hall with a single hammerbeam roof built in 1611 by the Yorkshire carpenter Thomas Holt.[59] The drawing by John Thorpe reproduced in Plate 17 shows another example with a double hammerbeam (on the right).

Another London building type with which carpenters were much concerned was the playhouse or theatre. Some theatres were circular in plan and the fact that the most famous of all was named The Globe shows how the round shape was seen as a microcosm of the world. There was comparable meaning associated with the two round buildings mentioned in Chapter 7, in Yorkshire and Kent. However one of those examples contained a chapel (*Figure 7.2*) and both seem to have been microcosms that had religious intention. By contrast, plays put on at The Globe were a microcosm of the life of the world in a humanistic, Renaissance context and there were allusions also to the architecture of Roman ampitheatres.[60]

There is good documentation for the construction of three of the several theatres built in London after 1570, in each case identifying the carpenters in charge of building works. The most informative is the contract for building the Fortune theatre, which states that the new building was to be designed after the same manner as the Globe 'late erected' (in 1598-9) except that it was to be square in plan rather than round. The contract was signed by the promoters, Henslowe and Alleyn, on the one part and by 'Peter Streete citizen and carpenter of London' on the other, and specified that the new theatre was to be 80ft square in plan externally with an open courtyard 55ft square inside. The foundation of piles and brick was to be 'wroughte one foote' at least above ground level. The frame was to be of three storeys, of which the lowest was to be 12ft in height, the second storey 11ft and the third or upper storey 9ft.[61] The structure was to be rather like that of an ordinary house with long vertical timbers at the back, but with the upper floors jettied forward rather in the same way as the house in Ludlow discussed earlier (*Figure 8.4*). However, it would be much narrower from front to back than most houses.

The architect Walter Godfrey once reconstructed this building from the detail in the contract, producing a convincing set of drawings,[62] but there was a jetty on only one floor in his version, whereas another reading of the contract suggests that there were jetties to both upper galleries. One reason for adopting a form of construction similar to domestic buildings may be that the design was derived from the traditional inn courtyard where companies of players sometimes gave performances. Another consideration is that the proprietors of at least one theatre thought of converting it into tenements if it did not succeed as a playhouse. It is also noteworthy that the contract specified that the layout of the stage and the positions of the staircases were 'prefigured in a Plott' or plan.[63]

Thus the contract was accompanied by a plan which, as so often, does not survive. Peter Streete, the carpenter, agreed to erect the Fortune using new timber of larger scantling than at the Globe theatre. The job was to be completed by July 1600 for a total cost of £440. Notes on the back of the contract show that between January and April, 1600, Peter Streete was in the country, close to the Thames in Berkshire, with a team of carpenters and other workmen purchasing and preparing the timber. Components of the timber frame for the theatre were then transported down river, probably to the Bridewell wharf where Streete had a regular arrangement for bringing timber into London.[64]

CARPENTER'S DRAWINGS IN SUMMARY

Although drawings for the Fortune Theatre mentioned in the contract no longer exist, very occasional drawings by carpenters do survive, including the one mentioned above by the Herefordshire carpenter John Abel and the example from Worcester discussed in Chapter 6. Apart from such work on paper or parchment, the other kinds of drawings that carpenters made were, firstly, outlines on framing floors, which we can only know about by deduction and reconstruction (*Figure 8.8*) and, secondly, setting-out lines on the timber itself, of which contrasting examples in this chapter are the decorative design by Thomas Cleese (*Figures 8.1, 8.2*), and the structural detail marked on roof trusses by unknown carpenters in Yorkshire.

Some of the conclusions drawn here about setting-out methods can be deduced from the study of buildings of the period and by reviewing the sources used by Moxon and other writers, but many further pieces of the jigsaw have fallen into place as a result of the project, completed in 1997, to reconstruct Shakespeare's Globe theatre as authentically as possible. Much research on Elizabethan setting-out methods was done by the master carpenter responsible, Peter McCurdy, backed by the work of Richard Harris at the Weald and Downland Museum.[65] However, setting out the timber frame of the Globe was complicated because, what looked from a distance like a round building, was actually a 20-sided polygon measuring about 100ft (30.5m) across. Marking out joints at the awkward angles this entailed was itself a challenge, especially when the researchers aimed to understand how it would have been done by the Elizabethan carpenter Peter Streete.

Although research on the Globe has demonstrated techniques and methods of drawing that were *available* to English carpenters around 1600, often by reference to the French books noted earlier, there is still uncertainty about which methods were *actually used* in particular instances. Some of the roofs on which red ochre lines have been found provide valuable clues, but only after more examples have been found and analysed will firm conclusions be possible about the techniques actually used by carpenters in different regions of England. What does seem clear, though, is that in some instances at least, timber frames and roof trusses were made on framing floors which, as places for drawing full-size outlines of parts of buildings, were the equivalent of the masons' tracing floors. Examples of the latter which survive seem untypical, however. Probably the majority of masons' tracing floors were at ground level and in some documented cases were in temporary shelters close to the building site. Both carpenters' and masons' floors would often have a beaten earth surface, the durable plaster surfaces at York and Wells being untypical. Hence it is not surprising that nothing survives of framing floors, except that sometimes the lines marked on structural timbers correspond to lines once drawn out on such surfaces.

CHAPTER 9

THE PERSISTENCE OF MEDIEVAL DRAWING TECHNIQUES

(full-size drawings after 1660)

FULL-SIZE DRAWING: A CONTINUING TRADITION

The chapel of Pembroke College, Cambridge, begun in 1663 and completed in 1665, has a simple rectangular plan with a handsome west elevation facing onto one of the main streets of Cambridge. The elevation has four Corinthian pilasters and a pediment in which is a carved shield and garlands or swags of fruit and foliage. It is surmounted by tall carved urns at the corners of the building, and a cupola in the centre (*Figure 9.1*)

This is a very different architectural design from any considered so far. Indeed, the building is usually regarded as an early work by Christopher Wren whose uncle, Bishop Matthew Wren, had commissioned the chapel as his gift to the college and as the place where he would be buried. However, there are no drawings for the building by Wren and the only document to connect him with it is a memorandum in his hand about the supply and transport of marble paving for the floor.[1] Some detailed drawings by craftsmen do exist, and also a contemporary wooden model of the building, although there is nothing to show who made it.[2]

Information available about craftsmen who built the chapel comes from contracts for woodwork and brickwork, but there is no documentation for stonework or sculpture. The woodwork contract dated 1664 names three joiners, Cornelius Austin, Richard Billops and the latter's son, William Billops. These men were to supply timber in the form of 'wainscott well seasoned all and without ... cracks'. They were then to set this up 'according to a certaine forme or draught ... with 14 seats on each side the chappell' with panelling behind and a large cornice above.[3]

Figure 9.1 Pembroke College Chapel, Cambridge: west elevation with urn finials on the skyline and carved garlands and cartouche in the pediment. The drawing is only approximately to scale, with the scale bar showing 5 metres.

The drawing referred to as a 'forme or draught' was not kept with the contract and this seems to be another instance, like many referred to in previous chapters, where plans are mentioned in contracts but are now missing. However, there is a drawing now preserved at All Souls College, Oxford, which has been published as an 'elevation of stalls in a chapel'.[4] The stalls are very similar to the seating at Pembroke College and, although this is probably not the missing contract drawing, it may be a preliminary version or a copy. There are annotations on the drawing and the handwriting has been identified as belonging to Edward Pearce (or Pierce)[5] a craftsman of considerable versatility who later worked for Wren a good deal, notably on St Paul's. During 1663-65 Pearce is known to have been working for Sir Roger Pratt, building a house Pratt had designed at Horseheath, about 12 miles from Cambridge.[6] This makes it entirely feasible for him to have been called in to advise at Pembroke College.

The drawing for the stalls is in pencil and pen on paper, but there are two other drawings which show details of the chapel. They are set out on a plastered wall in another building at Pembroke College which was just being completed as work on the chapel began, and inside it was an unfurnished room which the masons were apparently allowed to use as their tracing house. This is now known as the Thomas Gray Room. When eventually it was furnished, panelling was installed and the drawings were thereby hidden and effectively preserved (and forgotten for nearly three centuries).[7]

The two architectural drawings on the walls of this room include an outline of a garlanded shield or cartouche within a triangular shape recognisable as part of the pediment on the chapel's west front. There is also a drawing of a flaming urn. A third mural is a portrait depicting a man in Jacobean dress and is executed partly in red chalk. The urn drawing seems to be related to the urns that stand as finials on the corners of the chapel but has freer, more spontaneous, lines particularly in the way the flames are depicted. This drawing was chosen for analysis because, in a recent restoration, the original urns were lifted off the building and replaced, and so were available for study at ground level (where they serve as garden ornaments). Their shapes have been altered by quite severe weathering of the stone, but it was still felt to be worthwhile to make a scale drawing of one of them. This is illustrated alongside an accurate copy of the flaming urn drawing (*Figure 9.2*).

Close inspection of the drawing (*Plate 41*) showed that it was carefully set out in pencil with a ruled centre line and one compass-drawn circle defining the curves of the bowl of the urn, with another establishing the height of its rim and the outline of the drapery. In Figure 9.2, the circle centres, noticeable as tiny holes in the plaster, are marked A and B. This illustration also shows that, although the stone urn differs quite markedly from the drawing, the heights of many features above the base are similar.

Thus the drawing on the wall can be regarded as another example of a full-size outline of an architectural detail, to compare with the medieval examples quoted. Unlike some others, though, this drawing was clearly not used for making templates, since the drawing differs so much from

Medieval Architectural Drawing

Figure 9.2 Measured drawing of an urn finial from Pembroke College Chapel, Cambridge (left) compared with a copy of the urn drawing on the wall of the Thomas Gray Room redrawn to the same scale (right). Construction lines in the drawing include a centre line and two circles, centred at A and B. The drawing on the left includes effects of weathering, especially on the drapery attached to the bowl of the urn.

the final carved shape. Apart from that, mural drawings were not well adapted for working with templates, which usually had to be laid out on a horizontal surface. So, as with some other examples where large drawings were made on walls rather than floors, the Pembroke drawings must have been used for working out the details of the design at full scale. Similarly the drawings at Acton Court, Gloucestershire, cited earlier, were probably used for preliminary design work on an oriel window and several variants in the angle of the base of the window were tried out in the drawing. By contrast, the mural drawing on the wall of Old Basing Church, Hampshire, of almost the same date as the Acton Court drawings (c.1550) is so closely similar to the completed west window that this may have been a drawing from which templates were made.[8]

The persistence of medieval drawing techniques

When more detailed comparison is made between the drawing at Pembroke and the carved stone urn, it can be observed that the drawing has flowing curves which would have been difficult to carve in stone and, in the completed work, the flames are rendered almost as if they were burning from a neatly trimmed wick. The drawn urn also has a more slender stem than would seem safe for a carving that was to be placed on top of a building exposed to extremes of wind and weather, and the executed design is more cautiously proportioned.

Hence, the drawing on the wall seems to represent an early stage in the process of designing the urns when some key dimensions were established, but with a freer shape than was really feasible. One might expect that the next stage in the design would have been to translate this preliminary design into a working drawing that would be laid out horizontally on a floor or table so that templates could be made to guide the carving of the four identical stone urns for the corners of the chapel.

Templates of some sort must have been used to achieve the regular shapes of the four urns, but we may question how the templates were made. A related question is whether the striking difference between the flowing lines of the drawing and the rather stolid execution of the finished urns indicates that different craftsmen were involved. Flaming urns were a motif quite often seen on wall monuments in churches, where the carver would sometimes show them in relief. In that situation, flowing lines could be used to represent the flames. The drawing on the wall at Pembroke looks very much like the first thoughts of a craftsman who had been used to designing wall monuments. Either he or another craftsman must have revised the design to make it more practicable as a three-dimensional form.

This raises the further question of who the craftsman was. Since Edward Pearce quite probably provided designs for the chapel seating and since he is known to have worked in stone as well as in wood, it would not have been surprising if he had made preliminary designs for the flaming-urn finials and the pediment sculpture. Scale drawings of his in pencil and ink on paper show that he designed many monuments with flaming urns, often in relief.[9] However, it may be wrong to assume that all the drawings in the Thomas Gray Room are by the same artist. Even if the urn design is by Pearce, the other drawings (including the portrait) may not to be. In the drawing with garlands and swags intended for the pediment, the shield or cartouche is given a fleshy shape which is unlike Pearce's usual style and could be closer to the work of Jaspar Latham, a contemporary London carver.[10] However, recent research at the college has suggested that Edward Pearce not only designed seating for the chapel, but was almost certainly responsible for other details, including the pediment with its carved detail and urns. In that case all the mural drawings are probably his.[11]

LATER INSTANCES OF FULL-SIZE DRAWINGS

Uncertainty about who made the mural drawings at Pembroke College or undertook the carving is less significant than the evidence provided by this example of the continued practice of drafting out full-size designs. Another, somewhat earlier seventeenth-century example is at Apethorpe Hall, Northamptonshire. Whereas drawings hidden behind panelling at Penbrooke College were unrelated to the room in which they were located, the drawings similarly hidden in the long gallery at Apethorpe represent the panelling which hid them. They are full-size drawings on the plastered wall showing the design in detail. The panelling was carefully devised to accomodate a series of large portraits (now dispersed) and the drawing would have contributed to the design process by allowing the effect to be judged before construction began.

Later examples of full-size drawings have been documented, for example in the work of the architect John Carr of York (1723-1807). He would make neat presentation drawings to a variety of scales, and working plans marked with dimensions were pasted on boards for use on site. However Carr also made a variety of larger-scale drawings for architectural detail, including some that were full size which he called 'directions at large' (i.e. directions to the workmen) or drawings 'in great'. Such drawings could be in ink, although Carr would carry chalk with him and, when visiting a building under construction, would sometimes draw in chalk on the nearest convenient surface.[12]

During the Gothic revival of the nineteenth century, reproduction of detail for traceried windows led to some renewal of methods of drawing at full scale. For example, there are drawings and templates made for restorations at York Minster in 1802-16 by William Shout.[13] At St Alban's Abbey a full-size drawing of a rose window was made on a wall during construction of the new west front under Lord Grimthorpe, possibly by Grimthorpe's foreman.[14]

In the twentieth century, the neo-Gothic detail of Liverpool Cathedral was drawn out full size on very large sheets of paper. Recent restorations of large medieval windows at Lincoln and York have entailed similar use of full-scale drawings and templates. Such experiences have prompted the comment that our perceptions of how medieval masons used tracing floors to make templates reflect experience of how modern restorers work, and that may often be misleading.[15] Templates may sometimes have been made more directly, without so much dependence on preliminary drawings.

This may be reflected in the word template itself which appears to be relatively modern. Medieval sources usually refer to the patterns of wood, paper, or metal to which this term refers as 'moulds', and many craftsmen in later centuries continued to use this term, with 'templet' coming in later as a synonym. That in turn gave way to the modern spelling in formal contexts. A twentieth-century textbook for training stone masons uses the word 'mould' alongside the later terms.[16]

Research on Elizabethan and later timber-framed buildings, mentioned in Chapter 8, has identified some of the methods once used in setting out timber structures, but one point that has emerged here is that a conventional full-size drawing on a framing floor is not always sufficient, because it is inevitably flat and two-dimensional. Carpentry joints are three-dimensional forms and, when marking up timbers to show the joints in a fully-framed building, blocks must be placed on the drawing to represent the third dimension and the timbers are then laid on these.

Apart from masons and carpenters, shipwrights are notable among other artificers who regularly made full-size drawings of what they were building, often using chalk on a wooden floor for laying out the lines of a ship. The large wood-floored drawing offices in which such drawings were set out were referred to as 'mould lofts', which is another reminder of the old name for a template.

A mould-loft floor used for drawing from 1758 onwards still exists at Chatham Dockyard (Kent). The lines of Nelson's flagship *HMS Victory* are thought to have been set out here, but in 1835 boards for a new floor were laid on top of the original ones. Both floors remain, although only the latter surface can now be seen.

The method of working in the mould loft during the nineteenth century was to enlarge a 1/48 scale drawing to full size, chalking or scribing the lines onto the floor. The curve of the hull would then be shown in detail, and templates or moulds would be made from softwood battens to fit these curves. After that, the moulds or templates were ready for use as guides to the selection and shaping of timbers for the hull. The mould loft at Chatham was in use until the 1890s, by which time the lines of iron ships were being laid out there, and it was then replaced by a new mould loft on another site.[17]

In medieval architecture, the intricate stonework required to make large traceried windows could probably only have been made with sufficient accuracy by using full-size drawings. From that time until the advent of computer-aided methods of design and manufacture, whenever a structure had to be made with great precision, it was often an advantage to make drawings at full scale. For example, during the 1850s American civil engineers favoured a type of bridge based on what was known as the McCallum or Macallum truss, because this made an exceedingly stiff structure, but 'it was so complicated that it was customary to make full-sized drawings on a smooth floor, from which patterns were taken for the framers'.[18]

While such examples may be a little unexpected, cross-fertilisation between house carpenters and shipwrights during the sixteenth to eighteenth centuries is not so surprising because, in times of war, house carpenters were recruited – or pressed – to work as ships' carpenters or at shipbuilding yards. Then, in peacetime, retired ships' carpenters would sometimes take up work on land.[19]

The use of full-size drawings in mould lofts or on framing floors was one technique that house carpenters and shipwrights had in common, and for which there is a continuous history from the earliest period in the Middle Ages discussed here into the seventeenth, eighteenth and nineteenth centuries. Even earlier, builders in other civilisations used full-size drawings laid out on floors or paving, including the Roman craftsmen who built the Pantheon.

INTERPRETING SURVIVING DRAWINGS

There is occasionally some difficulty in understanding medieval drawings on walls and tracing floors, not only because they survive in fragmentary form, often with several sets of lines overlapping, but also because medieval drawing conventions are unfamiliar. One aspect of this is that in many instances, only half of a symmetrical design was drawn out, but a more fundamental difference in conventions may be observed where an elevation was combined with a plan or section in a single drawing.

An outstanding example is on the tracing floor at Wells Cathedral and seems to refer to the cathedral cloister which was rebuilt from about 1420 onwards. It was discussed in Chapter 3, where Figure 3.1 indicates the large number of overlapping lines and curves that are seen when an attempt is made to record every single line or mark on the tracing floor. By contrast, Figure 3.4 is an attempt to interpret some of what is on the tracing floor by omitting apparently irrelevant lines and reconstructing a little of what is missing by use of dashed lines. The point of this illustration was to show how the original drawing apparently combined a design for window tracery with a plan of the vaulting ribs in one bay of the cloister walk.

Another way of representing this particular drawing at Wells is provided here in Figure 9.3. This includes less in the way of interpretative lines so the window tracery is less easily recognisable. However, the illustration (which reproduces just over a quarter of the whole area of the tracing floor at Wells) still demonstrates curves that belong to an elevation (marked B) drawn out in close proximity to the group of straight lines at C that splay out from the circle on the right, and the additional curves at D which are harder to account for.

The explanation proposed in Chapter 3 is that these lines and curves together represent a typical bay in the cloister at Wells with an elevation of the window (B), a plan of the vault (C) and perhaps sections of different parts of the vault (D) combined in one image. In other words, several superimposed drawings together represent the three-dimensional form of this part of the cloister.

As more research is done at Wells, it is likely that other explanations will be found for some of the detail in this drawing, but any new understanding will almost certainly confirm the sophistication of what is attempted here in terms of representing several different aspects of a structure in one image. The point is worth repeating because the drawing seems to mark a high point in English architechtural drawing.

In discussing medieval architectural drawings that survive on parchment in continental Europe, James S. Ackerman notes that medieval masons in France were drawing plans and sections in the thirteenth century.[20] The impression left by English drawings is that while details of window tracery (including rose windows) were regularly drawn out as early as 1200, plans and sections were rarely represented by any kind of precise drawing until after 1350. When plan views of details do begin

Medieval Architectural Drawing

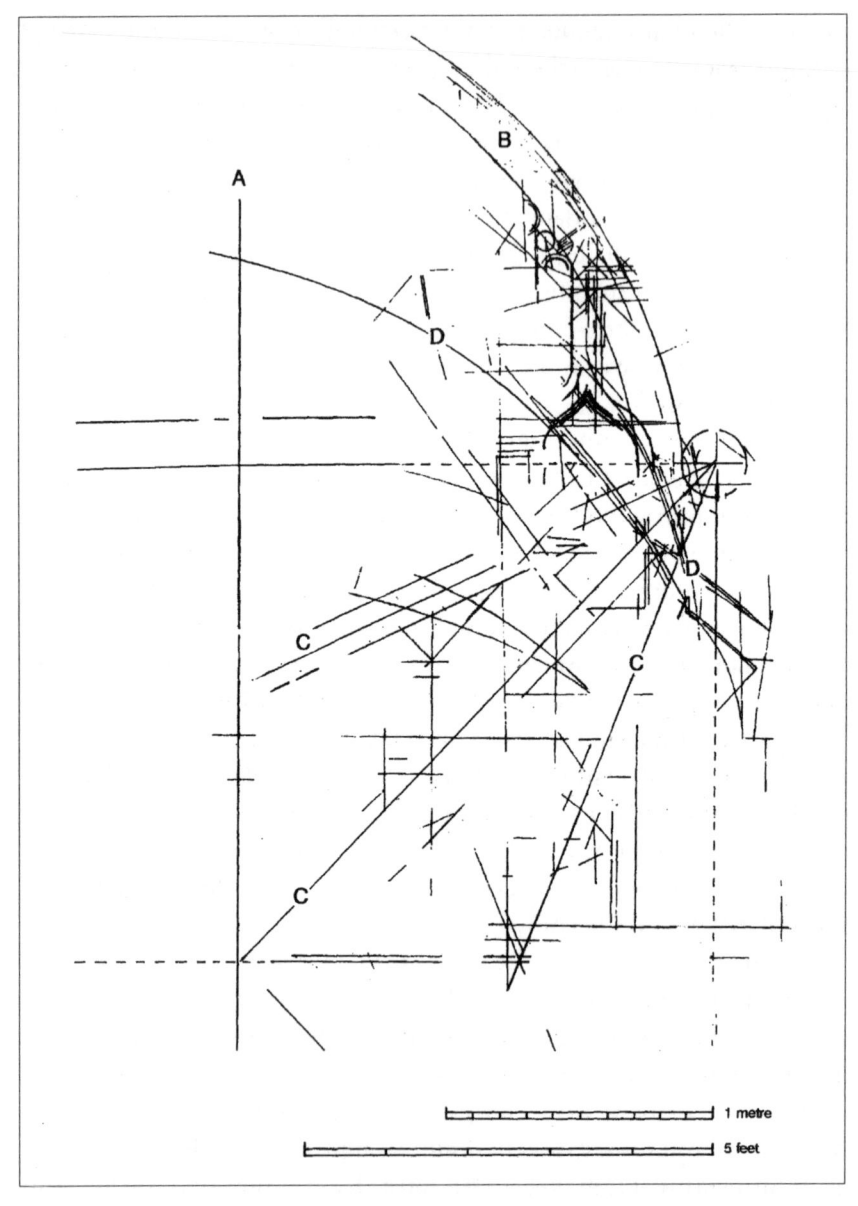

Figure 9.3 Drawings on th tracing floor at Wells Cathedral which combine fragmentary evidence of a window (B) with part of a plan showing diagonal vaulting ribs (C). The centre line of the window drawing is at A and some unexplained curves are at D.

to appear, they are nearly always combined with elevations, as in the example from Ashwell (Hertfordshire; *Figure 2.6*) dating from about 1360 and the present example from Wells which dates from around 1420.

The disadvantage of these precise and complex drawings is that they were always full size. Several other kinds of drawings have been discussed, including model drawings and prints used by carvers, pictorial representations of buildings and sketched elevations, of which the most elaborate was the detailed elevation of a timber-framed house apparently by a Worcester carpenter of the late fifteenth century (*Plate 29*).

However, the most important innovation for freeing builders from dependence on full-size drawing for working out the details of a projected building was acceptance of the conventions of scale drawing. This came later in England than on the Continent but, once scale drawing was understood and accepted, it enabled the architect to emerge as a designer who made drawings on paper, as distinct from the craftsman who often needed to do full-size drawings on the building site. There was not a sharp demarcation, however, and as this chapter has shown, a craftsman such as Edward Pearce was accustomed to making scale drawings on paper but would also sometimes make full-size drawings on site. A century later the architect John Carr (who had begun life as a stone mason) would sometimes draw detail full size when visiting building sites for which he was responsible.

DRAWING INSTRUMENTS

Although the emergence of scale drawing represents a decisive break with medieval practice, the continued, if less frequent resort to full-size drawing in the seventeenth and eighteenth centuries marks a degree of continuity in drawing practice. Another aspect of medieval architectural drawing that can seem to show continuity relates to drawing instruments. The thirteenth-century 'muse' that represents geometry on the painted ceiling of Peterborough Cathedral carries compasses and an L-shaped set-square (*Figure 3.12*), and these instruments sometimes appear on medieval masons' grave slabs. Other instruments used for measuring or drawing often accompany the square and compasses in illustrations of building craftsmen, including a measuring rod or staff, a straight-edge or ruler, and a level.

It is striking that the same instruments, the square and compasses, continued to be put into the hands of muses in eighteenth-century illustrations and they still appeared on monuments or wherever a symbol was needed for a mason's skills or an architect's achievements. However there was a significant change. While medieval masons were sometimes also shown with a measuring staff, it was often in the form of a slender pole which, when held vertically, seems to be about the height of a man. This could be used as a standard of length, possibly with some subsidiary lengths marked on it, but it did not have detailed subdivisions of feet and inches with identifying numerals.

Significantly different are measuring rods or rulers in post-medieval illustrations, even those in the hands of an iconic muse of architecture.[21] They now usually have graduations marked on them with some basic unit (a foot or an inch) divided into halves, quarters and sometimes eighths. Furthermore, as noted in Chapter 7, scale-bars appearing on maps often combined a pair of compasses not with a square, but with a ruler subdivided in this way. This change, emphasising the subdivided or graduated ruler, marks a real break with medieval tradition and is associated with the advent of scale drawing.

Medieval illustrations of craftsmen at work can rarely be taken at face value, however. The relative size of a human figure may be diminished and the instruments he or she carried are often deliberately exaggerated for effect. A square and compasses might be shown because of what they symbolised about geometry regardless of whether they were actually being employed for the job in hand. In the more realistic illustrations, though, the mason's measuring rod or staff appears to be about two metres long, and close analysis of one thirteenth-century French example by Nancy Wu led to the conclusion that the actual length in that instance was 1.92m (6ft according to one standard of length used in France at the time).[22]

Although masons' staffs were used as standards of length and were not graduated in feet and inches, it is likely that various significant lengths would be marked on them, such as the heights of plinths and window sills in the building currently under construction. Meanwhile, at some unknown time, carpenters began to mark straight-edges (and possibly set-squares) in inches. The evolution of such instruments is unclear until, in 1556, Leonard Digges illustrated a 'carpenter's ruler' that was not only subdivided into inches, but incorporated a ready reckoner as well (*Figure 7.5*).

Digges also illustrated a graduated measuring rod or staff that could take the place of the more traditional one. He suggested that 6ft and 10ft staffs could be more portable if made in two lengths plugged together, end-to-end.[23]

Although masons used similar instruments, the carpenter's ruler does seem to have been developed within one trade rather than the other, and in marking numbers and setting-out lines on timber carpenters also had their own methods. They used some tools for marking up timber that other craftsmen would not usually employ for such purposes, including knives, chisels and gouges. They also had the specialist tool known as the rase-knife (*Figure 4.9*).

Changes in drawing instruments from the late Middle Ages onwards were paralleled by increased availability of paper and improvements in drawing media. It should be recalled that in 1300, paper was still a novelty, newly introduced into Europe from the East, and was not used for drawing until the fifteenth century. At the same time, the high cost of parchment may at times have inhibited the production of drawings, or encouraged craftsmen to draw on scrap materials and on walls.[24] After 1500, however, paper increasingly became the usual material on which to draw, with preliminary lines often marked with a stylus or metal point to be inked in later and with pencils being used more often by 1600.

To sum up, although the practice of making full-size drawings persisted long after the Middle Ages, with some of the drawing instruments that had been employed by medieval craftsmen still being used, the advent of new attitudes to measurement, and of scale drawing, marked a major break with the past. One of its effects was to make it possible for a design to be completely worked out on paper, away from the site, leading to a greater separation between those who did the drawing and those who did the building. That, in turn, allowed architecture to become a gentlemanly profession separate from the work of craftsmen. However, there was not a sharp transition in which everybody changed their ways at once. Except for a minority of high-status buildings, craftsmen continued to play the major part in building design using a mixture of traditional and modern methods. Timber-framed buildings continued to be built by carpenters with hardly any use of the new drawing methods, nor any involvement of architects. John Abel in Herefordshire and the younger Dale in Cheshire were carpenters who may have begun to function rather like architects but, in general, medieval methods, including setting-out techniques, persisted among carpenters until after 1700.

Comparisons between medieval craftsmen's drawings and work done in later periods can sometimes seem to indicate a decisive improvement in technique. Eugene Ferguson once characterised it by arguing that the Renaissance in Europe was a time of prolific 'graphic invention'.[25] Included in this was the invention of linear perspective, innovations in technical drawing and the introduction of different projections for depicting three-dimensional images onto flat paper (such as scale drawings in architecture and map projections in cartography). Part of this movement in graphic invention was the understanding of dimensional accuracy which made for clearer drawings of buildings and enabled designers to visualise what they planned more adequately. The same innovations enhanced the precision with which visual ideas could be communicated and helped make it possible for architecture to be practised as a profession rather than a craft skill.

Nonetheless, while recognising the significance of these developments, we should recall that there were effective processes for design in all periods. Indeed, the earlier medieval craftsmen produced some of the greatest buildings of all time. The questions that ought to be asked in the light of this are more to do with how medieval craftsmen worked and how they visualised a proposed new structure, given that their drawing methods were so different. Some answers may be found in a better understanding of the geometry used by builders. That topic has been mentioned only briefly here because the tracing floors described in the main chapters show little evidence of the direct application of such methods as *ad quadratum* design. However, a closer study of small, apparently informal drawings to be found in a number of places (such as the church of St Cross Hospital, Winchester) reveals more exercises in this kind of geometry, including drawings of squares diagonally placed within larger squares. It is also possible that, as suggested in Chapter 3, design procedures using circles had more importance than some modern studies of *ad quadratum* geometry have hitherto recognised.

Even so, architectural drawings must be considered from other points of view not just as geometry. Although relatively few such drawings have survived, almost 20 from between 1200 and 1550 have been illustrated here (including four separate drawings from the tracing floor at York) and many more have been taken into account in the discussion. In addition, there are the setting-out lines for wall-paintings and carpentry that demonstrate relevant drawing techniques but are not themselves architectural drawings. The drawings show that, by the fourteenth century, some quite sophisticated techniques for visualising three-dimensional structures were being used, including the technique of combining elevations and plan-views in one set of outlines (*Figure 9.3*). Later, there were increasingly accurate presentations of elevations and plans on parchment until, eventually, concepts of drawing to scale emerged.

Of the drawings not discussed here, some were omitted because justice could not have been done to them in this rather broad-brush survey.[26] It seemed that they would be better appreciated through one of the more specialist approaches to the subject, of which two can be mentioned. Firstly, there is the use of evidence from drawings to achieve much deeper understanding of specific buildings, sometimes reconstructing architectural features which no longer exist. Such an approach has importance for the study of ruined monastic buildings,[27] but may also be applicable to understanding earlier phases of parish churches (especially some in Cambridgeshire now equipped with fifteenth-century windows but with sketches of earlier tracery on walls or piers; *Figure 2.4*). Secondly, there is research that looks comprehensively at every aspect of the work of the medieval mason, including masons' marks and graffiti drawings,[28] with a view to understanding the craftsmen's working lives and how their work was organised.

Both these approaches are beyond the scope of the present book, but both, in different ways, can help answer questions about the social processes underlying medieval building projects. For example, did improvements in drawing techniques make for a sharper distinction between master masons responsible for design and ordinary working masons? Did the superior status of master masons lead to the use of secluded, upper-floor rooms as tracing houses? And what were working relationships like between those who commissioned buildings and those who constructed them? For example, an exceptional drawing such as the clearly-presented fourteenth century window design at York (*Figure 2.9* at A) may have been prepared to facilitate discussion between stone masons and churchmen. On a different level, practices that entailed numbering sculptures or roof timbers with Arabic numerals, little known in the thirteenth century except among scholars, seem to indicate active interventions by churchmen.

This book has mainly attempted to answer more basic questions than these. Most basic of all is the suggestion sometimes made that medieval craftsmen often worked without drawings. It is possible to say on the basis of evidence discussed here that, where window tracery was concerned, masons were making detailed drawings from around 1200 onwards (Chapter 2). Drawings of other parts of buildings are more difficult to find until later, and early drawings by carvers of wood or stone, or by carpenters, almost never survive. However, there is evidence that stone carvers did use some drawings in the thirteenth century (Chapter 1), and by the end of the fifteenth century there is ample evidence for the use of model drawings and prints by woodcarvers (Chapter 6). In the absence of drawings for carpentry structures from before 1450, it has seemed better to see what can be learned from carpenters' setting-out lines and numbering systems (Chapter 4).

The other question addressed here was the evolution of drawing methods. The scope of drawings expanded from a preoccupation with window tracery to the representation of other details in plan and elevation. When drawing methods are examined on this level, despite interesting examples from the fifteenth century and around 1500, the most significant development can seem to be the introduction of scale drawing later in the sixteenth century. Even after this, however, some medieval techniques persisted into the seventeenth century, especially in carpentry, in architectural sculpture and in shipbuilding.

The drawings discussed in this book are of obvious interest for understanding medieval architecture, but they also raise many questions. Some of the latter are very detailed and concern design methods, geometry and even the media used for drawing (red ochre, metal points, pen and, later, pencil). Other questions are of wider social relevance and reflect on the working relationships between craftsmen, clerics, house-owners and others who paid for building work. As more detailed research is done and more drawings are discovered, the larger questions about the social background of medieval building design will inevitably be given fuller answers.

APPENDIX

Where to see medieval drawings
(and selected post-medieval examples)

Drawings on parchment or paper
The bibliographical references for each chapter identify libraries and record offices where the few surviving medieval architectural drawings on parchment or paper are preserved. The most important are in London (the British Library and the RIBA Smythson Collection at the Victoria and Albert Museum); in Cambridge (Corpus Christi and Magdalene Colleges); and at Worcester (Worcestershire Record Office).

Tracing floors
Apart from the above, the most important medieval architectural drawings are on the tracing floors at Wells Cathedral (Somerset) and York Minster. Both are in locations that are difficult to access and are not normally open to the public, though at York guided tours are occasionally organised by the Centre for School Visits at the Minster.

The principle of the tracing floor applied much later to shipbuilding can be seen in the mould loft at Chatham Historic Dockyard (Kent), which is a museum that is regularly open.

Drawings on the fabric of buildings
A distinction is needed between *architectural drawings* which may show recognisable designs for window tracery and other features, and *setting-out* markings on components of a building that provide reference lines for measurement, or show how an item was to be cut to shape, or indicate how joints should fit. In stone buildings, setting-out marks were often hidden within mortared joints and only show when a building is ruined or when individual components are displayed in museums (e.g. site museums at Knaresborough Castle and Byland Abbey, both in North Yorkshire).

Medieval drawings on the walls of churches typically consist of fine lines on rough stone surfaces that are hard to pick out. Two churches which are

Medieval Architectural Drawing

famous for them and where (at the time of writing) there are guidebooks on the medieval graffiti which help the visitor to find them, are Gamlingay (Cambridgeshire, *Figure 2.4*) and Ashwell (Hertfordshire, *Figures 2.5, 2.6*). However, the guidebooks concentrate on graffiti of general interest and omit some of the architectural or geometrical drawings (especially at Ashwell, where large cupboards obscure certain architectural drawings). A third such church is at Leighton Linslade (Leighton Buzzard, Bedfordshire) where the relevant volume of Pevsner provides enough detail for the drawings to be found.

Where drawings are more difficult to pick out, searching for them will be greatly aided if a torch is used to provide oblique light to small areas of wall. If there are masons' marks, they should soon be found this way, then having 'got one's eye in', if there are other marks or drawings on the walls, they should eventually be found. Medieval graffiti include sketches of people, heraldic devices, music notation, ships and windmills, subjects which are mostly ignored here. Locations of drawings in churches are surprisingly often piers (pillars) but they may sometimes be found on window reveals, door jambs and smooth areas of walling.

Buildings where there are drawings that include window detail, especially tracery, include the following:

> Byland Abbey, North Riding (now North Yorkshire), see Figure 2.2
> Ely Cathedral, Cambridgeshire, Galilee porch, see Figures 2.1, 2.3
> Cambridge University Museum of Archaeology and Anthropology, Downing Street, Cambridge (slab from St John's College, not on display, view by appointment)
> Gamlingay, Cambridgeshire, St Mary's Church (see Figure 2.4)
> Barrington, Cambridgeshire, All Saints' Church (drawings on piers)
> Offley, Hertfordshire, Church of St Mary Magdelene (window tracery designs on wall and carved on the font also)
> Ashwell, Hertfordshire, St Mary's Church, see Figure 2.6
> Old Basing, Hampshire, St Mary's Church, chapel (full-size drawing)
> Christchurch Priory, Hampshire, vestry (full-size, or nearly full-size drawings)
> Lincoln Cathedral, Longland Chapel and other locations (geometry related to window design)
> Leighton Linslade (Leighton Buzzard), Bedfordshire, All Saints' Church

Appendix

Buildings where there are other types of architectural or geometrical drawing include:

> Gloucester Cathedral, Lady Chapel (*Figure 5.2*) and Parliament Room
> Acton Court, Iron Acton, Gloucestershire (courtier's house with large architectural drawing; occasionally open to the public; *Figure 5.8*)
> Englishcombe Tithe Barn, Somerset (geometrical drawings, *Figure 7.1*)

It will be noticed that these examples tend to be concentrated in southern and eastern England, partly because there have been more investigations there than anywhere else. Many examples in that region not listed here can be found with the aid of the book by Violet Pritchard (*English Medieval Graffiti*, Cambridge University Press, 1967). However, other factors that influence the regional distribution include building stone and the activities of Victorian church restorers (who often removed plaster and scraped walls).

Not surprisingly, many of the best medieval drawings are in places where the building stone produced smooth surfaces that are not too hard and hence are easy to draw on with a scribing tool (e.g. the Bath stone at Englishcombe, Somerset, *Figure 7.1*). One reason why there are so many good examples in Cambridgeshire and Hertfordshire is that *clunch* was often the building stone here. This is an unusually hard form of chalk. It was used at Ashwell, where many drawings are to be seen, and is exemplified also by the slab with the thirteenth-century drawing at Cambridge. It occurs in other parts of southern England which ought to be investigated more thoroughly for mural drawings. In other regions where the local stone lent itself to the purposes of the mural draughtsman it is likely that more architectural or geometrical drawings will be discovered than have hitherto been reported.

Setting-out lines and marks in timber-framed buildings and roof structures
In examining timber structures (including roofs) it will often be best to start by looking for the carpenters' numbers, which are always close to joints. Most setting-out lines will be on the same face of the timber as the carpenters' numbers. In such towns as Ludlow (Shropshire) and Leominster (Herefordshire) there are post-medieval buildings in which quite elaborate carpenters' numbers can be examined on the exterior, from the street. Inside Castle Lodge, Ludlow, internal partitions on the

upper floors show setting-out lines for some early alterations as well as numbers.

In Worcester, a partly fifteenth-century house known as The Commandery has prominent carpenters' numbers on panels in the hall and on structural timbers around the head of a staircase, and is open as a museum.

At Cressing Temple, Essex, the two great barns are open to the public and show examples of carpenters' numbers. Upstairs in a separate granary block there are beams that show levelling marks. At both the Avoncroft Museum of Building (Worcestershire) and the Weald and Downland Museum (Sussex) it is possible to examine timber-framed buildings closely to find numbers, levelling marks and so on. At the Weald and Downland site, the Court Barn has ritual marks (apotropaic marks) in the form of overlapping circles.

Other setting-out marks discussed are either in inaccessible positions in roofs or in buildings for which there is no public access. Similar examples may now and then be found by taking whatever opportunities arise for looking inside barns or the attics of houses. Occasionally in northern England one is rewarded by seeing much of the triangle of the roof drawn out in red ochre centre lines, though more often a red line survives in only one place, perhaps on a king post. Again, it is necessary 'to get one's eye in' because what is often a faded brownish red does not contrast sharply with the natural colour of the timber. Old barns are often the most likely places, if they have not been converted into houses.

Underdrawing for wall paintings
When the setting-out lines for a wall painting were scribed on the wall with a metal point and the painting itself has decayed, the lines may potentially be confused with the geometrical drawings seen in some graffiti. Apart from that, drawing techniques used in paintings are worth study in themselves. A small number of the many examples are:

Polstead, Suffolk, St Mary (*Plate 24*)
Exeter Cathedral, Devon, sedilia (*Plate 8, Figure 3.10*)

Wheel of Fortune (and Wheel of Five Senses) paintings requiring much prior drawing with compasses are to be seen in the following buildings (churches and a house):

Appendix

Swaton, Lincolnshire, St Michael (east end of south aisle)
Kempley, Gloucestershire, St Mary (in the care of English Heritage; open regularly; *Plate 25*)
Leominster, Herefordshire, Priory (north side of nave, west end)
Longthorpe Tower, Longthorpe, Peterborough (house in the care of English Heritage; open by appointment only)

Stained glass
Stained glass has not been discussed in this book through lack of space, but the process of drawing, often on a whitewashed table and using cartoons, is of considerable interest in the wider context of medieval drawing techniques. There is much good material on glass at the Victoria and Albert Museum, London, and in the museum of stained glass within Ely Cathedral.

GLOSSARY

aisled barn or hall	building with lines of posts (or pillars) supporting the roof and demarcating aisles on both sides (or sometimes just on one side)
ashlar	masonry in large, square blocks with well-finished, even surfaces
ashlar piece (or post)	vertical timber in a roof connecting a rafter with a horizontal timber on top of the stone wall of the building (a term used specifically in the context of timber roofs on stone-walled buildings)
augur	hand-held tool for boring holes in timber (hence 'augur holes')
aumbry	cupboard or recess in the wall of a church for communion vessels
baluster	vertical support for a hand-rail, sometimes in the form of a short, fat pillar
brace	in timber framing, a length of timber at an angle running between horizontal and vertical members of a frame; it may be straight, curved, or curved with cusps
clunch	a hard variety of chalk used as a building stone (especially in Cambridgeshire)
cusp	projecting point at the meeting of two curves in the ornamentation of a Gothic window, brace or arch
cusping	series of cusps in the design of a window or arch
frater	dining hall in a monastery
halving	carpentry joint where two timbers cross and are reduced in thickness where they are in contact and pegged together
jetty	overhang of the upper storey of a house, where it is cantilevered out above the storey below

Glossary

lap-joint	carpentry joint where the end of one timber overlaps the surface of another and they are pegged together
model book	a book of patterns for carvers, glaziers and other artists to copy
mortice	socket cut in a timber to receive the tenon (tongue) cut in the end of another timber, hence 'mortice-and-tenon' joint
ogee	shape for a pointed arch in which curves reverse direction, tapering to a sharp point at the top (an arch shape introduced $c.1300$)
parclose screen	an openwork screen in a church, usually marking off a side-chapel
reredos	closed screen behind an altar, forming a visual backdrop to the altar
retrochoir	space east of the choir and behind the high altar in a large church or cathedral
scantling	prescribed size of timbers for use as rafters or in a frame
sedilia	seats for priests alongside the altar in a church; often ornamented with canopies above
scribed lines	lines drawn with a sharp point so as to leave a scratch or other impression in the surface on which a drawing is being made, but without leaving ink or pigment
setting-out lines (or drawings)	often refer to marks on timber or stone to guide the cutting of the material, the fitting of parts, or the levelling of the structure; may also indicate a preliminary outline for a drawing, painting or carving
soffit	the underside of a beam or arch with the surface facing towards the floor
triforium	gallery or arches at 'first-floor level' in a large church; typically where there is a row of arches above the main arches of the nave or choir (there is often a passage along the building here at the level of the aisle roofs)
voussoirs	wedge-shaped stones which together form an arch

NOTES

I   STONE CARVERS: IDENTITIES AND DRAWINGS

1. Nikolaus Pevsner, *The Leaves of Southwell* (London: King Penguin, 1945).
2. Jean Givens, 'The leaves of Southwell revisited' in Jennifer S. Alexander (ed.), *Southwell and Nottinghamshire: Medieval Art, Architecture, and Industry*, BAACT 21 (1998) pp. 60-6.
3. Lawrence Stone, *The Pelican History of Art: Sculpture in Britain: the Middle Ages* (Harmondsworth: Penguin, 1955) pp. 140, 151, 168.
4. Norman Summers, *The Chapter House, Southwell Minster* (Derby: English Life Publications, 1984).
5. Medieval craftswomen include Margaret de Gunton, in 1319-20 responsible for the carpentry of a church roof in Norfolk (Chapter 4), and Agnes Ramsey, daughter of the master mason William Ramsey, who carried on the family business and in 1358-9 was paid £106 for making a monument to Queen Isabella. L.F. Salzman, *Building in England down to 1540* (Oxford: Clarendon Press, 1967) p. 71, mentions a woman dauber (plasterer) at Ripon in 1392 and notes a man in this trade who was helped by his daughter.
6. Nikolaus Pevsner (note 1 above), p. 30.
7. Pamela Z. Blum, 'The sculptures of the Salisbury chapter house' in Laurence Keen & Thomas Cocke (eds.), *Salisbury Cathedral: Medieval Art and Architecture*, BAACT 17 (1996) pp. 68, 76.
8. Nikolaus Pevsner (note 1 above) p. 49.
9. ibid, p. 37.
10. Jean Givens (note 2 above), p. 64.
11. ibid.
12. Robert W. Scheller, *Exemplum: model book drawings and the practice of artistic transmission, c.900-c.1470*, trans. Michael Hoyle (Amsterdam University Press, 1995).
13. Paul Williamson, *Gothic Sculpture, 1140-1300* (New Haven and London: Yale University Press, 1995) p. 4.
14. On visual thinking and drawing see Arnold Pacey, *Meaning in Technology* (Cambridge (Mass.): MIT Press, 1999) pp. 42-8.
15. Nikolaus Pevsner (note 1 above), p. 25.
16. Lawrence Stone (note 3 above), p. 151.
17. Jennifer S. Alexander, 'Southwell Minster Choir: the evidence of the masons' marks' in Jennifer S. Alexander (ed.), *Southwell and Nottinghamshire: Medieval Art, Architecture and Industry*, BAACT 21 (1998) pp. 44, 47.
18. ibid, p. 45.
19. R.H.C. Davies, 'A catalogue of masons' marks as an aid to architectural history', *JBAA*, 3rd series, 17 (1954) pp. 43-75; also W. Harry Rylands, 'Masons' marks', *Transactions of HSLC* 43-44 (1893), pp. 123-200.
20. Nicholas Dawton, 'Gothic sculpture' in Rosemary Horrox (ed.), *Beverley Minster: an Illustrated History* (Friends of Beverley Minster, 2000), pp. 113-114.
21. P.J.P. Goldberg, 'The Percy tomb in Beverley Minster', *Yorkshire Archaeological Journal* 56 (1984) pp. 65-74.
22. Nicholas Dawton, 'The Percy Tomb workshop' in Christopher Wilson (ed.), *Medieval Art and Architecture in the East Riding*, BAACT 9 (1989) pp. 121-132; also Nicholas Dawton, 'The medieval monuments', in Rosemary Horrox (note 20 above), pp. 133-144.
23. A.F. Leach (ed.), 'Memorials of Beverley Minster, the Chapter Act Book, vol. II', *Surtees Society* 108 (1903), pp. 114, 124.

24. M.R. Petch. 'William de Malton, Master Mason', *Yorkshire Archaeological Journal* 53 (1981), pp. 37-44.
25. David O'Connor, 'The medieval stained glass of Beverley Minster' in Christopher Wilson (ed.), *Medieval Art and Architecture in the East Riding*, BAACT 9 (1989), pp. 62, 69.
26. Jennifer Alexander, 'Masons' marks and stone bonding' in Tim Tatton-Brown and Julian Munby, *The Archaeology of Cathedrals*, Oxford University Committee for Archaeology, Monograph 42 (1996), pp. 219-236, especially pp. 232-3.
27. Norman Summers (note 4 above), plate 30, p. 16.
28. Nicola Coldstream, *The Decorated Style* (University of Toronto Press, 1994), p. 101.
29. Günther Binding, *Medieval Building Techniques*, translated by Alex Cameron (Stroud: Tempus, 2001), pp.79-80.
30. David Carpenter, 'Westminster Abbey: some characteristics of its sculpture', *JBAA*, 3rd series, 35 (1972), pp. 1-14.
31. John Harvey, *English Medieval Architects* (revised edn, Stroud: Alan Sutton, 1984), appendix 1, p. 375.
32. Warwick Rodwell, *Wells Cathedral: excavation and structural studies, 1978-93* (Swindon: English Heritage, 2 vols., 2001),Vol. 1, pp. 176-7.
33. L.S. Colchester and J.H. Harvey, 'Wells Cathedral', *Archaeological Journal* 131 (1974), pp. 200-214.
34. Jerry Sampson, *Wells Cathedral West Front* (Stroud: Sutton Publishing, 1998), pp. 49-50.
35. L.S. Colchester (ed.), *Wells Cathedral: a History* (Shepton Mallet: Open Books, 1982), pp. 62-4, 99.
36. L.S. Colchester and J.H. Harvey (note 33 above), p. 204.
37. Paul Williamson (note 13 above), p. 106, implies that one of the Bristol heads is related to the one in the nave at Wells, but also sees a close similarity with a head in the lady chapel at Glastonbury Abbey.
38. Jerry Sampson (note 36 above), p. 82.
39. ibid, pp. 101-2.
40. ibid, pp. 99-100.
41. L.F. Salzman, *Building in England down to 1540* (Oxford: Clarendon Press, 1967), p. 32.

2 EARLY ARCHITECTURAL DRAWING

1. G.G. Coulton, *Art and the Reformation* (Oxford: Blackwell, 1928), pp. 178-9.
2. James S. Ackerman, *The Reinvention of Architectural Drawing, 1250-1550 (the 3rd Soane Lecture)* (London: Sir John Soane's Museum, 1998).
3. Robert Branner, 'Villard de Honnecourt, Reims, and the origins of Gothic architectural drawing', in Lynn T. Courtenay (ed.), *The Engineering of Medieval Cathedrals* (Aldershot: Ashgate, 1997), pp. 63-80 (reprinted from *Gazette des Beaux-Arts*, 1963, pp. 129-146). The 'lodge book' of Villard de Honnecourt is extensively reproduced by Francois Bucher, *Architector: the Lodge Books and Sketchbooks of Medieval Architects*,Vol. 1 (New York: Abaris, 1979).
4. A full account of the drawings at Clermont Cathedral is given by Michael T. Davis, 'On the drawing board', in Nancy Y. Wu (ed.), *Ad Quadratum: the Practical Application of Geometry in Medieval Architecture* (Aldershot: Ashgate, 2002), pp. 183-204.
5. Jennifer Alexander, 'Masons' marks and stone bonding', in Tim Tatton-Brown and Julian Munby (eds.), *The Archaeology of Cathedrals* (Oxford University Committee for Archaeology, 1996), pp. 219-236, especially p. 227.
6. Stuart Harrison and Paul Barker, 'Byland Abbey... the west front and rose window reconstructed', *JBAA* 140 (1987), pp. 134-151.
7. Kirsty Rodwell and Robert Bell, *Acton Court: the evolution of an early Tudor courtier's house* (London: English Heritage, 2004), pp. 271-5.
8. John Crook, 'New light on the history of St Mary's Church, Old Basing, Hampshire: an incised design', *JBAA* 154 (2001), pp. 92-132.

9. Stuart Harrison and Paul Barker (note 6 above). The date usually given for the west front of the abbey is in the 1190s, but the impression can be gained that the rose window itself was designed somewhat later.
10. D.H. Heslop (with contributions by Stuart Harrison), 'Excavations within the church at the Augustinian Priory of Gisborough, Cleveland', *Yorkshire Archaeological Journal* 67 (1995), pp. 51-126.
11. John Harvey, *Medieval Craftsmen* (London: Batsford, 1975), p. 120.
12. Stuart Harrison, 'Kirkstall Abbey: The 12th-century tracery and rose window' in Lawrence R. Hoey (ed.), *Yorkshire Monasticism*, BAACT 16 (1995), pp. 73-8.
13. David Lewer and Robert Dark, *The Temple Church in London* (London Historical Publications, 1997), p. 124.
14. Jean Bony, 'The stonework planning of the first Durham master', in Lynn T. Courtenay (ed.), *The Engineering of Medieval Cathedrals* (Aldershot: Ashgate, 1997), pp. 117, 129.
15. L.F. Salzman, *Building in England down to 1540* (Oxford: Clarendon Press, 1967), pp. 20-1.
16. Jennifer Alexander (note 5 above), p. 227.
17. The slab is now in the University of Cambridge Museum of Archaeology and Anthropology, accession number Z 15088, and a photograph has been published by Malcolm Hislop, *Medieval Masons* (Princes Risborough: Shire, 2000), p. 22. I am much indebted to Anne Taylor of the museum for information about the stone and a photograph.
18. John Crook (note 8 above), p. 129.
19. John Maddison, *Ely Cathedral: Design and Meaning* (Ely Cathedral Publications, 2000), pp. 56-7.
20. Nikolaus Pevsner, *BOE Bedfordshire, Huntingdon and Peterborough* (Harmondsworth: Penguin, 1968), p. 108. The church is All Saints, Leighton Linslade.
21. Violet Pritchard, *English Medieval Graffiti* (Cambridge University Press, 1967); also Doris Jones-Baker, 'English medieval graffiti', *The Local Historian* 23 (1) (February 1993), pp. 4-19.
22. Authors who have written about St Mary's Church, Ashwell include Walter Millard, 'The Church of St Mary, Ashwell', *Journal of the RIBA*, 3rd series, 19 (1911-12), pp. 17-21; RCHME, *Inventory of the Historical Monuments of Hertfordshire* (London: HMSO, 1910), pp. 38-40; Reginald Hine, *Relics of an Un-Common Attorney* (London: Dent, 1951), p. 208; David Sherlock, *Ashwell Church: Medieval drawings and writings* (Ashwell Parish Church, 1978).
23. Audrey Erskine, Vyvyan Hope and John Lloyd, *Exeter Cathedral: a short history* (Exeter Cathedral, 1988), p. 45; John Harvey (note 11 above), p. 116.
24. L.F. Salzman (note 15 above), pp. 20-1.
25. Use of lampblack for this purpose is mentioned by John Harvey (note 11 above) p. 120.
26. Arnold Pacey, 'The tracing floor and masons' loft at York Minster'. Report for York Minster Works Office with contributions by Alison Armstrong, 2003, based on a study of 2001.
27. John Harvey (note 11 above), p. 64.
28. L.F. Salzman (note 15 above), p. 178.
29. Louise Cochrane, *Adelard of Bath: the first English scientist* (London: British Museum Press, 1994), p. 64.
30. John Harvey (note 11 above), p. 77.
31. L.S. Colchester and J.H. Harvey, 'Wells Cathedral', *Archaeological Journal* 131 (1974), pp. 200-214, especially p. 214.
32. John Maddison (note 19 above), p. 56.
33. John Maddison, 'Master masons of the Diocese of Lichfield', *Transactions of the Lancashire and Cheshire Antiquarian Society* 85 (1988) pp. 107-72.
34. R.A. Brown, H.M. Colvin and R.A. Taylor, *The History of the King's Works, vols. 1-2, The Middle Ages*, Vol. 1 (London: HMSO, 1963), p. 254. The contract is quoted in full by L.F. Salzman (note 15 above), pp. 439-41.
35. Tim Tatton-Brown, 'Building the tower and spire of Salisbury Cathedral', in Lynn T. Courten (ed.), *The Engineering of Medieval Cathedrals* (Aldershot: Ashgate, 1997); on how 'the lines of the spire were laid out', see p. 348.

36. Stuart Harrison and Paul Barker (note 6 above), pp. 141-2.
37. Alexander Holton, 'The working space of the medieval master mason: the tracing houses of York Minster and Wells Cathedral', *Proceedings of the Second International Construction History Congress* (London: Construction History Society, 2006), pp. 1579-97.
38. The complicated series of design changes made while the chapter-house complex was under construction is described by Sarah Brown, *York Minster: an Architectural History, c.1220-1500* (Swindon: English Heritage, 2003), pp. 66-71.
39. John Harvey, 'The tracing floor of York Minster', *Friends of York Minster, Annual Report* 40 (1968), pp. 1-8. Reprinted in Lynn T. Courtenay (ed.), *The Engineering of Medieval Cathedrals* (Aldershot: Ashgate, 1997), pp. 81-6; but Harvey did not envisage the use of chalk or charcoal for drawing on the tracing floor.
40. L.F. Salzman (note 15 above), pp. 155-6.
41. M.W. Barley, *The English Farmhouse and Cottage* (London: Routledge, 1961), p. 83.
42. L.S. Colchester and John Harvey (note 31 above), p. 214 and note.
43. Alexander Holton (note 37 above), p. 1586.
44. R.A. Brown, H.M. Colvin and A.J. Taylor (note 34 above), Vol. 2, p. 759.
45. L.F. Salzman (note 15 above), p. 156.
46. John Harvey (note 11 above), pp. 145-6.
47. R.A. Brown, H.M. Colvin and A.J. Taylor (note 34 above), Vol. 2, p. 689.
48. Nikolaus Pevsner, *BOE Yorkshire: The West Riding* (2nd edn, revised Enid Radcliffe, 1967), p. 298.
49. R.A. Brown, H.M. Colvin and A.J. Taylor (note 34 above), Vol. 2, p. 689.
50. ibid; also Sarah Brown (note 38 above), p. 117.
51. Alexander Holton (note 37 above), p. 1586. Examination of masons' tooling visible on fragments of stone in the rubble tends to confirm the point, as reported in Arnold Pacey (note 26 above), pp. 1-2.
52. Laboratory examination (but not chemical analysis) by Alison Armstrong, reported in Arnold Pacey (note 26 above), pp. 1-3.
53. John Harvey (note 11 above), pp. 145-6.
54. A basic description and plan of the Wells tracing floor is given in L.S. Colchester and J.H. Harvey (note 31 above), pp. 212-14.
55. Warwick Rodwell, *Wells Cathedral: Excavation and Structural Studies* 1 (London: English Heritage, 2 vols., 2001), pp. 141, 146 gives dates for the porch, but alterations to roofs and parapets are more fully examined by Cecil A. Hewett, *English Cathedral and Monastic Carpentry* (Chichester: Phillimore, 1985), pp. 205-7.
56. L.S. Colchester (ed.), *Wells Cathedral: A History* (Shepton Mallet: Open Books, 1982), pp. 81-9.
57. John Harvey (note 39 above), p. 8. Reprinted in Lynn T. Courtenay (ed.), *The Engineering of Medieval Cathedrals* (Aldershot: Ashgate, 1997), p. 85.
58. ibid, p. 6; in reprinted version, p. 83.

3 GEOMETRY IN MEDIEVAL DRAWING

1. For studies of building plans in relation to the geometry of the square, see Nancy Y. Wu (ed.), *Ad Quadratum: the Practical Application of Geometry in Medieval Architecture* (Aldershot: Ashgate, 2002); for emphasis on the geometry of the circle, see Painton Cowen, *The Rose Window: Splendour and Symbol* (London: Thames & Hudson, 2005), pp. 241-257.
2. Trinity College, Cambridge, Ms. R.17.1, f 284v/285.
3. John Newman, *BOE, North East and East Kent* (Harmondsworth: Penguin 1969), p.208.
4. L.F. Salzman, *Building in England down to 1540* (Oxford: Clarendon Press, 1967), p. 20; also Newman (note 3 above), p. 175.
5. Robert Branner, 'Villard de Honnecourt, Reims, and the origin of Gothic architectural drawing', in Lynn T. Courenay (ed.), *The Engineering of Medieval Cathedrals* (Aldershot: Ashgate, 1997), pp. 64-5.
6. John James, *The Template-makers of the Paris Basin* (West Grinstead Publishing, 1989), p. 34.

7. James S. Ackerman, *The Reinvention of Architectural Drawing, 1250-1550* (London: Sir John Soane's Museum (the 3rd Soane Lecture), 1998), pp. 7-8.
8. ibid; also Klára Benešovská and Ivo Hlobil, *Peter Parler and St Vitus's Cathedral* (Prague Castle Administration, 1999), p. 10.
9. Jerry Sampson, *Wells Cathedral West Front* (Stroud: Sutton Publishing, 1998), p. 142.
10. John Maddison, *Ely Cathedral: Meaning and Design* (Ely Cathedral Publications, 2000), pp. 15-16.
11. Roberta Gilchrist, *Norwich Cathedral Close* (Woodbridge: Boydell Press, 2005), p. 38.
12. Eric Fernie, 'The ground plan of Norwich Cathedral and the square root of two', *JBAA* 129 (1976), pp. 77-86. This paper is further discussed in Nancy Y. Wu (note 1 above), pp. 1-10, 83-121.
13. Nigel Hiscock, 'A schematic plan for Norwich Cathedral' in Nancy Y. Wu (note 1 above), pp. 98-100.
14. Christopher Norton, 'The design and construction of the Romanesque Church of St Mary's Abbey, York', *Yorkshire Archaeological Journal* 71 (1999), pp.73-88.
15. For a simple explanation of *ad quadratum* design see Malcolm Hislop, *Medieval Masons* (Prince's Risborough: Shire, 2000), pp. 16-20.
16. Various standards for the foot length are separately discussed by Ellen M. Shortell and Stephen Murray in Nancy Y. Wu (note 1 above), pp. 127-8, 171-2. For the foot used at Notre Dame, see Painton Cowen (note 1 above), p. 258.
17. Christopher Norton (note 14 above), pp. 83-5.
18. Jerry Sampson (note 9 above), pp. 136-8.
19. Christopher Wilson, *The Gothic Cathedral: the architecture of the Great Church, 1150-1530* (London: Thames & Hudson, 1990), p. 172.
20. L.S. Colchester and J.H. Harvey, 'Wells Cathedral ... Appendix: the Wells Tracing Floor', *Archaeological Journal* 131 (1974), p. 214.
21. L.S. Colchester, *Wells Cathedral* (London: Unwin Hyman, 1987), pp. 59-61. My own measurements of the drawings on the tracing floor were made in September 2001 and my studies of windows in the Vicars' Close and the cloister a year later.
22. Warwick Rodwell, *Wells Cathedral: Excavation and Structural Studies, 1978-93* Vol. 1 (Swindon: English Heritage, 2 vols., 2001), pp. 245-50.
23. John Harvey, 'The building of Wells Cathedral' in L.S. Colchester (ed.), *Wells Cathedral: a History* (Shepton Mallett: Open Books, 1982), pp. 92-4.
24. Audrey Erskine, Vyvyan Hope and John Lloyd, *Exeter Cathedral: a Short History* (Exeter, 1988), pp. 45, 47, 49.
25. James S. Ackerman (note 7 above), pp. 7-8.
26. Nigel Hiscock (note 13 above), p. 100.
27. John Harvey, *English Medieval Architects* (London: Batsford, 1954; revised edn, Stroud: Alan Sutton, 1984).
28. Adrian Hastings, *Elias of Dereham: Architect of Salisbury Cathedral* (Dean & Chapter of Salisbury, 1997), pp. 6-10.
29. Tim Ayers (ed.), *Salisbury Cathedral: the West Front* (Chichester: Phillimore, 2000), pp. 14-15.
30. Virginia Jansen, 'Salisbury Cathedral and the episcopal style of the early thirteenth century', in Laurence Keen and Thomas Cocke (eds), *Salisbury Cathedral: Medieval Art and Architecture*, BAACT 17 (1996), pp. 32, 36.
31. Jerry Sampson (note 9 above), p. 142.
32. Frederick Stallard with Paul Bush, *The Geometric Skeleton of Peterborough Cathedral* (Glossop: Paul Bush, 1994).
33. R.A. Brown, H.M. Colvin, and A.J. Taylor, *The History of the King's Works* (London: HMSO, vol. 1, 1963), p. 153.
34. Eric Fernie, 'The Romanesque church of Selby Abbey' in Lawrence R. Hoey (ed.), *Yorkshire Monasticism*, BAACT 16 (1995), pp. 40-9.
35. B.G. Morgan, *Canonic Design in English Medieval Architecture* (Liverpool University Press, 1961).
36. J.S. Ackerman, 'Ars sine scientia nihil est': Gothic theory of architecture at the Cathedral of Milan', *Art Bulletin* 31 (1949), pp. 84-111.

Notes

37. Jon Cannon, 'The absent figure: on authorship and meaning in the fourteenth-century eastern arm of St Augustine's Bristol', *AMS Transactions* 48 (2004), pp. 21-48.
38. ibid, pp. 32-3.
39. Nikolaus Pevsner, *BOE, Herefordshire* (Harmondsworth: Penguin, 1963), pp. 34, 247.
40. Nicola Coldstream, *The Decorated Style: Architecture and Ornament, 1240-1320* (University of Toronto Press, 1994), pp. 71, 144-5, 173-4.
41. Veronica Sekiles, 'A group of masons in early fourteenth-century Lincolnshire' in F.H. Thompson (ed.), *Studies in Medieval Sculpture* (London: Society of Antiquaries, 1983), pp. 151-164. See also W.D. Wilson, 'The work of the Heckington lodge of masons', *Lincolnshire History and Archaeology* 15 (1980), pp. 21-7.
42. Many medieval illustrations of compasses being handled by masons are cited (and often reproduced) by Günther Binding, *Medieval Building Techniques,* trans. Alex Cameron (Stroud: Tempus, 2001).
43. Jennifer Alexander has classified the many small drawings in buildings in a different but complementary manner, pointing out the significance they had for the mainly non-literate community that produced them; Jennifer Alexander, 'Masons' marks and stone bonding' in Tim Tatton-Brown and Julian Munby (eds), *The Archaeology of Cathedrals* (Oxford University Committee for Archaeology, 1996), pp. 219-236.
44. Erskine, Hope and Lloyd (note 24 above), p. 34.
45. Audrey M. Erskine (ed.), 'The accounts of the fabric of Exeter Cathedral, 1279-1326', *Devon and Cornwall Record Society*, new series 24 (1981), p. 202.
46. E.W. Tristram, *English Wall-painting of the Fourteenth century* (London: Routledge, 1950), pp. 27-8, 93, 95, 99, 107.
47. Caroline Babington, Tracy Manning, and Sophie Stewart, *Our Painted Past: Wall Paintings of English Heritage* (London: English Heritage, 1999), pp. 58-9.
48. E. Clive Rouse and Audrey Baker, 'The wall paintings at Longthorpe Tower near Peterborough', *Archaeologia* 96 (1955), pp. 1-57.
49. RCHME, Record of the spiral drawing at Wells, National Monuments Record, photograph no. BB70/7430.
50. Fieldwork at St Mary's Church, Ashwell, August 1977, July 2000 and April 2001. I am indebted to the rector (Rev. Jacqui Birdseye) and verger for facilitating the third visit, and to Pamela Maryfield for help with interpretation.
51. Reginald L. Hine, *Relics of an Un-common Attorney* (London: Dent, 1951), p. 213.
52. Colin Platt, *King Death: the Black Death and its aftermath in late-medieval England* (London: UCL Press, 1997), p.3.
53. Timothy Easton, 'Ritual marks on historic timber', Weald & Downland Open Air Museum, Spring Magazine 1999, pp. 22-8.
54. Reginald L. Hine (note 51 above), pp. 206-15; additional insights have been gleaned from Reginald Hine's papers held by the Society of Antiquaries, London, and from David Sherlock, *Medieval Drawings and Writings in Ashwell Church* (Ashwell Parish Church, 1978), p. 8.
55. Mary Nattrass, 'Witch posts and early dwellings in Cleveland', *Yorkshire Archaeological Journal* 39 (1956-58), pp. 136-146.
56. For the date of the Peterborough ceiling, see Ian Tyers and Cathy Groves, 'Tree ring dates ... Peterborough', *VA* 31 (2000), pp. 119; and *VA* 32 (2001), pp. 87-8; Paul Bush, *The Painted Ceiling of Peterborough Cathedral* (Glossop: Bush, 1997).
57. Günther Binding (note 42 above), pp. 53, 77. John Harvey (note 27 above) discusses the identity of Richard of Gainsborough at greater length, p. 113.
58. A survey of this sort was initially made in 1970 (Arnold Pacey, *The Maze of Ingenuity* (London: Allen Lane, 1974), fig. 13, p. 82). Repeating it with the extra resources provided by Binding (note 42 above), a similar selection of instruments is found.
59. Lawrence R. Hoey (note 34), p. 108.

4 CARPENTERS' MARKINGS

1. John Fitchen, *The Construction of Gothic Cathedrals: a Study of Medieval Vault Erection* (London: Oxford University Press, 1961).
2. Cecil A. Hewett, *English Cathedral and Monastic Carpentry* (Chichester: Phillimore, 1985), pp. 88, 113.
3. Edward Roberts, *Hampshire Houses, 1250-1700: their Dating and Development* (Hampshire County Council, 2003), pp. 7-8. Further information on the career of Thomas of Witney is from John Harvey, *English Medieval Architects* (revised edn, Stroud: Alan Sutton, 1984), pp. 338-41; and from Richard K. Morris, 'Thomas of Witney at Exeter, Wells and Winchester' in Francis Kelly (ed.), *Medieval Art and Architecture at Exeter Cathedral*, BAACT 11 (1991), pp. 57-84.
4. J.M. Fletcher and P.S. Spokes, 'Origins and development of crown-post roofs', *Medieval Archaeology* 8 (1964), pp. 152-83.
5. Cecil A. Hewett (note 2 above), p. 88.
6. John Harvey, 'The building of Wells Cathedral' in L.S. Colchester (ed.), *Wells Cathedral: a History* (Shepton Mallet: Open Books, 1982), p. 86; Cecil Hewett (note 2 above), pp. 6, 11-12, 85.
7. Sarah Brown, *York Minster: an Architectural History, c.1220-1500* (Swindon: English Heritage, 2003), pp. 294-7.
8. R.R. Laxton, C.D. Litton, and R.E. Howard, 'Dendrochronology of roof timbers in Lincoln Cathedral', *English Heritage Research Transactions* 7 (2001), p. 40.
9. Mortice-and-tenon joints were used by Roman carpenters, but had to be reintroduced during the Middle Ages. In England, their use has been demonstrated from c.1180, e.g. in a series of aisled halls and barns. See John Walker, 'Late twelfth and early thirteenth century aisled buildings', *VA* 30, (1999), pp. 21-53.
10. John Harvey, *Medieval Craftsmen* (London: Batsford, 1975), pp. 198-9. Nikolaus Pevsner and Bill Wilson note that the church at Caister was re-roofed in 1330 'under a famous contract', but the roof was replaced again in 1785. *BOE Norfolk (1): Norwich and the North East* (Harmondsworth: Penguin, 2nd edn, 1997), p. 424.
11. There are three contracts altogether: two dated 1319 for St Margaret's Church, Norton (Norton Subcourse), and one of 1330 for Holy Trinity, Caister. John Harvey (note 10 above), pp. 199-200.
12. ibid.
13. Daniel Miles, 'Analysis of an archaic roof at Wistanstow, Shropshire', *VA* 28 (1997), pp. 105-6.
14. Adrian V.B. Gibson, 'Constructive geometry in the design of the 13th-century barns at Cressing Temple', *Essex History and Archaeology* 25 (1994), pp. 107-112; continued in 27 (1996), pp. 182-6.
15. Laurie Smith, 'The geometrical designer at Cressing Temple', *Essex History and Archaeology* 27 (1996), pp. 190-2.
16. D. Andrews, A. Gibson, T. Robey, P. Ryan and M.C. Wadhams, *Cressing Temple: A Guide* (Essex County Council, 1997), p. 12.
17. Laurie Smith (note 15 above), pp. 191-2.
18. D.W.H. Miles and Henry Russell, 'Plumb and level marks', *VA* 26 (1995), pp. 33-8.
19. I am indebted to Brenda Watkin for checking my drawing of Water Hall; for more details of this house, see Vernacular Architecture Group, *Essex: Spring 2003* (conference handbook), p. 4.6.
20. Nikolaus Pevsner and Edward Hubbard, *BOE Cheshire* (Harmondsworth: Penguin, 1971), p. 227.
21. For 'position marks' on medieval stonework see G.G. Coulton, *Art and the Reformation* (Oxford: Blackwell, 1928), pp. 160, 162. For similar marks on timber the best introduction is Richard Harris, *Discovering Timber-framed Buildings* (Prince's Risborough: Shire Publications, 1978, 3rd edn, 1993), p. 15.
22. Christa Grössinger, *The World Upside-down: English Misericords* (London: Harvey Miller, 1997), pp. 23-4.

Notes

23. Timothy Easton, 'Ritual Marks on Historic Timber', Weald and Downland Open Air Museum, Spring Magazine 1999, pp. 22-28.
24. Audrey Erskine, Vyvyan Hope and John Lloyd, *Exeter Cathedral: a short history* (Exeter Cathedral, 1988), p. 34.
25. Charles Tracy, *English Gothic Choir Stalls, 1200-1400* (Woodbridge: Boydell Press, 1988), p. 27; Christa Grössinger (note 22 above), p. 23.
26. Christa Grössinger (note 22 above), pp. 40-2.
27. Charles Tracy (note 25 above), pp. 32-3.
28. Christa Grössinger (note 22 above), pp. 42-3.
29. D.W.H. Miles and Henry Russell (note 18 above).
30. For other insights into the use of the saw and axe in conversion of timber, see J.C. Kirk, 'Butts Cottage ... Conversion of trees to timber in the rural Sussex Weald', *VA* 35 (2004), pp. 12-20.
31. John McCann, 'Carpenters' assembly marks' in Paul Oliver (ed.), *Encyclopedia of Vernacular Architecture of the World* Vol. 1 (Cambridge University Press, 3 volumes, 1997), pp. 520-1; also, John McCann, 'Reading the timber', *Period Home,* Vol. 2, no. 4 (December/January 1981-2), pp. 23-4.
32. Gustav Milne, 'Timber Building Techniques in London, *c.*900-1400', *London and Middlesex Archaeological Society, Special Paper 15* (1992), pp. 34-5.
33. Several examples are illustrated without comment by R.R. Laxton, C.D. Litton, and R.E. Howard (note 8 above).
34. D.W.H. Miles, *The Tree-ring Dating of the Roof Carpentry of the Eastern Chapels, North Nave Triforium and North Porch, Salisbury Cathedral,* English Heritage Centre for Archaeology, Report 94 (2002), pp. 40, 43.
35. Dan Miles, 'Irish oaks and Arabic numerals', *Current Archaeology* 188 (October 2003), pp. 368-9.
36. Jerry Sampson, *Wells Cathedral West Front: Sculpture and Conservation* (Stroud: Sutton Publishing, 1998), pp. 53, 98; J.T. Irvine, 'Memorandum relative to the Arabic numerals ... in the west front at Wells', *Proceedings, Somersetshire Archaeology and Natural History Society* 34, part (i) (1888), pp. 62-3
37. Adrian Hastings, *Elias of Dereham: architect of Salisbury Cathedral* (Dean & Chapter of Salisbury, 1997), p. 22; also John Harvey, *English Medieval Architects* (revised edn, Stroud: Sutton Publishing, 1984), pp. 83-4.
38. Louise Cochrane, *Adelard of Bath: the first English Scientist* (London: British Museum Press, 1994).
39. L.S. Colchester (note 6 above), p. 111.
40. Jane Penoyre, *Traditional Houses of Somerset* (Tiverton: Somerset Books, 2005), fig. 6.5, p. 122.
41. W.D. Peckham, 'Sutton Rectory', *Sussex Archaeological Collections* 65 (1924), pp. 54-68.
42. Recorded by RCHME and quoted by Charlotte Bradbear and Stephen Croad, 'Emergency recording ... Gloucestershire', *AMS Transactions* 43 (1999), pp. 127-8.
43. Cecil Hewett (note 2 above), pp. 108-110.
44. Edward Roberts, 'A thirteenth-century king-post roof at Winchester, Hampshire', *VA* 27 (1996), pp. 65-8.
45. Sarah Brown (note 7 above), fig. 2.28, p. 68, illustrating timbers on which paired circles can be seen.
46. Information from John McCann and Beth Davies, to whom I am very grateful. See John McCann, 'Reading the timber', *Period Home,* Vol. 2, no. 4 (December/January, 1981-2), pp. 23-4. For the roof carpentry, see Cecil Hewett (note 2 above), p. 230; and N.W. Alcock, 'Bushmead Priory, Bedfordshire: a thirteenth-century hall and roof', *JBAA,* 3rd series 33 (1970), pp. 50-6.
47. For a house at Elstow with a similar carpenter's mark see John Bailey, 'The development of medieval buildings adjoining the abbey at Elstow', *Bedfordshire Archaeology* 24 (2001), especially p. 66.
48. Sarah Brown (note 7 above), pp. 116-17.

49. J.T. Smith, 'The early development of timber-framed buildings', *Archaeological Journal* 131 (1974), especially pp. 238, 245-6.
50. Laurie Smith (note 15 above), pp. 190-2.
51. Cecil Hewett (note 2 above), pp. 118-119.
52. John Maddison, *Ely Cathedral: Design and Meaning* (Ely Cathedral Publications, 2000), pp. 65, 70.
53. ibid, pp. 69-70, discussing Hewett's analysis.
54. R.A. Brown, H.M. Colvin and A.J. Taylor, *The History of the King's Works*, Vol. 1 (London: HMSO, 1963), pp. 529-30
55. Lynn T. Courtenay, 'The Westminster Hall roof and its 14th-century sources', *JSAH* 43 (1984), pp. 295-309; Lynn T. Courtenay and R. Mark, 'The Westminster Hall roof: a historiographic and structural study', *JSAH* 46 (1987), pp. 374-93.
56. Cecil A. Hewett, *English Historic Carpentry* (Chichester: Phillimore, 1980), pp. 188, 203-4.
57. Gene Waddell, 'The design of Westminster Hall roof', *Architectural History* 42, 199, pp. 47-67.
58. Lynn T. Courtenay, 'The Westminster Hall roof: a new archaeological source', *JBAA* 143 (1990), pp. 95-107.
59. Part of a wall post from Westminster Hall now in the Museum of London clearly shows the numeral XII (with a tag) in two places, and less clearly in a third. I am much indebted to John Clark of the museum for access to this timber and for his comments.

5 LATER MEDIEVAL ARCHITECTURAL DRAWINGS

1. L.F. Salzman, *Building in England down to 1540* (Oxford, Clarendon Press, 1967), p. 15; also Philip Lindley, 'The commissioning process' in Richard Marks and Paul Williamson (eds), *Gothic: Art for England 1400-1547* (London: V&A Publications, 2003), pp. 89-91.
2. Walter H. Godfrey, 'An Elizabethan builder's contract', *Sussex Archaeological Collections* 65 (1924), pp. 212-223.
3. John H. Harvey, *Henry Yevele, c.1320-1400: the Life of an English Architect* (London: Batsford, 1944), pp. 39, 72-3.
4. William Worcestre, *Itineraries*, edited from the MS. at Corpus Christi College, Cambridge, by John Harvey (Oxford: Clarendon Press, 1969), pp. xvii, 59n, 116-17, 239.
5. ibid, p. 289.
6. Eric C. Fernie, 'Introduction' in Nancy C. Wu (ed.), *Ad Quadratum: the Practical Application of Geometry in Medieval Architecture* (Aldershot: Ashgate, 2002), p. 3.
7. The contract is reproduced by L.F. Salzman (note 1 above), pp. 430-2.
8. William Worcestre (note 4 above), pp. 131, 313-317.
9. Andrew Foyle, *Bristol*, Pevsner Architectural Guides (New Haven and London: Yale University Press, 2004), p. 111.
10. David Verey and Alan Brooks, *BOE Gloucestershire, 2: The Vale and the Forest of Dean* (New Haven and London: Yale University Press, 2002), p. 432. I am also indebted to Kirsty Rodwell for information about this example.
11. David Welander, *The History, Art and Architecture of Gloucester Cathedral* (Stroud: Alan Sutton, 1991), pp. 266, 274-5; also appendix 8, pp. 563-6.
12. R.H.D. Short, 'Graffiti on the reredos of the lady chapel of Gloucester Cathedral', *Transactions of the Bristol and Gloucestershire Archaeological Society* 67 (1946-7), pp. 21-36.
13. John Harvey, *English Medieval Architects* (revised edn, Stroud: Alan Sutton, 1984), p. 146.
14. L.F. Salzman (note 1 above), pp. 126-7; also Jennifer Alexander, 'Masons' marks and stone bonding' in Tim Tatton-Brown and Julian Munby (eds), *The Archaeology of Cathedrals* (Oxford University Committee for Archaeology, 1996), pp. 219-236
15. An example of a drawing on vellum is a design for a canopied funerary monument, possibly intended for erection in the Henry VII Chapel, Westminster Abbey, and attributed to William Vertue, *c.*1515. British Library, London, MS. Cotton, Augustus II 1. Illustrated and discussed in Richard Marks and Paul Williamson (note 1 above), pp. 88, 166-7.
16. Pepysian Library, MS. PL 1916, Magdalene College, Cambridge.

17. M.R. James, 'An English medieval sketchbook, no. 1916 in the Pepysian Library', *Walpole Society* 13 (1924-25), pp. 1-17
18. Christa Grössinger, *The World Upside Down: English Misericords* (London: Harvey Miller, 1997), pp. 58, 64; see also Robert W. Scheller, *Exemplum: Model-Book Drawings and the Practice of Artistic Transmission*, trans. Michael Hoyle (Amsterdam University Press, 1995), pp. 201-8.
19. M.R. James (note 17 above); also John H. Harvey (note 3 above), p. 14 and figs 12, 13, and 14.
20. M.R. James (note 17 above), folio 17b, width 5ins (127mm), 'drawn with a dry point'.
21. Nikolaus Pevsner, *BOE Bedfordshire, Huntingdon and Peterborough* (Harmondsworth: Penguin, 1968), p. 108.
22. The slab is now in the University of Cambridge Museum of Archaeology and Anthropology, accession number Z 15088; a photograph has been published by Malcolm Hislop, *Medieval Masons* (Prince's Risborough: Shire, 2000), p. 22. The slab has also been illustrated by G.G. Coulton, *Art and the Reformation* (Oxford: Blackwell, 1928), p. 178 (reprinted Cambridge University Press, 1958).
23. John Crook, 'New light on the history of St Mary's Church, Old Basing, Hampshire: an incised design', *JBAA* 154 (2001), pp. 92-132; the drawing at Christchurch is discussed on pp. 127-9.
24. W.D. Wilson, 'The work of the Heckington lodge of masons, 1315-1345', *Lincolnshire History and Archaeology* 15 (1980), pp. 21-8, especially p. 27.
25. Nikolaus Pevsner and John Harris, *BOE Lincolnshire* (Harmondsworth: Penguin, 1964), plate 28 and p. 660.
26. G.G. Coulton (note 22 above), p. 179; M. Pavitt, *Medieval and Other Graffiti* (Gamlingay: Friends of St Mary's, 1998), p. 4; Reginald L. Hine, *Relics of an Un-Common Attorney* (London: Dent, 1951) mentions the Gamlingay drawing, p. 213, and Hine's rubbing of it is among his papers held by the Society of Antiquaries, Burlington House, London, Boxes 788/1-3.
27. John Crook (note 23 above), pp. 120, 124.
28. J.H. Harvey, 'The tracing floor of York Minster', *Friends of York Minster, 40th Annual Report* (1968), pp. 1-8; reprinted in Lynn T. Courtenay (ed.), *The Engineering of Medieval Cathedrals* (Ashgate, Aldershot, 1997), pp. 81-6.
29. Arnold Pacey, 'The tracing floor and masons' loft at York Minster'. Report for York Minster Works Office with contributions by Alison Armstrong, 2003, pp. 2-3.
30. RCHME, *An Inventory of the Historical Monuments of the City of York, Volume V, the Central Area* (London: HMSO, 1981), pp. 36-40 and Plate 27.
31. Illustrations are provided in Arnold Pacey (note 29 above), figs 17, 18.
32. John Bilson, 'St Mary's Church, Beverley', *Yorkshire Archaeological Journal* 25 (1920), pp. 357-425.
33. John Harvey, *English Medieval Architects* (revised edn, Stroud: Alan Sutton, 1984), p. 110.
34. John Bilson (note 32 above), pp. 415-16.
35. John Harvey (note 33 above).
36. L.F. Salzman (note 1 above), p. 342; for Knaresborough, see R.A. Brown, H.M. Colvin and R.A. Taylor, *The History of the King's Works, vols. 1-2, The Middle Ages*, Vol. 2 (London: HMSO, 1963), pp. 687-9.
37. Jennifer S. Alexander, 'Southwell Minster Choir: the evidence of the masons' marks', in Jennifer S. Alexander (ed.), *Southwell and Nottinghamshire: Medieval Art, Architecture and Industry*, BAACT 21 (1998), pp. 44-59.
38. Kirsty Rodwell and Robert Bell, *Acton Court: the Evolution of an early Tudor Courtier's House* (London: English Heritage, 2004), especially pp. 170-3, 271-8.
39. ibid, pp. 9-11, 26, 125-6.
40. ibid, pp. 170-3.
41. Malcolm Airs, *The Tudor and Jacobean Country House* (Stroud: Alan Sutton, 1995), p. 91.
42. Kirsty Rodwell and Robert Bell (note 38 above), pp. 274-8.
43. ibid, quoting Ian Friel, pp. 275-6; also A.B. Emden, 'Graffiti of medieval ships from the

Church of St Margaret at Cliffe, Kent', *The Mariner's Mirror: Journal of the Society for Nautical Research* 8 (1922), pp. 167-173.
44. YVBSG Report 1371, on 159 Church Street, Whitby.
45. An example of a windmill graffito in the church at Newnham, Hertfordshire, is to be found among Reginald Hine's papers held by the Society of Antiquaries (note 26 above), Box 788/1, graffito no. 287.
46. Jennifer S. Alexander (notes 14 and 37 above) and Kirsty Rodwell (note 38 above). I am also indebted to both authors for lectures they have given and queries they have answered.

6 HOUSE CARPENTERS AND CHURCH CRAFTSMEN

1. The drawing is part of the MS. Register of Bishop Jerome de Ghinucci, property of the Diocese of Worcester, deposited in the Worcestershire Record Office (WRO 716.093).
2. F.W.B. Charles and K. Down, 'A sixteenth century drawing of a timber-framed town house', *Transactions of Worcestershire Archaeological Society*, 3rd series, 3 (1970-72), pp. 67-79.
3. ibid, pp. 68-9, 73; also D.F. Stenning, 'Timber-framed shops, 1300-1600: comparative plans', *VA* 16 (1985), pp. 35-9.
4. Rape of Hastings Architectural Survey, 'A row of Wealdens in Battle' and 'Building accounts for a house', *Historic Buildings in East Sussex* 1 (1) (1977), pp. 3-5 and 1 (3) (1979), pp. 55-6.
5. F.W.B. Charles and K. Down (note 2 above), p. 69
6. Nikolaus Pevsner, *BOE, Shropshire* (Harmondsworth: Penguin, 1958), p. 272; compare John Newman and Nikolaus Pevsner, *BOE, Shropshire* (new edn, New Haven and London: Yale University Press, 2006).
7. D.H. Miles and D. Haddon-Reece, with Madge Moran, 'Shropshire dendrochronology project', *VA* 25 (1994), pp. 32, 34; further discussed by Daniel Miles, 'The interpretation, presentation and use of tree-ring dates', *VA* 28 (1997), pp. 40-56, especially p. 52.
8. Madge Moran, *Vernacular Buildings of Shropshire* (Logaston: Logaston Press, 2003), p. 240.
9. ibid, p. 239.
10. Vince Hemingway and Irene Hemingway, *The Greyfriars, Worcester* (guidebook), (National Trust, 2002).
11. J.B. Lawson, 'John Sandford of Shrewsbury and Pitchford', *Transactions of Shropshire Archaeological Society* 64 (1985), pp. 119-120.
12. RCHME, *City of York, Volume V, An Inventory of the Monuments in the Central Area* (London: HMSO, 1981), entry for nos. 41, 43, 45 Goodramgate, pp. 136-8, plates 6, 122.
13. Heather Swanson, *Building Craftsmen in Late Medieval York* (York: Borthwick Papers 63, 1981); names of many carpenters working in late medieval York can be identified in F. Collins (ed.), 'Register of the Freemen of York', *Surtees Society* 96 (1887).
14. John Leyland, *The Itineraries of John Leyland, 1535-43*, 5 vols, ed. Lucy Toulmin-Smith (London; Bell, 1907). Vol. 1, p. 60; also, Jack Binns, *Heroes and Villains: a Biographical Journey through Scarborough's Past* (Pickering: Blackthorn Press, 2002), p. 51.
15. Christopher Hall, John Petty, Peter Bartle and Arnold Pacey, 'The Newcastle Packet, Scarborough', YVBSG Report 1644 (2003).
16. ibid. I am indebted to Christopher Hall for showing me Frank Tugwell's drawings.
17. R.E. Clarke, *Relics of Old Scarborough* (Scarborough: J. Chapman, 1899).
18. Richard Marks and Paul Williamson (eds), *Gothic: Art for England, 1400-1547* (London: V&A Publications, 2003), p. 294.
19. Christa Grössinger, *Humour and Folly in Secular and Profane Prints in Northern Europe* (London: Harvey Miller Publishers, 2002), pp. 1-2.
20. ibid, p. 42, 45-6, 90-3.
21. I am indebted to Christa Grössinger (private communication) for this comment on the lettering.
22. Christa Grössinger, *The World Upside-down: English Misericords* (London, Harvey Miller Publishers, 1997), pp. 58-64, 67-9.
23. M.D. Anderson, *History and Imagery in British Churches* (London: John Murray, 1971), p. 214.

24. J.S. Purvis, 'The use of continental woodcuts and prints by the Ripon school of carvers', *Archaeologia* 85 (1936), pp. 107-128.
25. M.D. Anderson, *Misericords: Medieval Life in English Woodwork* (Harmondsworth: King Penguin, 1954), p. 18.
26. Christa Grössinger (note 22 above), p. 21.
27. John Harvey, *English Medieval Architects* (revised edn, Stroud: Alan Sutton 1984), entry for Dam, Jacob (fl. 1457-79).
28. Christa Grössinger (note 19 above), p. 183.
29. James Raine (ed.), 'The fabric rolls of York Minster', *Surtees Society* 35 (1859), p. 74.
30. Sarah Brown, *York Minster: an Architectural History, c.1220-1500* (Swindon: English Heritage, 2003), pp. 209, 214-15 (where Dam is referred to by his alias, David Carver).
31. Charles Tracy, *English Gothic Choir Stalls, 1400-1540* (Woodbridge: Boydell Press, 1990), pp. 19-20.
32. Nikolaus Pevsner, *BOE, Yorkshire: The North Riding* (Harmondsworth: Penguin, 1966), pp. 35, 67.
33. J.S. Purvis, 'The Ripon carvers and the lost choir stalls of Bridlington Priory', *Yorkshire Archaeological Journal* 29 (1929), pp. 157-200.
34. J.S. Purvis (note 24 above), p. 112 quotes the standard width and thickness of a desk-end as 15 x 3½in. The present author has found desk-ends at Wensley (North Riding) which approximately conform to these measurements, whereas the Aysgarth and Ripon desk-ends comprise a plank measuring 13½in (342mm) x 4½in (114mm) thick to which other features at the front are attached, giving a greater overall width.
35. F. Collins (note 13 above), p.220.
36. J.T. Fowler (ed.), 'Memorials of Ripon, 4', *Surtees Society* 115 (1908), pp. 173, 294-6; also 'Memorials of Ripon, 3', *Surtees Society* 81 (1889), pp. 198-206.
37. Charles Tracy (note 31 above), pp. 19, 26.
38. M.D. Anderson (note 25 above), p. 18.
39. Christa Grössinger (note 22 above), pp. 68-9.
40. Richard Pollard and Nikolaus Pevsner, *BOE, Lancashire: Liverpool and the South West* (New Haven and London: Yale University Press, 2006), pp. 580-1
41. M.D. Anderson (note 23 above), pp. 168-172.

7 CIRCLES AND SCALE DRAWINGS

1. Martin Cook, *Medieval Bridges* (Prince's Risborough: Shire Archaeology, 1998), p. 47.
2. Maurice Howard, *The Early Tudor Country House: Architecture and Politics 1490-1550* (London, George Philip 1987), p. 142.
3. R.W. Hoyle, *The Pilgrimage of Grace* (Oxford University Press, 2001), pp. 50, 219.
4. Peter Leach, *BOE, Yorkshire, the Northern West Riding* (New Haven and London: Yale University Press, forthcoming).
5. This local tradition is not supported by any early written sources, and scholarly authors ignore it, but the story is often repeated in guide-books and also, notably, by Alan Bennett, *Untold Stories* (London: Faber, 2005), pp. 225, 414.
6. Another instance is the screen from Jervaulx Abbey (*Plate 32*), moved to the parish church at Aysgarth by a group of 20 men, including probably joiners working in Aysgarth church at the time, who were able to dismantle the screen and re-assemble it without damage. T.D. Whitaker, *An History of Richmondshire* (London, 2 vols, 1823); Harry Speight, *Romantic Rich mondshire* (London: Elliot Stock, 1897).
7. H.M. Colvin, John Summerson, Martin Biddle, J.R. Hale and Marcus Merriman, *The History of the King's Works*, Vol. 4, part 2 (London: HMSO, 1982), pp. 207-8. On Barking Abbey, see Alfred W. Clapham and Walter H. Godfrey, *Some Famous Buildings; being the Results of Recent Research in London and Elsewhere* (London: Caxton House, 1913), pp. 199-214.
8. Malcolm Airs, *The Tudor and Jacobean Country House: a Building History* (Stroud: Alan Sutton, 1995), p. 75.

9. Maurice Howard (note 2 above), pp. 136, 144.
10. Nikolaus Pevsner, *BOE, North Somerset and Bristol* (Harmondsworth, Penguin, 1958), p. 190. Also Cathy Groves and Jennifer Hillam, 'Tree-ring dates from Sheffield University', *VA* 26 (1995), pp. 57-8.
11. Bob Meeson, 'Ritual marks and graffiti: curiosities or meaningful symbols?', *VA* 36 (2005), pp. 41-8.
12. Malcolm Airs (note 8 above), pp. 6-7.
13. Mark Girouard, *Robert Smythson and the Elizabethan Country House* (New Haven and London, Yale University Press, 1983), p. 25.
14. Malcolm Airs (note 8 above), p. 9.
15. Richard T. Spence, *Lady Anne Clifford* (Stroud: Sutton Publishing, 1997), pp. 8-11, 98, 181.
16. Mark Girouard (note 13 above),
17. Richard T. Spence, 'Mining and smelting in Yorkshire by the Cliffords', *Yorkshire Archaeological Journal* 64 (1992), pp. 157-183.
18. Malcolm Airs (note 8 above), p. 13.
19. Kirsty Rodwell and Robert Bell, *Acton Court: the evolution of an early Tudor courtier's house* (London: English Heritage, 2004), pp. 18, 24-26, 193.
20. John Harvey, *English Medieval Architects* (revised edn, Stroud: Alan Sutton, 1984), p. 308.
21. Both drawings are illustrated in Richard Marks and Paul Williamson (eds), *Gothic: Art for England 1400-1547* (London: V&A Publications, 2003), pp. 166-7, 244 (catalogue items 27, 109).
22. Mark Girouard, 'Three Gothic drawings in the Smythson Collection', *RIBA Journal* 64 (1956), pp. 35-6; Mark Girouard, 'The Smythson Collection of the RIBA', *Architectural History* 5 (1962), pp. 61, 167.
23. Barrie Dobson, 'Two ecclesiastical patrons' in Richard Marks and Paul Williamson (note 21 above), pp. 234-6.
24. F.W.B. Charles and Kevin Down, 'A sixteenth century drawing of a timber-framed house', *Transactions of the Worcestershire Archaeological Society*, 3rd series, 3 (1970-72), pp. 67-79.
25. John Summerson (ed.), 'The book of architecture of John Thorpe in Sir John Soane's Museum', *Walpole Society* 40 (1964-66), pp. 76-7.
26. Nikolaus Pevsner, *BOE, Hertfordshire* (Harmondsworth: Penguin, 1953), pp. 246-8.
27. John Summerson, *The Pelican History of Art: Architecture in Britain, 1530-1830* (Harmondsworth: Penguin, 4th edn, 1963), p. 26.
28. Malcolm Airs (note 8 above), p. 90.
29. John Summerson (note 25 above), pp. 1-13.
30. Malcolm Airs (note 8 above), p. 91.
31. ibid, pp. 7, 37, 212; the drawing collection remains at Hatfield House, but there are facsimiles in the British Library, London.
32. James S. Ackerman, *The Reinvention of Architectural Drawing, 1250-1550* (the 3rd Soane Lecture) (London: Sir John Soane's Museum, 1998), p. 14.
33. ibid, p. 20. Also see the account of perspective drawing in Samuel Y. Edgerton, *The Renaissance Rediscovery of Linear Perspective* (New York: Basic Books, 1975).
34. John Shute, *The First & Chief Groundes of Architecture* (London: Thomas Marshe, 1563); Eileen Harris, *British Architectural Books and Writers, 1556-1785* (Cambridge University Press, 1990), p. 513.
35. Malcolm Airs (note 8 above), p. 36.
36. William Worcestre, *Itineraries*, edited from the MS. at Corpus Christi College, Cambridge, by John Harvey (Oxford: Clarendon Press, 1969), p. 59 and note.
37. Günther Binding, trans. Alex Cameron, *Medieval Building Techniques* (Stroud: Tempus, 2004), see illustrations 254, 266 and 418, pp. 83, 135.
38. Items displayed at the *Mary Rose* Museum, Portsmouth.
39. Leonard Digges, *A Boke Named Tectonicon* (London: John Daye, printer, 1556 (reprinted 1561, 1562, etc. I have used the 1562 edition.))
40. J.A. Bennett, 'Geometry and surveying in early-seventeenth-century England', *Annals of Science* 48 (1991), pp. 345-354; on the simplified theodolite of Digges, p. 346.

Notes

41. Leonard Digges (note 39 above), chapters 10, 11, 14 (pages are not numbered).
42. Eileen Harris (note 34 above), pp. 41, 182-3.
43. ibid. Also E.G.R. Taylor, *The Mathematical Practitioners of Tudor and Stuart England* (Cambridge University Press, 1954), pp. 166-7
44. A.W. Skempton, 'Thomas Digges'. In Alec Skempton et al. (eds), *Biographical Dictionary of Civil Engineers*, Vol. 1, 1500-1830 (London: Thomas Telford, 2002), pp. 181-3.
45. H.W. Robinson, *Marine Cartography in Britain: a History of the Sea Chart to 1855* (Leicester University Press, 1962), pp. 146-7 and plates 4 and 8.
46. P.D.A. Harvey, 'Estate surveyors and the spread of the scale map in England, 1550-1580', *Landscape History* 15 (1993), pp. 37-49.
47. On surveyors of building works, see Mark Girouard (note 13 above), pp. 21-2. Examples regarding seventeenth-century stone bridges can be found in records of the West Riding Quarter Sessions, e.g. a dispute about the surveyors' accounts, West Yorkshire Archive Service, Wakefield, QS1/19/5/6/3.
48. E.G.R. Taylor (note 43 above); J.A. Bennett (note 40 above).
49. Dover map, National Archives, MPF1/122; discussed by A.H.W. Robinson (note 45 above). For biographical information on John Symons, see John Summerson (note 27 above), p. 25.
50. Symons drew plans of the former Havering Palace, Romford, see H.M. Colvin et al. (note 7 above), p. 152; and plans of the Great House, Chelsea: Alfred W. Clapham and Walter H. Godfrey (note 7 above), pp. 80, 82-3, 148, 150.
51. A.W. Skempton (note 44 above), p. 182.
52. Matthew Baker's MS. 'Fragments of early English shipwrightry' in the Pepys Library, Magdalene College, Cambridge is discussed by Ken Baynes and Francis Pugh, *The Art of the Engineer* (Guildford: Lutterworth Press, 1981).
53. John Summerson (note 25 above), pp. 7-8, 12-13.
54. ibid, drawing catalogued as T2. I am indebted to Mark Girouard for examining the original drawing with me at Sir John Soane's Museum.
55. Mark Girouard, 'The Smythson Collection of the RIBA', *Architectural History* 5 (1962), where pp. 79, 81, 89, 93 show drawings with decorated scale bars and compasses, whereas pp. 74, 76, 78, 97 have simple single-line bar scales.
56. Walter H. Godfrey, 'An Elizabethan builder's contract', *Sussex Archaeological Collections* 65 (1924), pp. 212-223.
57. Malcolm Airs (note 8 above), p. 151.
58. Alfred W. Clapham and Walter H. Godfrey (note 7 above), illustrations of three plans by John Symons from the Hatfield collection, pp. 82-3, 149.
59. John Summerson, *Inigo Jones* (Harmondsworth: Penguin, 1966), pp. 22, 36. For a fuller analysis of Jones's draughting techniques, see Gordon Higgott in J. Harris and G. Higgott (eds), *Inigo Jones, Complete Architectural Drawings* (London, 1989).
60. Malcolm Airs (note 8 above), pp. 41, 44.
61. John Summerson (note 27 above), pp. 26-7; and Malcolm Airs (note 8 above), pp. 21-2, 48-9.
62. Mrs Baldwin-Childs, 'The building of the Manor House at Kyre Park, Worcestershire, 1598-1618', *The Antiquary* 21 (January-June 1890), pp. 202-5.
63. Mrs Baldwin-Childs, 'The building of the Manor House ... continued', *The Antiquary* 22 (July-December 1890), pp. 24-6, 50-3.
64. Mark Girouard, (note 13 above), pp. 276, 313n, 317n.
65. T.W. Hanson, 'Halifax builders in Oxford', *Halifax Antiquarian Society Transactions* (1928), pp. 253-320, pp. 258-320, especially pp. 258-9 for the 'form' and pp. 287-8 for 'daubing'.

8 SETTING OUT CARPENTRY AND DRAWING IN RED

1. Malcolm Airs, *The Tudor and Jacobean Country House: A Building History* (Stroud: Alan Sutton, 1995), pp. 38, 40, 54.

2. Gordon Batho, 'Notes and documents on Petworth House, 1574-1632', *Sussex Archaeological Collections* 96 (1958), pp. 108-135.
3. Leonard Digges, *A Boke Named Tectonicon* (London, 1556 (reprinted 1561, 1562, etc.)).
4. Herbert Davis and Harry Carter (eds), 'Introduction' in Joseph Moxon, *Mechanick Exercises on the Whole Art of Printing (1683-4)* (London: Oxford University Press, 2nd edn, 1962), p. xxv.
5. Joseph Moxon, *Mechanick Exercises, or, the Doctrine of Handy-Works*, 2 volumes (London, 1677-84), see Vol. 1, preface and p. 92. (I have also used a facsimile of the 3rd edn, 1700, published by the Early American Industries Association, New York, 1970).
6. André Félibien, *Des Principes de l'Architecture, de la Sculpture, de la Peinture* (Paris: Coignard, 1676). I am indebted to Professor Derek Long for allowing me to compare illustrations in his copies of Moxon and Félibien (2nd edn 1690).
7. Anthony Blunt, *Philibert de l'Orme* (London: Zwemmer, 1958), pp. 3-7, 108, 122-4.
8. Eileen Harris, *British Architectural Books and Writers, 1556-1785* (Cambridge University Press, 1990); on pp. 38-9 Harris claims that there was no adequate English publication on structural carpentry before Francis Price's *Treatise on Carpentry* (London, 1733).
9. Jeremy Lake, *The Great Fire of Nantwich* (Nantwich: Shiva, 1983), p. 99, discussing 'Accounts and memorandums of Richard and Thomas Minshull', Cheshire Record Office, MF 14.
10. James W.P. Campbell, 'The carpentry trade in seventeenth-century England', *Georgian Group Journal* 12 (2002), pp. 215-237, quoting guild regulations in Norwich; also see Lake (note 9 above), pp. 98-9.
11. James Hall, *A History of the Town and Parish of Nantwich* (privately published 1883; reprinted Manchester: E.J. Morton, 1972), p. 294.
12. Michael Faraday, *Ludlow: a Social, Economic and Political History, 1085-1660* (Chichester: Phillimore, 1991).
13. David Lloyd, Peter Howell and Margaret Richards, *The Feathers: Ludlow Research Paper No. 5* (Ludlow Historical Research Group, 1986), pp. 62-3.
14. David Lloyd, *The Concise History of Ludlow* (London: Merlin Unwin, 1999).
15. Madge Moran, *Vernacular Buildings of Shropshire* (Logaston: Logaston Press, 2003), pp. 85, 249-50.
16. The original accounts for the Preacher's House were among records lost during World War II, but a partial transcript made before the war is held by Ludlow Historical Research Group. Surveys of the Preacher's House, Ludlow, and the house in Raven Lane were carried out by David Cant and Arnold Pacey, and reports have been lodged with Ludlow Historical Research Group.
17. Lake (note 9), p. 61; also Hall (note 11).
18. Nikolaus Pevsner and Edward Hubbard, *BOE: Cheshire* (Harmondsworth: Penguin, 1971), pp. 255-7.
19. Lake (note 9), p. 119 mentions the rebuilding of The Crown after 1583 as costing £313. An examination by the author and Dr David M. Farrar has shown that the building was altered later to incorporate the long gallery and that there are similarities with Little Moreton Hall. The difference is that in The Crown the long gallery gave access to chambers or lodgings, like the open-sided galleries overlooking some traditional inn yards.
20. Information kindly provided by Gwyneth Guy, biographer of John Abel.
21. Ron Shoesmith and Ruth Richardson, *A Definitive History of Dore Abbey* (Logaston: Logaston Press, 1997, new edn 2000), p. 168.
22. ibid, pp. 177, 179.
23. Pevsner and Hubbard (note 18), p. 20.
24. W.F. Price, 'Notes on the Parish Church of St Wilfred, Standish', *Transactions of HSLC* 55-56 (1903-4), pp. 238-86; T.C. Porteous, *The History of Standish* (Wigan, 1927), p. 67.
25. Malcolm Airs, 'Lawrence Shipway, freemason', *Architectural History* 27 (1984), pp. 368-73.
26. For Richard Southworth and John Rigby, carpenters, see W.F. Price (note 24 above), pp. 245, 259. For John Southworth, carpenter, see Lancashire Parish Register Society, Wigan Registers, Vol. 1 for 1580-1625, (Liverpool, 1899), pp. 210, 254.

Notes

27. William A. Singleton, 'Traditional house-types in rural Lancashire and Cheshire', *Transactions of HSLC* 104 (1952-53), pp. 75-92, especially pp. 90-2.
28. The museum is the History Shop, Library Street, Wigan; for an illustrated description of Crooke Hall, see *Victoria County History of the County of Lancaster*, Vol. 6 (1923), pp. 202-3.
29. These houses are well described by Garry Miller, *Historic Houses in Lancashire: the Douglas Valley 1300-1700* (Barrowford: Heritage Trust for the North West, 2002), pp. 93, 195.
30. The carpenter's numbers in Arabic numerals in these houses were cut with a rase-knife that was set to mark circles of fixed diameter, and when a carpenter introduced a new rase-knife, the different diameter in his numerals was (and is) very clear. For background on the rase-knife, see R.A. Salaman, *A Dictionary of Tools* (London: Allen & Unwin, 1975).
31. Lancashire Parish Register Society, Wigan Registers, Vol. 1 for 1580-1625 (Liverpool, 1899); for Rigby, see pp. 159, 249. There is just a chance that whilst the carpenter with initials IR was John or James Rigby, RR was a Robinson. See the will and probate inventory of Robert Robinson or Robertson of Ince, near Wigan, in Lancashire Record Office. Robinson died in 1620, and a later Richard Robinson was a joiner.
32. Arnold Pacey, 'Some carpenters' marks in Arabic numerals', *VA* 36 (2005), pp. 69-71. Giant's Hall is also discussed by Miller (note 29 above), pp. 46, 195.
33. David Cant and Arnold Pacey (with Alison Armstrong), reports on Club House Farm, Shevington, and Holland's House, Dalton, 2005-6, deposited in the archives of the North West Traditional Buildings Preservation Trust, Barrowford, Nelson, Lancashire.
34. Alison Armstrong (with others), 'Lyon Lane, Eastburn', YVBSG Report no. 1702.
35. Much of the research on these matters is discussed in relatively ephemeral journals including *Mortice and Tenon* (nos 1-7, published in the 1990s), and newsletters of the Essex Historic Buildings Group (to 2006).
36. Richard Harris, 'The grammar of carpentry', *VA* 20 (1989), pp. 1-8.
37. Trevor Hodgson and David Gulliver, *The History of Cononley: an Airedale Village* (Cononley: Kiln Hill, 2000), p. 35.
38. 'Gunthwaite Hall Barn, Penistone, West Yorkshire', *Cornerstone* (SPAB) 26 (1) (2005), pp. 30-1.
39. Arnold Pacey, 'The Great Barn of Bolton Priory', *Medieval Yorkshire* 34 (2005), pp. 15-21. The carpenters who built the northern end of the barn are thought also to have reconstructed the roof of Addingham church, three miles to the south.
40. Dendrochronology sampling by Robert Howard, University of Nottingham, May 2005, discussed by Stephen Moorhouse, 'Sources of timber for the Great Barn at Bolton Abbey', *Medieval Yorkshire* 34 (2005), pp. 23-8.
41. Arnold Pacey (note 39 above).
42. Walter Rose, *The Village Carpenter* (Cambridge University Press, 1937; reprinted, Hertford: Stobart Davies, 1995), p. 4.
43. John Harvey, *Medieval Craftsmen* (London: Batsford, 1975), p. 68.
44. Displayed in the *Mary Rose* Museum, Portsmouth, July 2000.
45. Edward Roberts, *Hampshire Houses, 1250-1700* (Hampshire County Council, 2003), p. 58. Another example of red ochre paintwork, originally from Kent, is a fifteenth-century house from North Cray, now at the Wealden and Downland Museum, Singleton, West Sussex.
46. I am very grateful to Brenda Watkin for information here and also for her report on Paul's Hall.
47. I am indebted to Gwyneth Guy for this information. The outbuildings at Court House Farm, Pembridge, are mentioned by Nikolaus Pevsner, *BOE Herefordshire* (Harmondsworth: Penguin, 1963 (reprinted 2001)), p. 268.
48. Somerset and South Avon Vernacular Buildings Study Group, quoted by D.H. Miles and Henry Russell, 'Plumb and level marks', *VA* 26 (1995), pp. 33-38, especially p. 36.
49. Alison Armstrong and Arnold Pacey, *High Bradley: Architecture and History* (privately published 2001), pp. 66-71.
50. YVBSG reports nos. 1625 (dated 2002) and 1722 (dated 2006) on Lower Winskill Farm, Langcliffe, near Settle, and on Cuckoo Nest Farm, Addingham Moorside, near Ilkley.

51. YVBSG report no. 1714 (dated 2006) on Bounty Barn, Starbotton. This is one of several remote barns falling into dereliction which contains valuable evidence of carpenters' setting-out methods. Such barns are not 'listed buildings' and their conservation is something of a challenge. See: R.F. White and P.R. Wilson (eds), *Archaeology and Historic Landscape of the Yorkshire Dales*, YAS Occasional Paper No. 2 (2004), pp. 145-156.
52. RCHME, *City of York, Volume III, An Inventory of the Monuments in the South-West* (London: HMSO, 1981), pp. lxix, lxxiv-lxxv, where carpenters' marks are said to be rare in the south-west of the city. We have recorded more in the central area in Coppergate and in Lady Peckett's Yard, behind 12-14 Pavement.
53. Sarah Brown, *York Minster: an Architectural History, c.1220-1500* (Swindon: English Heritage, 2003), pp. 171, 174.
54. The house is at 30 East Stockwell Street, Colchester; I am indebted to Dave Stenning for telling me about it and to Tony Barker for helping me examine it (July 2006).
55. J.T. Smith and M.A. North (eds), *St Albans, 1650-1700: a Thoroughfare Town and its People* (Hatfield: University of Hertfordshire Press, 2003), pp. 8-9, 154-5.
56. I am indebted for this comment to Mr Ian Garwood, Surveyor to the Middle Temple. I am also very grateful to him for showing me the hall and for taking photographs.
57. Michael G. Murray, *Middle Temple Hall: an Architectural Appreciation* (London: Middle Temple, 2000), p. 4.
58. Airs (note 1 above), p. 54.
59. T.G. Jackson, *Wadham College, Oxford: its Foundation, Architecture and History* (Oxford: Clarendon Press, 1893), p. 47. (Thomas Holt probably came from Methley, near Wakefield, not York.)
60. J.R. Mulryne and Margaret Shewring (eds), *Shakespeare's Globe Rebuilt* (Cambridge University Press, 1997), pp. 148-9.
61. ibid, appendix, pp. 180-182.
62. Walter H. Godfrey, 'The Fortune Theatre, London' in A.W. Clapham and W.H. Godfrey (eds), *Some Famous London Buildings ... Recent Research* (London: Caxton House, 1913), pp. 13-28.
63. Mulryne and Shewring (note 60 above), p. 181.
64. ibid, p. 56.
65. Peter McCurdy, co-author with Jon Greenfield of 'Shakespeare's Globe Theatre: the construction of two experimental bays' in Andrew Gurr, J.R. Mulryne and Margaret Shewring (eds), *The Design of the Globe* (University of Warwick, 1993), pp. 53-88; see also references to Peter McCurdy's work in Mulryne and Shewring (note 60 above), pp. 97 etc., and to the contribution of the Weald and Downland Museum, p. 104.

9 THE PERSISTENCE OF MEDIEVAL DRAWING METHODS

1. Peter Meadows, 'Sir Christopher Wren and Pembroke College Chapel', *Georgian Group Journal* 4 (1994), pp. 55-7. On Bishop Wren's burial in the chapel, see Jayne Ringrose, 'Matthew Wren makes his will', *Pembroke College Annual Gazette* 67 (1993), pp. 21-6.
2. The model was described in 1923 as a recent discovery: Ellis H. Minns and Maurice Webb, 'Pembroke College Chapel, Cambridge' in R. Dircks (ed.), *Sir Christopher Wren, AD 1632-1723: Bicentenary Memorial Volume* (London: Hodder and Stoughton, 1923), pp. 229-232.
3. The contract was published by R. Willis and J.W. Clark, *The Architectural History of the University of Cambridge*, Vol. 1 (Cambridge University Press, 3 vols, reprinted 1988), pp. 155-6.
4. The drawing appears in *Wren Society* 9 (1932), plate 43.
5. The identification has been made by Dr Gordon Higgot (pers. comm.), to whom I am most grateful.
6. R.L. Poole, 'Edward Pierce the Sculptor', *Walpole Society* 11 (1922-3), pp. 33-45; also Howard Colvin, *A Biographical Dictionary of British Architects, 1600-1840* (3rd edn, New Haven and London: Yale University Press, 1995).

7. Denys Spittle, 'The Thomas Gray Room', *Pembroke College Annual Gazette* 39 (1965), pp. 10-12.
8. John Crook, 'New light on the history of St Mary's Church, Old Basing, Hampshire: an incised design', *JBAA* 154 (2001), pp. 92-132.
9. Drawings of funerary monuments by Edward Pearce in the British Museum, accession numbers 189 to 192 prefixed 1881-6-11-. There is a scale bar on many of these drawings, usually unlabelled, but clearly indicating feet and inches. Other drawings by Pearce in Sir John Soane's Museum do not have the urn detail. All these drawings were once attributed to Talman but are now known to be by Pearce and many have been published in *Wren Society* 17 (1940), plates 22-24.
10. The attribution of the drawing with the cartouche to Jaspar Latham has been suggested by Geoffrey Fisher of the Courtauld Institute. For London work by Pearce and Latham, see Simon Bradley and Nikolaus Pevsner, *BOE, London: the City Churches* (London: Penguin, 1998), pp. 53, 102, 117.
11. I am indebted to Dr A.V. Grimstone for comments on this point (which imply that Christopher Wren was consulted at a relatively late stage in the process of planning the chapel). A book on the subject by Dr Grimstone is forthcoming.
12. Brian Wragg, *The Life and Works of John Carr of York*, edited by Giles Worsley (York: Oblong, 2000), pp. 60, 63, 95.
13. William Shout's drawings are in York Minster Library.
14. Robert Branner cites the St Albans drawing in Lynn T. Courtenay (ed.), *The Engineering of Medieval Cathedrals* (Aldershot: Ashgate, 1997), pp. 67, 68.
15. Alexander Holton, 'The working space of the medieval master mason: the tracing houses of York Minster and Wells Cathedral', *Proceedings of the Second International Construction History Congress* (London: Construction History Society, 2006), pp. 1579-97.
16. E.G. Warland, *Constructional Masonry* (London: Pitman, 1946 (reprinted 1947)), p.42.
17. Information from the Chatham Historic Dockyard Trust.
18. Editorial comment, *Transactions, American Society for Civil Engineers* 7 (1878), p. 340. I am indebted to Dr Sara Wermiel for pointing this out.
19. A rather surprising eighteenth-century example is Mary Lacy, a house-builder who had earlier worked as a shipwright; see Peter Guillery, 'The further adventures of Mary Lacy', *Georgian Group Journal* 10 (2000), pp. 61-9.
20. James S. Ackerman, *The Reinvention of Architectural Drawing, 1250-1550* (The 3rd Soane Lecture) (London: Sir John Soane's Museum, 1998), pp. 7-8.
21. William Halfpenny, *The Art of Sound Building* (London: The Author, 1725), frontispiece.
22. Nancy Y. Wu (ed.), *Ad Quadratum: The Practical Application of Geometry in Medieval Architecture* (Aldershot: Ashgate), pp. 183, 193-4, 194n.
23. Leonard Digges, *A Boke Named Tectonicon* (London: Thomas Daye, 1556).
24. Robert W. Scheller, *Exemplum: Model Book Drawings and the Practice of Artistic Transmission in the Middle Ages*, trans. Michael Hoyle (Amsterdam University Press, 1995), pp. 4-6.
25. Eugene S. Ferguson, *Engineering and the Mind's Eye* (Cambridge (MA): MIT Press, 1992), pp. 3, 75.
26. Some medieval drawings have also been omitted for copyright reasons.
27. Stuart Harrison and Paul Barker, 'Byland Abbey ... the west front and rose window reconstructed', *JBAA* 140 (1987), pp. 134-151.
28. Jennifer Alexander, 'Masons' marks and stone bonding' in Tim Tatton-Brown and Julian Munby (eds), *The Archaeology of Cathedrals* (Oxford University Committee for Archaeology, 1996), pp. 219-236.

INDEX

(Italics denote information in illustrations or captions on the page indicated).

Abbey Dore (Herefordshire) 195
Abel, John (carpenter) 195, 196, 211, 225
Acton Court (Gloucestershire) 135, 167, 216, 231
Adelard of Bath 44, 106-7
ad quadratum design 59, 64, *73*, 73-4, *92*, *93*
Akroyd, John and Martin (masons) 186
Alberti, Leone Battista 171
Apethorpe Hall Northamptonshire 218
apotropaic marks, *see* ritual marks
Arabic numerals 107, 154, *154*, 192, 196
architectural drawings, illustrations of *34*, *36*, *38*, *39*, *40*, *66*, *127*, *128*, *136*, *140*, *169*, *182*, colour plates *6*, *11*, *17*, *18*, *20*, *23*
 at Wells 66, *222*, colour plate *6*
 at Worcester 140, colour plates 29, 30
 at York 54, 57, *131*, *132*
 see also drawings, setting-out lines
Arundel (Sussex) 108, 117, 184
Ashwell (Hertfordshire) church 42, 44, 58, 71, 230, 231
 drawings 40-2, *40*, *41*, *82*, 82-4
assembly marks 97, 98, *see also* carpenters' numbers
Aysgarth (North Riding) *155*, *156*, colour plate *32*

Bacon, Sir Nicholas 185
Baker, Matthew (shipwright) 181
Ballflower 49, 58
banker masons 22-4
barns, aisled *93*, 203, *204*
Bath Abbey 163
Battle Abbey (Sussex) 143
Beamsley Hospital (West Riding) 165, *166*
Bebb, Francis (carpenter) 193-4, colour plate *35*
Belchamp St Paul's (Essex) 205
Bentley, John (mason) 185-6
Berkeley Castle (Gloucestershire) 76, colour plate *7*
Berty, Thomas (mason) 168
Beverley Minster (East Riding) 16, 24-6, *25*, *31*, *64*, 133-4
Bishop's Cleeve (Gloucestershire) 108
Bodleian Library, Oxford 185, 186
Bolton Priory (West Riding) 203, *204*
Borley (Essex) 205
Boudon, Hugh de (mason) 49, 50
Bridlington Priory (East Riding) 27
Bristol 75, 76, 86,118, 119
 St Stephen's Church 120, *121*, colour plate *12*

Bristol Cathedral 28-30, *29*, 75, 76,157-8, *158*
Bromflet, William (*alias* William Carver) 156
Burghley, Lord 180, *see also* Cecil, William
Bury St Edmunds 63, 117, 133
Bushmead Priory (Bedfordshire) 108, 109, 110-112
Byland Abbey (North Riding) 35-7, 42, 44, 45, 58, 230, colour plates 19, 20

Caister (Norfolk) 90, 115, 118
Cambridge 38, 125, 127, 152, 213-18, 230, 231
 King's College Chapel 134
Canterbury Cathedral 60, 88, colour plate *23*
Canterbury, Thomas of (mason) 37
carpenters 37, 87, 96-9,139
carpenters' circular marks *103*, *105*, *110*
carpenters' numbers 96-8, 99, *103*, *107*, 104-115
carpenters' ruler 175-7
Carr, John (architect) 218
carvers 19-22, 100-1, 148,152-8
Castle Acre Priory (Norfolk) 33
Caundish, Richard (military engineer) 178
Cavendish, Richard (scholar) 167
Caxton, William 153
Cecil, William 180, 181, 185
chalk, use in drawing 22, 47, 54, 56, 58, 67, 86, 137, 205, 215, 218, 219
Chapman, John (mason) 163
Chatham Dockyard 219
Chertsey (Surrey) 113, 163
Chester 165
Chipping Norton (Oxfordshire) 86
Christchurch Priory (Hampshire) 38, 127, 230
Churche's Mansion, Nantwich 192, colour plate *34*
circles, in drawing 77-8, 79, 92, *103*, colour plates 24, 25
Cleese, Thomas (carpenter) 190-1, 212
Clermont-Ferrand (France) 35
Clifford, Lady Anne 165
Colchester (Essex) 208
Compasses 42, 78, 164, 177, 191-2
Cononley (West Riding) 203
contract drawings 117, 125, 214
Corfe (Dorset) 47
Coverham Abbey (North Riding) 162
Cressing Temple (Essex) 92, 93-4, 115, 232

Cross, Benedict (mason) 120, *121*, 138
Crowland (Lincolnshire) 84

daisy-wheel patterns 78, 81
Dale, Richard (carpenter) 195, 196
Dam, David (*alias* David Carver) 153, 156
Dartington Hall (Devon) 137
de l'Orme, Philibert 189
de Muet, Pierre 188
dendrochronology 143, 163
Dereham, Elias of 72-3, 106-7
devices, Elizabethan 165, 166
Digges, Leonard 174-5, 188, 224
Digges, Thomas 177, 178
Dore Abbey (Herefordshire) 86, 195
Dover Harbour (Kent) 177, *180*, 181
drawings 18-19, 71, 85, 167-8, 171-2
 base-lines in 43, 56, 57, 58, 66, 67, 102,126, 128
 centre lines in 64, 65, 66, 122, *123*
 full-size 59, 62, 168
 charcoal, chalk and ink in 47, 86, 140-1, 203-5
 see also architectural drawings, scale drawings, setting-out lines
Dürer, Albrecht 148
Durham Cathedral 37

Eastburn (West Riding) house at 200, 203, colour plate *37*
Ely Cathedral (Cambridgeshire) 62, 63, 71, 72, 88, 232
 drawings at 33, *34*, 38-9, 44-6, 58
 octagon 88, *112*, 112-14
Ely, Nicholas of (mason) 73
Englishcombe (Somerset) barn at 163, *164*, 231
Estrich boards 43
Euclid 44, 167
Ewerby (Lincolnshire) church at 76, 77, *128*, colour plate *28*
Exeter Cathedral (Devon) 42, 69, 87, 99, 100, 118
 Sedilia 79, 79-80, colour plate *8*

Farnham, Surrey 113
Fastoff, Sir John 118
feet, measurements in 64, 118, 119
Félibien, André 188, 189
Fernie, Eric 74, 119
Fletcher, John 88
Forman, John (mason) 130, 133-4, 138, 182
Fortune Theatre, London 210-11

254